PROCEEDINGS OF THE 2017 INTERNATIONAL CONFERENCE ON E-LEARNING, E-BUSINESS, ENTERPRISE INFORMATION SYSTEMS, & E-GOVERNMENT

Editors

Hamid R. Arabnia
Azita Bahrami, Leonidas Deligiannidis
Fernando G. Tinetti

Associate Editors

Lamia Atma Djoudi, Ashu M. G. Solo

CSCE'17
July 17-20, 2017
Las Vegas Nevada, USA
americancse.org

This volume contains papers presented at The 2017 International Conference on e-Learning, e-Business, Enterprise Information Systems, & e-Government (EEE'17). Their inclusion in this publication does not necessarily constitute endorsements by editors or by the publisher.

Copyright and Reprint Permission

AMERICAN
COUNCIL ON
SCIENCE AND
EDUCATION

Foreword

It gives us great pleasure to introduce this collection of papers to be presented at the 2017 International Conference on e-Learning, e-Business, Enterprise Information Systems, and e-Government (EEE'17), July 17-20, 2017, at Monte Carlo Resort, Las Vegas, USA.

An important mission of the World Congress in Computer Science, Computer Engineering, and Applied Computing, CSCE (a federated congress to which this conference is affiliated with) includes *"Providing a unique platform for a diverse community of constituents composed of scholars, researchers, developers, educators, and practitioners. The Congress makes concerted effort to reach out to participants affiliated with diverse entities (such as: universities, institutions, corporations, government agencies, and research centers/labs) from all over the world. The congress also attempts to connect participants from institutions that have **teaching** as their main mission with those who are affiliated with institutions that have **research** as their main mission. The congress uses a quota system to achieve its institution and geography diversity objectives. "* By any definition of diversity, this congress is among the most diverse scientific meeting in USA. We are proud to report that this federated congress has authors and participants from 64 different nations representing variety of personal and scientific experiences that arise from differences in culture and values. As can be seen (see below), the program committee of this conference as well as the program committee of all other tracks of the federated congress are as diverse as its authors and participants.

The program committee would like to thank all those who submitted papers for consideration. About 65% of the submissions were from outside the United States. Each submitted paper was peer-reviewed by two experts in the field for originality, significance, clarity, impact, and soundness. In cases of contradictory recommendations, a member of the conference program committee was charged to make the final decision; often, this involved seeking help from additional referees. In addition, papers whose authors included a member of the conference program committee were evaluated using the double-blinded review process. One exception to the above evaluation process was for papers that were submitted directly to chairs/organizers of pre-approved sessions/workshops; in these cases, the chairs/organizers were responsible for the evaluation of such submissions. The overall paper acceptance rate for regular papers was 24%; 22% of the remaining papers were accepted as poster papers (at the time of this writing, we had not yet received the acceptance rate for a couple of individual tracks.)

We are very grateful to the many colleagues who offered their services in organizing the conference. In particular, we would like to thank the members of Program Committee of EEE'17, members of the congress Steering Committee, and members of the committees of federated congress tracks that have topics within the scope of EEE. Many individuals listed below, will be requested after the conference to provide their expertise and services for selecting papers for publication (extended versions) in journal special issues as well as for publication in a set of research books (to be prepared for publishers including: Springer, Elsevier, BMC journals, and others).

- *Prof. Abbas M. Al-Bakry (Congress Steering Committee); University President, University of IT and Communications, Baghdad, Iraq*
- *Prof. Nizar Al-Holou (Congress Steering Committee); Professor and Chair, ECE Department; Vice Chair, IEEE/SEM-Computer Chapter; University of Detroit Mercy, Detroit, Michigan, USA*
- *Prof. Hamid R. Arabnia (Congress Steering Committee); Graduate Program Director (PhD, MS, MAMS); The University of Georgia, USA; Editor-in-Chief, Journal of Supercomputing (Springer); Fellow, Center of Excellence in Terrorism, Resilience, Intelligence & Organized Crime Research (CENTRIC).*
- *Dr. Azita Bahrami (Co-Editor, EEE); President, IT Consult, USA*
- *Prof. Dr. Juan-Vicente Capella-Hernandez; Universitat Politecnica de Valencia (UPV), Department of Computer Engineering (DISCA), Valencia, Spain*
- *Prof. Kevin Daimi (Congress Steering Committee); Director, Computer Science and Software Engineering Programs, Department of Mathematics, Computer Science and Software Engineering, University of Detroit Mercy, Detroit, Michigan, USA*
- *Prof. Zhangisina Gulnur Davletzhanovna; Vice-rector of the Science, Central-Asian University, Kazakhstan, Almaty, Republic of Kazakhstan; Vice President of International Academy of Informatization, Kazskhstan, Almaty, Republic of Kazakhstan*

We would like to extend our appreciation to the referees, the members of the program committees of individual sessions, tracks, and workshops; their names do not appear in this document; they are listed on the web sites of individual tracks.

As Sponsors-at-large, partners, and/or organizers each of the followings (separated by semicolons) provided help for at least one track of the Congress: Computer Science Research, Education, and Applications Press (CSREA); US Chapter of World Academy of Science; American Council on Science & Education & Federated Research Council (http://www.americancse.org/); HoIP, Health Without Boundaries, Healthcare over Internet Protocol, UK (http://www.hoip.eu); HoIP Telecom, UK (http://www.hoip-telecom.co.uk); and WABT, Human Health Medicine, UNESCO NGOs, Paris, France (http://www.thewabt.com/). In addition, a number of university faculty members and their staff (names appear on the cover of the set of proceedings), several publishers of computer science and computer engineering books and journals, chapters and/or task forces of computer science associations/organizations from 3 regions, and developers of high-performance machines and systems provided significant help in organizing the conference as well as providing some resources. We are grateful to them all.

We express our gratitude to keynote, invited, and individual conference/tracks and tutorial speakers - the list of speakers appears on the conference web site. We would also like to thank the followings: UCMSS (Universal Conference Management Systems & Support, California, USA) for managing all aspects of the conference; Dr. Tim Field of APC for coordinating and managing the printing of the proceedings; and the staff of Monte Carlo Resort (Convention department) at Las Vegas for the professional service they provided. Last but not least, we would like to thank the Co-Editors of EEE'17: Prof. Hamid R. Arabnia, Dr. Azita Bahrami, Prof. Leonidas Deligiannidis, and Prof. Fernando G. Tinetti.

We present the proceedings of EEE'17.

Steering Committee, 2017
http://americancse.org/

Contents

SESSION: LATE PAPERS - BANK RISK MANAGEMENT

SESSION

E-LEARNING, LEARNING METHODOLOGIES, AND EDUCATION

Chair(s)

TBA

ISBN: 1-60132-454-5, CSREA Press ©

A Survey of Learning Management Systems and Synchronous Distance Education Tools

Khondkar Islam, Pouyan Ahmadi, and Salman Yousaf
George Mason University
kislam2, pahmadi, syousaf3@gmu.edu

Abstract— Although compelling assessment has been quite frequently examined in recent years, more studies are required to yield a better understanding of several Distance Learning (DL) methods where Learning Management Systems (LMSs) significantly affect student learning process. Most studies in this area do not consider the effect of varying web-facilitated DL application tools. To address these drawbacks, the objective of our study is to compare two LMSs and four synchronous distance education tools (SDET). The comparisons confirm the superiority of Moodle Integrated Synchrotrons Teaching Conferencing (MIST/C) which seems to be the most practical, convenient and modest distance education tool offered in the market today because it is open source and has a second mirrored whiteboard for simulteaching that is not available with any other system.

Keywords— *Learning Management System, distance learning, synchronous distance education*

I. INTRODUCTION

Distance education (DE) is an effective mode of learning, if the delivery and exchange of education content are facilitated properly. Web-based DE application tools used by students and faculty are key components required to achieve this, by making the learning process easy and effective while eliminating unnecessary difficulty. Some of these tools are difficult both to learn and use, and thus turn out to be an obstacle for faculty and students [1]. A survey of popular DE application tools being used today is presented in this paper to compare their key features, ease-of-use and learning curve. This includes comparisons of two learning management systems (LMSs): one developed by a commercial institution, and the other an open source. Comparisons of four synchronous distance education tools (SDETs) are also included here: one commercial product and three are open source.

A. DE LMS and SDET Requirements

DE LMS and SDET must offer a user-friendly graphical user interface, simple navigation options, and have enhanced security features to deter unauthorized access to the system and files [2]. The system should not be bandwidth intensive, and be able to process audio and video streaming in a distributed network setting. Course creation and management has to be easy, and the system must support common file types. There has to be an option to reuse course contents so instructors are able to reuse contents in other sections of the same course or during another semester with minor modifications.

The virtual environment provided by DE LMS and SDET has to appear sufficiently real to create an atmosphere where faculty and students feel they are interacting in person. This raises the learning motivation of students and teaching enthusiasm of instructors that promote class participation using the *discussion board* and *chat* room. It is therefore necessary for the LMS and SDET to have easy-to-use and effective interactive communication options such as the discussion board, chat room, email, etc. [2].

Early research suggests web users need to be provided with an effective usable environment because it drives substantial savings and achieves better performance. In academia, effective LMS and SDET need little instructor time to set up and manage the course, while improving the learning experience of students. It is important for the LMS and SDET to be not cluttered with too many appealing usage options, as that can be confusing for students and the instructor. Only features that meet course objectives and are relevant to a sound-learning environment for designing an effective course should be included in the LMS and SDET. Since usability is critical, the LMS and SDET must be easy to use and to learn, and must offer options that are easy to remember. Considering web usability, tools must have web pages that are easy to navigate and must display information in an organized manner so users do not have to struggle to find what they are looking for. Pedagogical usability enables users to learn effectively and retain the skills and knowledge learned; it is integrated with technology usability, which is referred to ease of use and usefulness of the technology [1]. Students do not have a high degree of pedagogical usability when technology usability is poor.

B. Communication Tools

Zaina et al [2] describe *chat* as a synchronous communication tool that allows students to receive immediate feedback on a subject, which helps to understand group reflection of the subject matter. The researchers view *discussion board* as an asynchronous communication tool where faculty and students post messages to share and debate ideas. Positive aspects of the discussion board are that it allows fusion among the group and lets them evaluate and think about a post before responding to it. In addition, the messages are saved and can be re-visited by the class at any time. It can be beneficial if chat conversations are also saved in the event a chat message is needed at a later time.

C. Grade Book Component

The *grade book* is a critical component of DE. Since students do not interact with the instructor in person, it is important for the faculty to be transparent with student grades. The grade book feature in most LMSs and SDETs lets the instructor post scores of home assignments, lab work, exams, etc. that the student is able to see, and monitor progress in class. This tool has to be easy to use and easy to understand by the instructor and students [1].

D. Knowledge Assessment

Zaina et al. [2] say knowledge assessment is essential in DE and is possible via examinations. The LMS and SDET must offer an effective tool to the instructor for developing exams with a time window to take the exam. This tool has to offer statistics of each question that gives a snapshot of how many students answered the question correctly. It enables the instructor to have a better understanding of the areas where students are deficient, and serves as useful information for the instructor to emphasize more on deficient areas to address lacking, and make necessary changes to the course content. A controversial aspect of knowledge assessment is the ability to administer proctored examinations to online students. While some educators see this as a requirement, others do not believe it has been achieved yet in a cost-effective way.

E. Administrator Role

Most LMSs and SDETs have an administrator whose task is to publish or set up the course, register users and address technical problems with the system. The responsibilities of the administrator should be restricted to just these tasks, because it would be difficult and time consuming for the instructor and students to depend on the administrator with course related matters, which should be the responsibility of the instructor. It would also overwhelm the administrator with problem tickets and lead to inefficient usage of the LMS and SDET [2].

The next section compares functionalities of Blackboard (BB) [3] and Moodle LMS to determine which one is better.

F. Blackboard and Moodle

Unal et al [1] conducted a study on usability of BB and Moodle LMSs. 135 students participated during fall 2008 and spring 2009 semesters. Their study shows Moodle, an open source LMS, was favored by participants over commercial LMS, BB. Only the Discussion Board module of BB fared slightly better than Moodle. Apart from quantitative comparison of participants' responses, the authors analyzed components of both LMSs that students found useful or better than the other.

Blackboard Corporation, founded in 1997, developed BB. It has thousands of deployments in over 60 countries and is available in 8 major languages [1]. Martin Dougiamas founded Moodle in 2001 and has over 70,000 active deployments in 222 countries translated into 75 languages [4]. The Moodle LMS is open source software and has a flexible modular design that allows users to select and implement extensions from thousands of available options to design their customized version of Moodle [1].

Unal et al. [1] asked participants about their experiences with Moodle and BB, and provide feedback on the following components:

- Course format and layout of both LMS
- Announcements of BB and News Forum of Moodle
- Course Documents of BB and Lessons of Moodle
- Assignment Manager of BB and Assignment/Activity of Moodle
- Discussion Board of BB and Discussion Forum of Moodle
- Collaboration Tools of both LMS
- Communications of BB and Moodle
- My Grade of both LMS

Course format and layout of BB is quite different from Moodle because it has a layout for the instructor that is in standard compartmentalized format and cannot be changed. It has different sections for each tool that has options for the instructor to manage the course, users, and course contents. Moodle on the other hand takes a different approach because it offers the instructor to select from one of the three different formats: weekly, topics and social. Weekly format has activities organized week by week, topics is similar to weekly where each week is referred to a topic. Social format is used as the social forum. There are three columns in the default layout of Moodle. There is one broad column in the middle with two narrow side columns. For this experiment, weekly format was used with course material in the broad column. The study found students favored course format and layout of Moodle over BB.

Announcements of BB and *News Forum* of Moodle are the most used modules. In BB, announcements section is on the homepage where posts can be made and seen. In Moodle, News Forum is used for general announcements and is located at the top of the center section. The participants preferred using the News Forum of Moodle over the Announcements module of BB.

The LMS component that is used to deliver course content is critical for an online course. BB has *Course Documents* module to provide course material in text, image and video formats. In Moodle, the *Lessons* module is used for this purpose where a lesson has a series of interactive pages. The student must select an answer in order to proceed to the next page. Students preferred the Lessons module of Moodle over the Course Documents module of BB.

ISBN: 1-60132-454-5, CSREA Press ©

Discussion is an important component of LMS. *Discussion Board* of BB is composed of forums where students are able to select a discussion board by clicking on the name of the board to add new topics or post a reply. Moodle's Discussion Board creates a discussion thread automatically when an instructor creates the forum. Students are able to reply to the thread and other postings. Students rated the discussion board of BB and Moodle about equal.

Assignment Submission feature allows students to upload assignments to the LMS. In this area, the instructor posts assignment with submission link for students to submit assignments by the due date. The survey revealed students favored Moodle over BB for assignment submission.

Collaboration and group work is important for an online class to be effective. BB and Moodle have similar elements to allow the instructor to create groups and assign students to individual group manually so they are able to share documents and send emails to each other, groups or the entire class. A Wiki module is available with both LMSs surveyed and was used by students to work together on a document, and track changes made to the document. Moodle offers an additional feature over BB, which is the option to post profile pictures. This automatically places the student's profile picture where his/her name appears. This feature created an environment for students to get to know each other in the online environment because the profile picture linked to a profile page with description, location and email address of the student. The study found students preferred the collaboration and communications tools of Moodle over BB.

Grade book module of a LMS or SDET is important since it allows instructors to post, update or remove grades of all students in addition to the option to import or export the grade book to an external application. The student is able to view his/her own grade using this module. BB and Moodle have similar grade book functions providing categorization and statistical reports. The cited comparison found students favoring the grade book of Moodle over that of BB.

This survey clearly shows Moodle to be as effective as BB that can be used as an alternative for online courses. Moodle also offers better technology usability, leading to a greater level of pedagogical usability, and has low total cost of ownership since it is an open source LMS that does not call for licensing expenses of commercial systems. Table 1 outlines the comparison of Moodle and BB.

Table 1: Comparison of BB and Moodle LMS [1]

	BB	Moodle
Format & Layout	✘	✔
Announcement	✘	✔
Course Docs	✘	✔
Assignment Manager	✘	✔
Discussion	✔	✔
Collaboration	✘	✔
Communication	✘	✔
Gradebook	✘	✔

G. Synchronous DE: Network EducationWare (NEW)

Snow et al. [5] state engineering and technology sectors are dominated by classroom lecture presentation based instructions. This includes lectures by an instructor in the classroom using blackboard and an overhead projector for presentation slides. The smart classroom concept has become popular in recent years because it allows computer generated lecture presentation to be combined with annotations for display to the student audience either in the classroom or to a remote location via the Internet. Using this approach, pre-recorded lectures are used for asynchronous delivery and live classes are made possible for synchronous DE delivery and exchange. It is critical to deliver quality DE material and lectures via the Internet in order to achieve an effective synchronous learning experience. Good quality synchronous DE delivery and exchange can be reached if the students are able to receive spoken and graphical content without significant delay, are able to ask and respond to questions, and are able to interact with each other during the class period.

NEW is an open source SDET that was developed by computer scientists of the Center of Excellence in Command, Control, Communications, Computing and Intelligence (C4I Center) at George Mason University. It is able to support both synchronous and asynchronous modes of quality DE content delivery. NEW is beneficial to students and instructors that is not bandwidth intensive in delivering high quality presentation without video because it is able to do so over 56 kb/s connections. This is made possible because instructor audio is compressed and streamed at 20 kb/s with quality of service (QoS) to guarantee audio delivery with higher priority. Since NEW limits individual page size to 64 KB to ensure low delay, it automatically converts larger slide pages to JPEG images to adhere to this size restriction. It does not require expensive or special hardware platform and complex software, and is easy-to-use and administer. In addition to these positive traits, the application software is entirely open source that allows users to use the source code for education purposes, and freely distribute and use the code in educational and governmental settings. The server side uses MySQL database. Apache web server with PHP scripting language is used by NEW's web portal that provides access to users for DE content. NEW is able to deliver audio graphics materials composed of lecture presentation slides, annotations made on the slides, and presenter's voice to the end clients with a few seconds delay. Without video, approximately 5 MB/h of NEW recordings is required for each class time [5].

Once authenticated by the web server, students use a web portal to access live classes and pre-recorded lectures and slides with NEW. The class is presented by the instructor with a NEW client running on his/her workstation. It is easy-to-use because it is not necessary to learn several controls. Key controls to master are the recorder, whiteboard and floor control. *Recorder* is in a button layout that is used to start a recording and for playbacks. *Whiteboard* looks like a computer drawing tool on which slides are presented.

ISBN: 1-60132-454-5, CSREA Press ©

Instructor is able to make annotations on the slides that make the learning experience effective and interesting. Annotation graphics are not network capacity intensive because only a few hundred bytes are generated per object. However, the freehand tool generates significant network traffic since few hundred bytes are generated per written character. The NEW client is rate limited, which prevents annotations to interfere with audio. JPEG images, HTML, ASCII text and video can be displayed on the whiteboard [5].

NEW operates in client-server mode where students and instructors run the clients, and the server is responsible for setting up connections, user authentication and content delivery. NEW is inexpensive to set up and operate because the capital outlay is minimal as it needs a basic Linux with Java application server (which can run virtually on MS Windows or Mac OS X) with a 1.8 GHz Pentium III processor, 1 GB memory and a 100 Mb/s network connection to support 40 simultaneous end clients. It is quite simple to install and operate NEW server-side components since most of this is automated. Video function can be used by end clients with 200 kb/s or greater network connectivity. Network level multicasting cannot be used due to its limited deployment over the Internet. NEW uses the open source Transport Layer Multicaster (TLM) that allows it to use TCP to connect client and server behind Network Address Translation (NAT) gateways and firewall systems [5].

OpenSSL, an open source Secure Sockets Layer (SSL) package was added to NEW to handle authentication, and content encryption to meet the security needs of users. NEW may be adapted for use by non-English speaking users since it uses Unicode to support several languages for its display components and controls. The developers have been working to expand NEW's footprint via their on-going effort to port NEW client component suite to Linux/UNIX and Mac OS X operating systems.

H. Moodle Integrated Synchronous Teaching/Conferencing (MIST/C)

Pullen et al. [6] have gone beyond NEW to combine asynchronous and synchronous modes to achieve more effective delivery and exchange of DE content to students. They do so by taking advantage of software integration capabilities of a high quality asynchronous DE LMS, Moodle to combine with their existing SDET (NEW) as a basis for the design and implementation of a new synchronous online teaching system called MIST/C.

Like NEW, under control of a master client MIST/C offers audio, video, whiteboard interfaces, floor control, recorder and a playback unit. Similar to NEW, it is not bandwidth intensive because it is able to operate over a 56 kb/s Internet connection without video and can support video via a better network connection.

Recommendations of George Mason University's Volgenau School of Engineering DE Committee were considered on the features that are necessary in hybrid synchronous/asynchronous online teaching environment to draw upon the functional requirements of MIST/C as outlined in Table 2 [7] below:

Table 2: MIST/C functional requirements [7]

Customizations	*Accessible, expandable and improvable*
Whiteboard	*Able to accept graphic files in real time*
Authoring formats	*PowerPoint, PDF, Keynote, OpenOffice- all participants able to annotate slides during session*
Video	*Common computer formats like mpg, avi, mov and camera*
Recording of sessions	*Automatic on server including chat and be able to render as mpeg for podcasting*
Interactions	*Testing, polling and hand raising, and voice and chat*
Student Tracking	*Login status and participation statistics*
Configurable to screen	*By user and application window capture*
Breakout	*Able to partition class into separate groups*

Changes were made to NEW so that MIST/C runs not only on Windows OS platform, but also on Linux and Mac OS X platforms. *Auto reconnect* feature was added where the Master Client informs the instructor and automatically reconnects to the server during network connection failure, without disrupting face-to-face live class or the recording session. It also automatically uploads the client recording to the server at end of class if approved by the instructor. Another useful feature, *server-side recording and download*, has been made possible where class sessions are automatically recorded on the server, in addition to the client. In the event client-side recording misses a segment of the class session, server will post that missing segment from the server-side recording to Moodle for the students or download it for other use.

The MIST/C development sought to create the simplest possible user interface. Considerable changes were made to the interface in MIST/C over NEW by integrating independent window for each active component such as audio, video, whiteboard, floor control, record control, play control, and master client into a small control window on the screen with toggle buttons to manage components as needed. A second *mirrored* whiteboard window is available for students to see full-size slides on the classroom projector; this is not cluttered with components seen on the master client primary whiteboard window. This feature is a significant advancement for simulteaching, where sets of students in different locations and in the classroom with the instructor are taught simultaneously, and is not available with any other synchronous teaching system.

The MIST/C *whiteboard* is an important component that is used to display static presentation slides and dynamic annotations. NEW supported single-page PDF, JPEG and

PostScript formats for the whiteboard, but now MIST/C supports multi-page PDF and crisper PNG slides, and is able to import any application running on the client machine to the whiteboard. The *floor control* now has a button for the voting interface that can be used by the instructor to post a question, and students are able to enter their vote in real time. Breakout rooms or groups may now be formed by the instructor using the *Breakout Group Manager* feature by a button on the floor control component so that students of a group may communicate only with members of that group. The instructor is able to either join a particular group to establish two-way communication with group members or maintain supervisory or oversight role to engage in one-way communication with members of all groups [7].

Next section, reports the results of comparison made in 2010 with the commercial product, Elluminate and an open source SDET, Dimdim.

I. Elluminate vs. Dimdim

Lavolette et al. [8] review Elluminate version 9.0 and Dimdim version 4.5, and present results in this paper. It is important to note, Dimdim is an open source SDET. Elluminate was acquired by BB in July 2010 [3] and renamed to Blackboard Collaborate. The researchers collect participant data based on their experience with the interface and features of both systems. Table 3 lists the features of Elluminate and Dimdim.

Table 3: Features of Elluminate 9.0 and Dimdim 4.5 [8]

Features	Elluminate 9.0	Dimdim 4.5
Communications Tools	No	No
Participants	Unlimited	20 or less
Voice chat	6 or less	4 or less
Text chat	Yes	Yes
Video	6 or less	1
Content Tools	No	No
Guided web browsing	Yes	Yes
Interactive whiteboard	Yes	Yes
Slide presentation	Yes	Yes
Polling and quizzing	Yes	No
Multimedia presentation	Yes	No
Application sharing	Yes	No
Desktop sharing	Yes	Yes (plugin required)
Simple feedback	Yes	Yes
Logistics Tools	No	No
Breakout rooms	Yes	No
Recording and playback	Yes	Yes
Password secured	Yes	Yes
Cross platform	Yes	Yes
Plugins required	Java	Flash

The survey had 12 Elluminate participants and five Dimdim participants attend a one-hour workshop using Google applications with Elluminate and Dimdim. After the session, they were provided with a set of questions for feedback. The researchers prepared the following five questions for the participants to determine advantages and disadvantages of each system [8]:

- Would you consider using Elluminate/Dimdim in your teaching?
- How easy or difficult was Elluminate/Dimdim to use?
- What was difficult about using Elluminate/Dimdim?
- What do you like about Elluminate/Dimdim?
- Do you have any other comments about Elluminate/Dimdim?

Table 4 lists advantages and disadvantages identified by the researchers in their survey of Elluminate and Dimdim.

Table 4: Advantages and disadvantages of Elluminate and Dimdim [8]

Features	Elluminate	Dimdim
Virtual meeting room	None	None
Advantages	Meeting room remains available if presenter logs out or network connection is disrupted.	None
Disadvantages	None	Closes meeting if host disconnects or logs out.
Advantages	No audio problems encountered; has a wizard to set up audio.	None
Disadvantages	None	At times during the workshop, participants experienced audio problems; does not have audio wizard.
Whiteboard	None	None
Advantages	None	Has thumbnail of slides next to the presentation space making it easier for the presenter to navigate slides; presentation slides have good resolution; presenter's mouse pointer automatically appear as laser pointer to other participants when the cursor is in the whiteboard space.
Disadvantages	Does not have thumbnails making it difficult to navigate slides; poor resolution of images; presenter must hold down mouse button to make it appear as laser pointer to other participants in whiteboard space.	None
Document Upload	None	None
Advantages	Offers choice of resolution when uploading slides; moderators can upload presentation.	Each presentation is uploaded as a separate document.
Disadvantages	Number of simultaneous moderators to upload document is unlimited; adds uploaded slides to the continuous list making it difficult to find start of the presentation that was just uploaded.	Does not offer choice of resolution, just one set resolution; only designated presenter by the host may upload the document.
Advantages	None	Only the intended recipient sees the private chat.
Disadvantages	Private chat is shared with intended recipient and all moderators; private chat appears in the same window as public chat and difficult to close.	Private chat box blocks part of the whiteboard and cannot be removed; main text-chat window closes when the presentation is changed.
Advantages	Easy to locate and use because they are clickable buttons on the interface.	None
Disadvantages	None	Difficult to find and use because they are hidden under multiple layers of menus.

From the results of [8], it is evident that both systems have positive and negative traits and it is entirely up to the user to make the final selection. It is however clear that the participants lean more toward Dimdim since it is free because it is an open source SDET. But since Elluminate has some additional features over Dimdim and because it is a popular commercial product that has been in the market since 2001 and is now incorporated into Blackboard, it is being used by many educational institutions whose participants feel comfortable using it. Dimdim was launched in 2007 and has limited coverage.

J.   Conclusion

MIST/C and Elluminate have many identical features and fare well in the user community. MIST/C appears to be the most cost-effective, easy-to-use and simple distance education tool available in the market today because it is open source and has a second mirrored whiteboard for simulteaching that is not available with any other system. The comparisons of this chapter validate its rich features and functionalities, which was critical in selecting MIST/C for use by individuals for delivery of DE content to remote users over limited bandwidth networks.

References

[1] Z. Unal and A. Unal, "Evaluating and comparing the usability of web-based course management systems," *Journal of Information Technology Education*, vol. 10, pp. 19–38, 2011.

[2] L. A. M. Zaina, G. Bressan, R. M. Silveira, I. Stiubiener, and W. V. Ruggiero, "Analysis and comparison of distance education environments," in *International Conference on Engineering Education*, Oslo, Norway, 2001.

[3] "About Bb." [Online]. Available: http://www.blackboard.com/About-Bb/Our-Story.aspx. [Accessed: 14-Apr-2013].

[4] "Moodle statistics as of November 2011," *Moodle*. [Online]. Available: http://moodle.org/stats. [Accessed: 05-Nov-2011].

[5] C. Snow, J. M. Pullen, and P. McAndrews, "Network EducationWare: an open-source web-based system for synchronous distance education," *IEEE Transactions on Education*, vol. 48, no. 4, pp. 705–712, 2005.

[6] J. M. Pullen and N. K. Clark, "Moodle-integrated open source synchronous teaching," in *16th Annual Joint Conference on Innovation and Technology in Computer Science Education*, Darmstadt, Germany, 2011, pp. 353–353.

[7] J. M. Pullen, N. K. Clark, and P. M. McAndrews, "MIST/C: open source software for hybrid classroom and online teaching," in *Technology for Education/758: Software Engineering and Applications*, Dallas, Texas, 2011.

[8] E. Lavolette, M. Venable, E. Gose, and P. Huang, "Comparing synchronous virtual classrooms: student, instructor and course designer perspectives," *Tech Trends*, vol. 54, no. 5, pp. 54–61, 2010.

Analyzing Post-Reading Questions from the Viewpoints of Cognitive Skills

Chiharu NAKANISHI [1], Kaori ANDO[2], Hodaka NAKANISHI[3], and Rie SUZUKI[4]

1. Music Department, Kunitachi College of Music, 5-5-1, Kashiwa-cho, Tokyo, 190-8520, Japan, nakanishi.chiharu@kunitachi.ac.jp

2. Faculty of Policy Studies, Chuo University, 742-1, Higashinakano, Hachioji-shi, Tokyo, 192-0393, Japan, k-ando.03n@g.chuo-u.ac.jp

3. Technology Transfer Center, Teikyo University, 2-11-1 Kaga, Itabashi-ku, Tokyo, 173-8605, Japan, nakanishi@med.teikyo-u.ac.jp

4. Department of Informatics, Tokyo University of Information Sciences, 4-1 Onaridai, Wakaba-ku, Chiba City, Chiba-Prefecture 265-8501 Japan, rsuzuki@rsch.tuis.ac.jp

Abstract-*The present study investigates the characteristics of post-reading questions in EFL / ESL reading textbooks for lower English proficiency students. Two types of textbooks were compared using Bloom's Revised taxonomy. The first textbooks aim at enhancing learners' critical thinking skills as well as their English skills whereas the other textbooks aim at improving learners' reading skills as well as their English skills. The focus of this investigation is on whether there are any differences in the cognitive skills that learners are expected to employ while using these textbooks and if so how they differ. The results illustrate that the two types of textbooks actually show different patterns of usage in the cognitive process. The cognitive skills enhancing textbooks use a variety of cognitive processes (12 of 19 subcategories). The reading skills improving textbooks use only 6 of them.*

Keywords: cognitive processes, Bloom's revised taxonomy, lower-/higher-order thinking skills, textbooks, lower-English proficiency, post-reading questions

1. Introduction

In any subject, it is essential to build not only lower-order but also higher-order thinking skills which is a part of the 21st century skills and competencies (OECD, 2009) [1]. Asking a right question at appropriate times activates students' cognitive skills and willingness to answer. Our present research focuses on the post-reading questions of EFL / ESL textbooks for students of lower English proficiency. Most of the EFL/ ESL teachers use textbooks and post-reading questions in textbooks. Analyzing cognitive processes of questions in textbooks is a source of useful information to provide teachers, material writers and teacher trainers who want to build students' cognitive skills. If the questions in textbooks are not adequate, teachers need to prepare other questions by themselves. To promote student cognitive skills, it is necessary to build teacher's competence of making appropriate cognitive questions. It is crucial to investigate what kind of cognitive skills are expected to be used in the post-reading questions of the present textbooks.

Some Japanese researchers have studied about the reading questions of textbooks. Tanaka said that the questions in textbooks are largely divided into two categories (fact-finding and inferential questions) (2010) [2]. Tanaka & Tanaka insisted that teachers should use inferential questions more which make students think deeply and actively (2015) [3]. Fukazawa reviewed post-reading comprehension questions in senior high school English textbooks in Japan. He found that most questions require only copying out the words directly from the passage and the answers to most questions were easily found or clearly written in the texts (2008) [4]. Hirai et al. (2014) [5] conducted a research on the questions and tasks of EFL junior and senior high school textbooks with the Bloom's Revised Taxonomy (Anderson et al. 2001) [6]. They found that approximately 40 to 80 percent of questions and instructions in the textbooks were categorized as a lower-level cognitive skills such as Level 1: Remember and Level 2: Understand.

ISBN: 1-60132-454-5, CSREA Press ©

2. The Present Study

2-1. The purpose of the study

The purpose of the present study is to investigate what kind of cognitive skills are built by the post-reading questions in EFL / ESL reading textbooks for students of lower English proficiency. We compare two types of textbooks. One is textbooks which claim to target at enhancing learners' critical thinking skills as well as their language skills (CTT: Critical Thinking Textbook) and the other type is textbooks which note to aim at improving learners' English skills and their reading skills (RST: Reading Skill Textbook). Questions to be asked are:

1) What is the average length of one unit and to what degree is readability considered in terms of English native speakers?

2) What are the themes and text styles of all units?

3) What are the formats and languages of the post-reading questions?

4) What cognitive processes are imposed on the post-reading questions by the framework of Bloom's Revised taxonomy?

2-2. Method

Five textbooks were analyzed in this study. Text A, "World English I" and Text B, "21st Century Reading 1" are published by Cengage Learning Inc., in America. Text A and B are used as EFL / ESL course books which aim to build communication skills and promote critical thinking (http://cengage.jp/). The present study focuses on the reading section of these textbooks.

Text C, D, and E are published by Nan'un-do Co. Ltd. in Japan and used as EFL reading textbooks. Text C, "Reading Tasks for College Students", Text D, "Sports Paradise" and Text E, "It's time to read" are noted to aim improving reading skills in the basic level on HP of the publisher (http://www.nanun-do.co.jp/). It must be noted that Text D is an ESP textbook which is consisted of 12 sports specific articles. Unlike the CTTs, they do not aim to promote cognitive skills. Thus, it is significant to observe whether any differences can be found in cognitive processes of the questions in these textbooks.

The research procedures were conducted in following the four steps.

2-2-1. Readability

The readability for English native speakers of the five textbooks was scaled. From each textbook, two chapters (totally 400-600 words) were extracted and placed into Text Readability Consensus Calculator. Text Readability Consensus Calculator uses 7 readability formulas to calculate the average grade level and text difficulty for English native speakers (http://www.readabilityformulas.com/free-readabilityformula-tests.php).

2-2-2. Themes and text styles

The reading passages were categorized and tallied per their themes and text styles.

2-2-3. Formats of post-reading questions

The formats of post-reading questions were categorized into five types, which are True/False, multiple choice, cloze, short answer, and others. Whether questions are given in the target language (English) or the first language (Japanese) was also analyzed.

2-2-4. Cognitive processes of post-reading questions

As a framework of analyzing post-reading questions, we used the 6 cognitive process categories and 19 subcategories by a Bloom's Revised Taxonomy of Educational Objectives (Anderson et al. 2001) [6]. Hereafter the framework that we used is abbreviated as Revised Taxonomy. In Revised Taxonomy, the cognitive processes were defined as the following 6 categories: Level 1 to 6: Remember, Understand, Apply, Analyze, Evaluate, and Create. Within these 6 categories, Anderson et al. (2001) [6] selected 19 subcategories. Table 1 provides cognitive processes and subcategories.

In the former researches, teaching and learning questions and activities were frequently sorted into 6 cognitive processes using frameworks by the original Bloom's taxonomy (1956) [7] or Revised Taxonomy. In the present research, sorting was done by 19 subcategories which provide more precise and useful information of cognitive processes.

Table1 The Cognitive Process Dimension
(Adapted from Anderson, 2001, pp.67-68)

Categories & Cognitive processes	Alternative Names	
1. Remember		Lower-order thinking
1.1 *Recognizing*	Identifying	
1.2 *Recalling*	Retrieving	
2. Understand		
2.1 *Interpreting*	Clarifying, paraphrasing, representing, translating	
2.2 *Exemplifying*	Illustrating, instantiating	
2.3 *Classifying*	Categorizing, subsuming	
2.4 *Summarizing*	Abstracting, generalizing	
2.5 *Inferring*	Concluding, extrapolating, interpolating, predicting	

ISBN: 1-60132-454-5, CSREA Press ©

2.6 Comparing	Contrasting, mapping, matching	
2.7 Explaining	Constructing models	
3. Apply		
3.1 Executing	Carrying out	
3.2 Implementing	Using	
4. Analyze		
4.1 Differentiating	Discriminating, distinguishing, focusing, selecting	
4.2 Organizing	Finding coherence, integrating, outlining, parsing, structuring	
4.3 Attributing	Deconstructing	Higher-order thinking
5. Evaluate		
5.1 Checking	Coordinating, detecting, monitoring, testing	
5.2 Critiquing	Judging	
6. Create		
6.1 Generating	Hypothesizing	
6.2 Planning	Designing	
6.3 Producing	Constructing	

For example, the post-reading questions were sorted into the following subcategories.

Example 1: "What does Peter do?" (Level 1: Remember 1.1 *Recognizing*) Students are expected to recognize the passage to answer the question. It is a fact-finding about the passage.

Example 2: "What are three things the buildings in the reading passages have in common?" (Level 2: Understand 2.6 *Comparing*, Level 4: Analyze 4.1 *Differentiating*) Sudetes are asked to compare the characteristics of buildings in the passage and distinguish the information. Two subcategories are used in one question.

Example 3: "How do you think people will get energy in the future? Solar, wind, fossil fuels, or another way? Discuss with a partner." First, students are expected to infer a way to get energy in the future (Level 2: Understand 2.5 *Inferring*), then, they are expected to attribute the background (Level 4: Analyze 4.3 *Attributing*), and finally they are expected to compare their opinion with other students (Level 2: Understand 2.7 *Explaining*, 2.6 *Comparing*).

We first sorted the questions independently and then compared the results. The results were mostly identical, but when they were different, we discussed and agreed on them.

3. Results
3-1. Readability

Totally 10 sample units of reading texts were extracted from 5 textbooks and examined. Table 2 shows number of words and readability (grade level and reading level). Depending on the textbooks, the lengths of the text vary from 190 to 300 words. Readability of the two CTTs (Text A and B) range between 6 and 8 and the average grade level for them are 7 or 6 respectively, while grade levels of the three RSTs vary greatly. Text C range 3 and 7, Text D range 8 and 11, and Text E range 4 and 8.

Table 2 Text Readability

	Unit	Number of Words	Grade Level	Reading Level
Text A	2	193	6	fairly easy to read
	7	200	8	standard / average
Text B	1	284	6	fairly easy to read
	9	307	7	fairly easy to read
Text C	1	229	3	very easy to read
	21	247	7	fairly easy to read
Text D	1	266	11	difficult to read
	12	274	8	standard / average
Text E	1	217	4	very easy to read
	20	240	8	standard / average

3-2. Themes and text styles

3-2-1. Themes

All the seventy-four chapters from the five textbooks were analyzed in order to observe whether the textbooks emphasize a limited number of themes or cover a variety of areas. The Nippon Decimal Classification (NDC), which is the most commonly used library classification system in Japan, was used to categorize the topics. Only the ten major classifications, General works, Philosophy, History, Social Sciences, Natural Sciences, Technology, Industry, the Arts, Languages, and Literature, were used in this study in order to minimize confusion. Table 3 shows the results.

Table 3 Topic Classification

n(%)

	0 General works	1 Philosophy	2 History	3 Social Sciences	4 Natural Sciences	5 Technology	6 Industry	7 The Arts	8 Languages	9 Literature	Total
Text A	0(0.0%)	1(8.3%)	4(33.3%)	2(16.7%)	2(16.7%)	2(16.7%)	0(0.0%)	0(0.0%)	0(0.0%)	1(8.3%)	12(100%)
Text B	0(0.0%)	0(0.0%)	1(10.0%)	4(40.0%)	1(10.0%)	3(30.0%)	0(0.0%)	0(0.0%)	0(0.0%)	1(10.0%)	10(100%)
Text C	0(0.0%)	1(4.5%)	2(9.1%)	6(27.3%)	1(4.5%)	1(4.5%)	1(4.5%)	1(4.5%)	2(9.1%)	7(31.8%)	22(100%)
Text D	0(0.0%)	0(0.0%)	0(0.0%)	0(0.0%)	0(0.0%)	0(0.0%)	0(0.0%)	12(100%)	0(0.0%)	0(0.0%)	12(100%)
Text E	0(0.0%)	1(5.0%)	1(5.0%)	4(20.0%)	1(5.0%)	4(20.0%)	0(0.0%)	2(10.0%)	0(0.0%)	7(35.0%)	20(100%)

It can be seen that all textbooks, apart from Text D, which is a sports-featured textbook as its title "Sports Paradise" suggests, include a variety of topics with each of them covering more than half of the ten classifications. Text C, in particular, deals with nine classifications and Text E also covers seven categories. Another thing to note is that the RSTs (Text C and E) and the CTTs (Text A and B) favor different classifications. Both two RSTs deal with Literature topics most frequently (Text C: 31.8%, Text E: 35.0%), whereas the two CTTs dedicate only one chapter to the topic of Literature.

3-2-2. Text styles

We focused on the text styles of the five textbooks to observe the characteristic features. Text styles were classified into four categories, which are Expository, Narrative, Conversation, and Letter. Expository style is to present the author's affirmation showing the examples of a certain theme. Narrative style is to state the incidents of a certain characters in chronological order and describe behaviors and feelings. On the other hand, Conversation style is to have a dialogue, most commonly more than two people shows the text of colloquial words (Tanaka et al., 2015)[8].

Table 4 Text styles

n(%)

	Total #	Expository	Narrative	Conversation	Letter
Text A	12	10(83.3)	2(16.7)	0(0)	0(0)
Text B	10	10(100)	0(0)	0(0)	0(0)
Text C	22	14(63.6)	8(36.4)	0(0)	0(0)
Text D	12	12(100)	0(0)	0(0)	0(0)
Text E	20	9(45.0)	9(45.0)	1(5.0)	1(5.0)

The results show that the text style of Expository is most frequently used in five textbooks except in Text E (RST). The Expository which is to define and explain an idea is the main style in all textbooks. Especially in Text B (CTT) and D (RST), 100% of Expository text style are used thoroughly. On the other hand, Text C (RST) is consisted of Expository (64%) and Narrative (36%). Text E (RST) has the characteristic features that 45% of Expository and Narrative styles are used equally and 5% of Conversation and Letter styles are used equally.

3-3.   Formats of post-reading questions

3-3-1. Formats of post-reading questions

Post-reading questions in the five textbooks were analyzed

here in order to see what kinds of question formats are commonly used in the textbooks. 528 questions in total were categorized into five different question types, these are True/False, Multiple Choice, Closed Questions, Short Answer, and Others. Table 5 shows the results.

Table 5 Format of post-reading questions

n(%)

	T/F	Multiple Choice	Cloze	Short Answer	Others	Total
Text A	46(31.9)	6(4.2)	34(23.6)	48(33.3)	10(6.9)	144(100)
Text B	10(6.4)	38(24.4)	28(17.9)	35(22.4)	45(28.8)	156(100)
Text C	3(5.6)	15(27.8)	5(9.3)	26(48.1)	5(9.3)	54(100)
Text D	48(50.0)	0(0)	48(50.0)	0(0)	0(0)	96(100)
Text E	46(59.0)	26(33.3)	0(0.0)	0(0)	6(7.7)	78(100)

It seems that the formats of the questions in each textbook vary from text to text, with Text A, B and C using all of the five question formats, whereas Text D and E use only two or three types respectively. However, one thing which can be noticed here is that all the textbooks have True/False questions. In fact, True/False was the most frequently observed question format in this study. 153 questions out of 528 (29.0%) were True/False questions. The second most used question format was closed questions (22.1%), followed by Short Answer questions (20.6%). Another interesting result is that two out of the three RSTs, which are Text D and E, do not have Short Answer questions at all, whereas both CTTs (Text A and B) use the Short Answer format to some extent. 33.3 % of Text A questions and 22.4% of Text B questions ask students to answer in a Short Answer format.

3-3-2. Language of post-reading questions and answers

Which language, whether the first language (Japanese) or the target language (English), is used in post-reading questions was observed in this part. Here the focus of the analysis is on the RSTs (Text C, D and E) as the two CTTs (Text A and B) are written in English and all the questions are stated in English and they do not specify which language students are expected to answer in most cases.

222 questions from these RSTs were sorted into four types, J→J, J→E, E→J or E→E. J→J type question asks students to read a question in Japanese and answer the question in Japanese. J→E means that students read a question in Japanese but

answer the question in English. E→J indicates that students read a question in English and answer in Japanese. E→E means students both read and answer a question in English. Table 6 illustrates the results.

Table 6 Post-reading questions

n(%)

Question→Answer Languages			
	J→J	J→E	E→J	E→E
Text A	0(0)	0(0)	0(0)	139(100)
Text B	0(0)	0(0)	0(0)	153(100)
Text C	28(51.9)	26(48.1)	0(0)	0(0)
Text D	0(0)	96(100)	0(0)	*48(50.0)
Text E	0(0)	72(100)	0(0)	0(0)

J: Japanese   E: English

* As for Text D, half of the questions are stated in both languages

The results show that all questions in the three RSTs are written in Japanese. Text D even provides Japanese translations when the questions are written using simple English. J→E is the most frequently used type with 194 out of 222 questions being this type (87.4%). Although all the questions are asked in Japanese, students are rarely asked to also answer in Japanese. Only 28 questions out of 222 (12.6%) asked students to answer in Japanese.

3-4. Cognitive processes of Post-reading questions

The post-reading questions in the five textbooks were classified into 6 cognitive process categories and 19 subcategories by the Revised taxonomy (Table 7). Among 528 questions, 72 questions were sorted into more than two subcategories. As a result, the number of 600 questions were analyzed.

Level 1: Remember 1.1 *Recognizing* questions are used in Text A (54.6%) and B (40.7 %) in CTTs, while Text C (43.8%), D (100%), and E (95.1%) in RSTs. 1.2 *Recalling* is found in Text B (13.8%), but it is not found in RSTs.

Level 2: Understand accounts for about one fourth of the questions in CTTs. Text A has 2.5 *Inferring* questions (12.6%) and 2.7 *Explaining* questions (5.5%). Text B has 2. 5 *Inferring* questions (7.8%) and 2.7 *Explaining* questions (6.6%). Whereas in RSTs, only Text C has 2.1 *Interpreting* questions (45.3%). All questions in *Interpreting* are translating from English to Japanese. Text D and E have 0 % from Level 2.

Level 3: Apply is less than 1 % in all five textbooks.

Level 4: Analyze is found Text A (13.7%), B (12.0%), C (10.9%), D (0%) and E (4.9%). 4.3 *Attributing* questions are used in Text A (11.5%) and B (8.4%). 4.1 *Differentiating* questions are secondly most used.

Level 5: Evaluate is less than 6 % in all five textbooks. Text B has *Checking* questions (1.8%) and *Critiquing* questions (3.6%), whereas Text A has 1.6% *Critiquing* questions. No RST has Level 5 questions.

There are no Level 6: There is no Create in all 5 textbooks.

Table 7 Post-reading questions in the levels of Revised Taxonomy

n(%)

Cognitive Processes		Remember		Understand							Apply		Analyze			Evaluate		Create		
Subcategories		1.1	1.2	2.1	2.2	2.3	2.4	2.5	2.6	2.7	3.1	3.2	4.1	4.2	4.3	5.1	5.2	6.1	6.2	6.3
	total #	Recognizing	Recalling	Interpreting	Exemplifying	Classifying	Summarizing	Inferring	Comparing	Explaining	Executing	Implementing	Differentiating	Organizing	Attributing	Checking	Critiquing	Generating	Planning	Producing
Text A	183	100(54.6)	7(3.8)	0(0)	3(1.6)	0(0)	0(0)	23(12.6)	11(6.0)	10(5.5)	0(0)	1(0.5)	4(2.2)	0(0)	21(11.5)	0(0)	3(1.6)	0(0)	0(0)	0(0)
Text B	176	68(40.7)	23(13.8)	0(0)	4(2.4)	0(0)	9(5.4)	13(7.8)	18(10.8)	11(6.6)	1(0.6)	0(0)	5(3.0)	1(0.6)	14(8.4)	3(1.8)	6(3.6)	0(0)	0(0)	0(0)
Text C	64	28(43.8)	0(0)	26(40.6)	1(1.6)	0(0)	1(1.6)	0(0)	0(0)	1(1.6)	0(0)	0(0)	6(9.4)	1(0.6)	0(0)	0(0)	0(0)	0(0)	0(0)	0(0)
Text D	96	96(100)	0(0)	0(0)	0(0)	0(0)	0(0)	0(0)	0(0)	0(0)	0(0)	0(0)	0(0)	0(0)	0(0)	0(0)	0(0)	0(0)	0(0)	0(0)
Test E	81	77(95.1)	0(0)	0(0)	0(0)	0(0)	0(0)	0(0)	0(0)	0(0)	0(0)	0(0)	19(4.9)	0(0)	0(0)	0(0)	0(0)	0(0)	0(0)	0(0)

4. Conclusion

The two CTTs (Text A and B) are similar to the three RSTs (Text C, D and E) in four ways. The first similarity is text theme. It is often true that contents and topics used in lessons have a huge impact on the development of students' understanding of the world (Katayama et al., 1994) [9], therefore it is important to carefully choose which topics to include. All textbooks, apart from Text D which is an ESP textbook, cover various kinds of topics rather than focusing on limited themes. This would be valuable for non-native English students in order to broaden their knowledge and develop their understanding of the world as English lessons are often the only exposure to the world for the students with lower English proficiency.

Secondly, concerning the style of text, expository is most

ISBN: 1-60132-454-5, CSREA Press ©

frequently adopted. Pena and Gillam (1999) [10] mention it relates to the students' zone of proximal development and effective learning strategies. The authors state that the Expository types are quite effective and related to achieve students' cognitive processes. Also Expository text structure awareness is one reading comprehension strategy that should be explicitly and systematically taught (Sweet & Snow, 2003) [11].

Thirdly, all the textbooks in this study employ the True or False question format. This format requires students only to look for information in the text, which usually does not involve higher-level cognition. However, this might need to be reconsidered. Hamaker (1986) [12] suggests the importance of using higher-order thinking questions, saying that they "may have a somewhat broader general facilitative effect than factual adjunct questions." (p.237)

Fourthly, among 19 subcategories of cognitive processes, Level 1 Remember (1.1 *Recognizing*) is most frequently used in terms of finding fact from a text. Many questions rely on recognizing literal information from a text and answer in a form of True / False or Cloze. It cannot be cognitively challenging, but it can be used to check comprehension of reading. Fact-finding or *Recognizing* questions are necessary for learners as first stage of comprehending a text. To answer Recognizing questions promptly is a prerequisite to proceed to second and third stage of reading (Takahashi and Takahashi, 1987) [13]. Generally, *Recognizing* questions appear to be easier to answer than other questions such as inferential questions (Fukazawa, 2008) [4], and students of low English proficiency are more likely to answer correctly. These questions might play a role to improve their self-efficacy and motivation to learn English in university.

In contrast, the CTTs and the RSTs are different in several aspects. Firstly, the CTTs are generally easier than the RSTs in terms of their readability. The CTTs also employ fewer kinds of text style. One might think textbooks must be difficult and use many kinds of text styles in order to be cognitively challenging. However, results of the present study suggest that this might be a wrong assumption.

The analysis of cognitive processes of learning questions showed different patterns in the CTTs and the RSTs. The CTTs use a variety of cognitive processes such as *Recognizing,*

Recalling, Exemplifying, Summarizing, Inferring, Comparing, Explaining, Differentiating, Attributing, and Critiquing. 12 of 19 subcategories are used. However, these subcategories mainly belong to lower-order thinking which are Level 1: Remember and Level 2: Understand. The subcategories of Level 2: Understand are mostly used (*Exemplifying, Summarizing, Inferring, Comparing,* and *Explaining*). Although the CTTs note to promote critical thinking, the percentage of using higher-order thinking skills which are *Attributing* (Level 4), *Checking* (Level 5), and *Critiquing* (Level 5), is very low. The RSTs emphasize on *Recognizing* questions. The total number of subcategories which are used in the three textbooks is 6, which is half of the CTTS. The two CTTS use *Recognizing* questions as a first step in checking comprehension of reading, before developing into a further stage, whereas the RSTs over emphasize the stage of *Recognizing.*

Another thing to be noted is that although all the texts from the CTTs and the RSTs are between 200 and 300 words, the numbers of their questions differ greatly. The CTTs have much more post-reading questions. The numbers of questions of CTTs, are as many as 144 and 156 respectively, but those of the RSTs are about 1/3 to 2/3 (Table 5). Also, the large number of post-reading questions in the CTTs are provided in order of cognitive levels.

[Example]

Frist Step: [Level 1: Remember (*Recognizing* question)]

Second Step: [Level 2: Understand (*Inferring, Summarizing,* and *Explaining* question)]

Third Step: [Level 3: Analyze (*Attributing* question) + Level 4: Evaluate (*Checking and Critiquing* question)]

The textbooks which have many questions are prone to being avoided by English lower proficiency students, but it seems that step by step questions as the above, are necessary to build higher-level of cognitive skills.

5. Teaching Implications

RST is a type of textbook which is widely used at university in Japan, however as shown in the present research, the post-reading questions in the RSTs seem not to be adequate to build a variety of cognitive skills. Therefore, it is important

ISBN: 1-60132-454-5, CSREA Press ©

for teachers to realize that they should carefully analyze the questions in a textbook and evaluate for themselves whether or not they deem the questions to be adequate or appropriate for their students, and to not just to blindly accept and use the questions given in textbooks. The Revised Taxonomy could be a useful tool in order to accomplish this.

6. Limit

This is the first step to see whether post-reading questions found in beginners' textbooks for university students can help leaners to develop various cognitive skills. It must be noted that only five textbooks were analyzed in this research and further research must be done in order to generalize the results. Additional research also needs to be done on how L1 and L2 used in not only questions but also answers can cognitively influence students.

7. References

[1] OECD. "21st Century Skills and Competences for New Millennium Learners in OECD Countries, EDU Working paper" no. 41. 2009. Retrieved fromhttp://www.oecd.org/officialdocu-ments/publicdisplaydocumentpdf/?cote=EDU/WKP(2009)20-&doclanguage=en,

[2] Takeo Tanaka. "Yoi hatsumon, warui hatsumon: jyugyo wo kaeru hatsumonn towa" [Good questions and bad questions: what are the questions to change classrooms]. Eigo Kyoiku, 59 (1), 10-13. 2010.

[3] Takeo Tanaka & Chisato Tanaka. "Eigo Kyoshi no tameno Hatsumon Technique" [Designing of English classrooms: Reading Comprehenshion, Focusiong on the quesiotns] Tokyo: Taishukan shoten. 2009.

[4] Seiji Fukazawa. "Dokkai wo sokushin-suru hatsumon zukuri no jyuyosei – Koto gakko eigo reading kyokashochu no setsumon-bunseki wo toshite"[Significance of Designing Questions to Enhance Reading Comprehension: Through the analysis of post-reading questions in senior high school English textbooks in Japan]. Bulletin of the Graduate School of Education, Hiroshima University. Part. II. 57, 169-176. 2008.

[5] Seiko Hirai (Ed.). "A Study of language education based on the theories of bilingualism: the effectiveness of CALP-oriented teaching methodologies" Report on study 23520699 Grants-in Aid for Scientific Research C. Japan Society for the Promotion of Science(JSPS), 2014.

[6] Lorin W. Anderson and David R. Krathwohl (Eds.). "A taxonomy for learning, teaching and assessing: A revision of Bloom's Taxonomy of educational objectives, abridged edition" New York: Longman. 2001.

[7] Benjamin S. Bloom, Max D. Engelhart, Edward J. Furst, Walker H. Hill, & David R. Krathwohl "Taxonomy of educational objectives: The classification of educational goals. Handbook I: Cognitive domain" New York: David McKay Company. 1956.

[8] Takeo Tanaka, Katsumasa Shimada & Hiroyuki Kondo. "Suiron hatsumon wo tori ireta eigo reading shido"[English Reading Guidance for Incorporating Inferential Questions] Sanseido Co Ltd., 74-87, 2015

[9] Yoshio Katayama, Eiichi Endo, Akira Sasaki & Mikio Matsumura. "Shin eigo ka kyouiku no kenkyu" [New Study on English Education]. Taishukan Publishing Co., Ltd, 1994.

[10] Ronald B. Gillam, Elizabeth D. Pena & Lynda Miler. "Dynamic Assessment of Narrative and Expository Discourse", Bulletin of the Topics in Language Discourse; Research Library 33-47, Nov.,1999.

[11] Anne P. Sweet and Catherine E. Snow (Eds.). Rethinking reading comprehension. New York: Guilford. 2003

[12] Christiaan Hamaker. "The Effects of Adjunct Questions on Prose Learning"; Review of Educational Research, 56 (2), 212-242. 1986.

[13] Tsuneo Takahashi & Masao Takahashi. "Eigo reading shido no kiso" [Basics of Teaching English Reading]. Tokyo: Kenkyusha. 1987

The Use of the Blackboard as a Knowledge Discovery System

Fathi Tenzakhti
Department of Management Information Systems
Prince Sattam Bin Abdulaziz University, Al Kharj, Saudi Arabia
Tenzakhti@yahoo.com

Abstract - *This study shows how one can use the blackboard as a knowledge discovery system at a higher education institute. The objective of such system is to monitor student progress and predict their performance in the course to identify at an earlier stage the students in need of the right advising or counseling before they drop out of the course. The system also serves to improve the teaching and assessment quality and assure its alignment with the learning outcomes of the course as the Blackboard discovery system provides information about course usage and activity as well as data on course items that have been aligned to goals.*

Keywords: Educational Computing System, Blackboard, Data Discovery System, Data mining, Data analysis.

1   Introduction

The use of the existing e-learning systems and tools in education is not enough for achieving a quality education. Even with the use of very good learning management systems like Moodle and Blackboard and the use of very sophisticated e-learning tools like web publishing tools such as blogs and WordPress , conferencing tools like videos, video conferencing, and communication tools like e-mail and instant messaging, we still need an information system that provides the educator and the management with a system that provides tools for creating and sharing knowledge as well as a multidimensional analytic capabilities that is needed to do all sorts of ad hoc analysis and decision making regarding student, educator and management performance [1, 3,5,7,13]. This system should somehow relate to existing intranets and be part of the Educational Computing System (ECS) which refers to education-oriented information technology that is critical to an educational institute's operations.

1.1   The Role of Knowledge Management in Higher Education

Academic environment is a treasure of knowledge and knowledge Management (KM) in higher education are the strategic management activities that support educators in using the institute's knowledge resource to effectively teach and research. These knowledge management practices can help capture, discover, share and apply knowledge in schools through the use of information and communication technologies. Therefore KM makes available for use satisfactory communication channels for educators to debate about important school topics and problems within the academic body, the students and the administration. The feedback from such a debate could be used to develop further strategies and plans to ameliorate school policy and improve teaching effectiveness [5]. These are some of the goals of a knowledge management in higher education [5]:

- KM is a knowledge platform that provides educators with a discussion forum where they can debate ideas concerning their teaching and research work and a place to post their course materials and tools for students to learn.
- KM allows experienced educators to transfer their knowledge to new educators and foster a knowledge sharing culture in the university.
- KM allows teachers and management to use data mining techniques to discover knowledge about student performance, strengths and weaknesses as well as career guidance.

One of the problems with such management information systems is its high cost. Not all higher education institutes are capable of purchasing such a system. One option is for these institutes to use existing system that provide some of the knowledge management system capabilities. The objective of these studies is to give a brief introduction to how such use can take place in a university environment and among educators. But before we embark, let us briefly define what knowledge is and what knowledge management systems are and what knowledge discovery (kd) is.

1.2 What is Knowledge Management and what is Knowledge Discovery?

Knowledge is the information, skills, and understanding that one has gained through learning, observation or experience.

Knowledge management (KM) is described as the tools, techniques, and strategies to retain, analyze, organize, create and share this knowledge [4]. KM associates three fundamental resources of any organization namely people, processes and technologies. The KM processes include knowledge discovery, knowledge capturing, knowledge sharing, and knowledge application [5]. Knowledge Discovery (KD) is the process of developing new tacit or explicit knowledge from data and information or from the synthesis of prior knowledge.

In this short paper, we will focus on how higher education institutes with no or limited access to knowledge management systems could use the blackboard for achieving some knowledge discovery. We will not talk about the other knowledge processes, namely knowledge capture, knowledge sharing, and knowledge application but we will briefly mention how blackboard can be related to educator's intranets as part of the Educational Computing System (ECS) to support these processes.

For example in the university where I am teaching there is no knowledge management system and not even a learning collaborative system. There is only a Virtual Learning Environment (the blackboard) that is available for both faculty members and students to manage the course tools and provide collaborations between students and educators. There are also educator's intranets for internal collaboration between the educators and a university web site that provides information about the services offered by the university and access to regulations, forms, and files that the user can use online or download to his computer. The question is "how can we use this Virtual Learning Environment to be able to achieve knowledge discovery?"

The rest of the paper is organized as follows. Section 2 reviews and discusses some existing research work related to knowledge management in higher education. Section 3 describes the knowledge discovery process and how it relates to students, educators, and management. Section 4 describes how the blackboard could be used as a knowledge discovery system. Finally section 5 concludes the paper and presents future directions.

2   Related Work

Knowledge management and knowledge management systems in higher education have been widely studied in the literature [1,5,6,10,11,13,14]

In [1], the author offers a data mining model for higher education system in the university. This model uses decision trees classification algorithm to evaluate student's performance. The model extracts knowledge to predict students' performance in final examination and help in identifying at an earlier stage the students in need of a special attention before the drop out of the school. This finding allows the educator to suggest the right advising/counseling. This is an interesting study except that it requires developing the model which might be expensive and time consuming as opposed to using an existing application like the blackboard which is part of most LMSs in the Saudi Arabia Universities. Besides, the blackboard provides other components of a KM system like knowledge capture and sharing. In addition, it does not describe how this model integrates with the existing component of the ECS.

The paper in [14] discusses how to integrate e-Learning systems and Knowledge Management Systems technology to improve the capture, organization and delivery of training courses and corporate knowledge. The author proposes a model for the phases of knowledge management that includes concepts and technology from e-Learning. He then uses the model to illustrate real world scenarios that add increasing amounts of knowledge management to an e-Learning environment. This study however does not address the knowledge discovery component of a KM system and how some of it can be achieved using e-learning systems like the blackboard. As in the previous study, this paper does not describe how this model integrates with the existing component of the ECS.

3. The Knowledge Discovery Process

In knowledge discovery, one develops new tacit or explicit knowledge from data or information. This new knowledge could also be the result of synthesizing (combining) prior knowledge. The knowledge discovery will explore the opportunities for knowledge discovery in educational data. It will use the data collected from the VLE, to predict future student performance and learn the underlying structure of student knowledge from these datasets. It will also explore the nature of educational data and what factors are important in determining student knowledge.

Examples of educator-student interaction that can lead to knowledge discovery are:
- Educators should supervise student to detect student behaviors that can lead to student dropping or failing the course.
- Educators perform data mining in student test scores in order to identify students' strengths and weaknesses. He then uses this knowledge to effectively design his instruction tools.

Examples of educator-educator interaction that can lead to knowledge discovery are:
- Educators meeting for time to time (e.g in department and College Board meetings) to assess the overall performance of the students and the amendments that might need to be made to the courses and curriculum.
- Educators assessing the key performance indicators in different subjects and different programs.
- Educators working collectively in research with the opportunity to learn from each other and to help each other.

Examples of student-student interaction that can lead to knowledge discovery are:

- Students participating in discussion boards by posting their views in the discussion forms.
- Students looking at other students research projects and learning from them.
- Students looking at the answers to the assessment and training questions and learning from them.

4.   The Blackboard as a Knowledge Discovery System

The Blackboard which is a Virtual Learning Environment (VLE) allows online access to learning materials and

ISBN: 1-60132-454-5, CSREA Press ©

activities. It offers some tools that are known to be used as part of a knowledge management system like wikis, blogs, discussion boards, e-mail, SMS, Journal, etc.. [5,12] as well as tools for outcomes rubrics, course analytics, assessment, communication and collaboration through real-time web conferencing and multimedia recording. This study shows how one can use the blackboard as a knowledge discovery system at CBAK to monitor student progress and predict their performance in the course in order to identify at an earlier stage the students in need of the right advising or counseling before they drop out of the course. The system will also serve to improve the teaching and assessment quality and assure its alignment with the learning outcomes of the course. Some of the services that black board offers that relate to knowledge management are:

- Publishing the material related to a course.
- Communication between educators and students.
- Collaborating between students and educators using wikis, blogs, and discussion forms.
- Course work submission.
- Online assessments and training of students.

The benefits of the black board are as follows:

- Allows easy, anytime anywhere access to course tools including handouts, web links, assessment, training material, reading material etc..
- Allows an easy way to announce course information and deadlines to the members of a course.
- Allows the educator to monitoring and tracking student's access and progress.

We will now discuss the knowledge management tools offered by blackboard and how it can be used for knowledge discovery. We will concentrate on the use of the blackboard to allow educators to supervise students to detect student behaviors that can lead to student dropping or failing the course and to perform data mining in student test scores in order to identify students' strengths and weaknesses.

4.1 How to Discover Knowledge using the Blackboard?

To discover knowledge from the blackboard, we mine the existing data concerning student performance and access in each assessment and in the course as a whole. The objective is to identify students' strengths and weaknesses and to use this knowledge to effectively design his instruction tools. The Blackboard has assessment analysis tools. These tools can be accessed from the course grade center or from the course evaluation center. We will start by the tools we could use from the grade center.

4.1.1 Grade Center

In the left menu bar, go to the grade center rubric and choose the type of assessment you want to analyze (Assignments, Tests, or all Assessments). You will be transferred to that grade center related to the chosen assessment where the grades displayed as a table. By choosing

the one of the assessment you want to analyze, a drop down menu will appear that allow you to do the following analysis:

1. Attempt Statistics.
2. View All Attempts.
3. Item Statistics.
4. Column Statistics.
5. Grade Report.

Attempt Statistics

This option will get you to a page whose title is Test Statistics and provides with the following information about the whole test:

- Total number of attempts for this Test
- Average Attempt Score
- Number of Graded Attempts
- Number Attempts that Need Grading

This option also provides information about the individual questions:

- For each multiple choice questions, it provides the percentage of students per choice (the percentage of students who selected the first choice, the percentage of students who selected the second choice..etc.). This is important as it tells you whether the question was a good question or no. When most students have selected an incorrect choice for a given question, you should find the clue to why this happened and what could have possibly gone wrong in the lecture or tutorial. It may also be that the question needs re-wording as it was misunderstood by the majority of students.
- In the multiple answer questions, the system gives you information about the percent of correct and incorrect answer for each answer. Here again if most of the students chose a wrong answer then this might be an indicator of a mistake in delivering the knowledge related to that part of the lesson.
- In the fill in the blanks, the system gives you information about the percentage of correct and partially correct answers and for each correct answer, the attempt count as percentage of total attempts. This might be a clue to a general misunderstanding of the blank if is not the correct one.

View All Attempts

This option will provide for each student the number of attempts, the date of the attempt, whether the attempt was completed or not and if so the duration of the attempt. This could be used to determine whether the time allotted to a test is a reasonable one.

Item Analysis

This option will provide test summary that includes test discrimination and test difficulty. Test discrimination is used to test good, fair and poor question effectiveness at discriminating those who know the content from those who do not. It explains the degree to which students with high test scores scored in good, fair, and poor questions [15]. An example of an analysis is this:

9 Good Questions Discrimination > 0.3
1 Fair Questions Discrimination = 0.1 to 0.3
1 Poor Questions   Discrimination < 0.1
0 Cannot Calculate

If the discrimination value is higher than 0, the question is a good one. If the discrimination is between 0.1 and 0.3, the question is a fair question and if the discrimination is less than 0.1, it is a poor question. In addition this option provides the degree of difficulty of the questions based on student scores. If 80% of the students were able to answer the question that it is an easy question. If 30% to 80% of the students answered a question, the question is a medium question. If only 30% of the student or less answered a question, it is a hard question. An example of an analysis is this:

4 Easy Questions   Difficulty > 80%
2 Medium Questions Difficulty = 30% to 80%
5 Hard Questions.   Difficulty < 30%

In the same window detailed information about each question is given. It provides for each question the discrimination value, the difficulty value, the average score along with the standard deviation and standard error. By clicking on any question in the list, the system gives more information about the question concerning for example the number of times a particular answer was chosen etc. One can also select to view the poor questions only. This will allow you to modify these questions or understand why their discrimination value is low. The same could be done about the difficulty of the questions. You can use this information to improve questions for future test or to adjust credit on current attempts Fig 1 illustrates the result of item analysis for one of the tests I was administrating to my student in the MIS department.

Column Statistics

This option allows users to view statistics about students' performance in a test. Students who are unavailable are not included in column statistics. The information provided with this tool is described in the table 1..

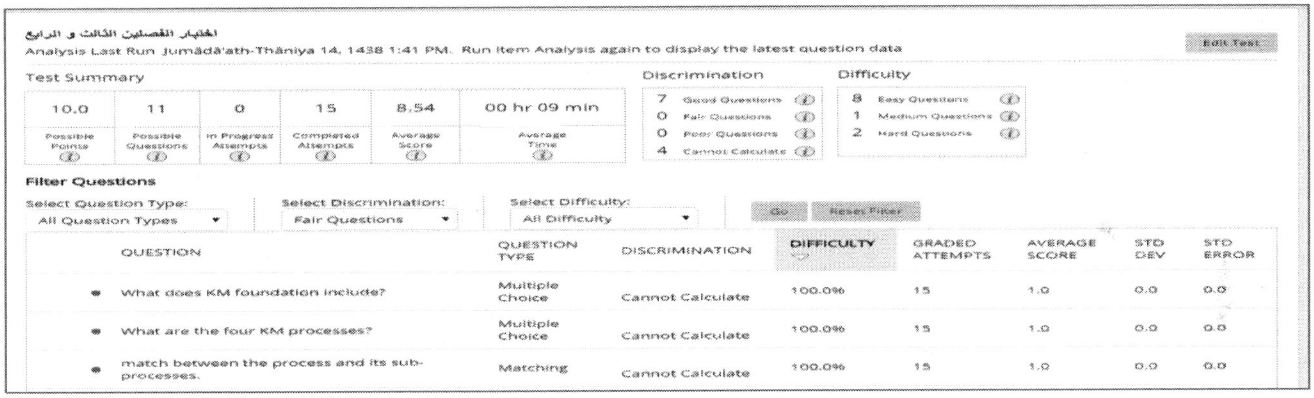

Fig 1. The result of an item analysis of one of my MIS tests

Table 1. Student's performance in a given assessment

Statistics		Status Distribution		Grade Distribution	
Count	11	Null	4	More than 100	0
Minimum Value	9.00	In Progress	0	90 - 100	9
Maximum Value	10.00	Needs Grading	0	80 - 89	0
Range	1.00	Exempt	0	70 - 79	0
Average	9.89			60 - 69	0
Median	10.00			50 - 59	0
Standard Deviation	0.31			40 - 49	0
Variance	0.10			30 - 39	0
				20 - 29	0
				10 - 19	0
				0 - 9	0
				Less than 0	0

ISBN: 1-60132-454-5, CSREA Press ©

Grade Report

In the Grade Center for any type of assessment or in the full grade center, one can click on the report menu and choose the create report option. Once the required information is filled, one can run the report. Example of the information one needs to provide includes the student names and the assessment you want to report on (one can choose multiple students and multiple assessments or all students and all assessments). The system will allow you to include some simple statistics concerning the course (Average, Mean). The result would be similar to what is illustrated in Fig 2

Print Report

Grade Center Reports can be printed using the browser's Print button. *More Help*

Quiz Report for عثمان محمد ال حسين الاسمري OTHMAN MOHAMMED ALASMARI.

GRADE INFORMATION

Item	Grade	Average	Median
First Quiz	4.50	3.10	3.00
Second Quiz	5.00	4.37	5.00
Third Quiz	5.00	4.13	5.00
Fourth Quiz	5.00	4.39	5.00
Fifth Quiz	-	3.39	3.50
Seventh Quiz	3.00	1.77	2.00
Sixth Quiz	-	3.00	3.00
Eigth Quiz	4.00	3.67	4.00
Ninth Quiz	-	3.17	3.00

Fig.2. This figure illustrates the grade report for the student Othman Mohammed Alasmari on 9 quizzes.

4.1.2 Evaluation Center

Blackboard has also an evaluation center that allows you to monitor student overall performance. The evaluation center includes the following:

1. Course Reports
2. Performance Dashboard
3. Retention Center

Course Reports

One can run several types of course reports to view information about course usage and activity. You can view summaries of course usage such as which course areas are used most frequently and course access patterns for specific students. Basically you can:

- Display a summary of all user activity inside content areas for a course. One could use this report to determine which students are active in your course and which content areas they use.

- Display overall activity within a single course, sorted by student and date. Data includes the total and average time spent per active student and the total amount and type of activity each student had in the course. Optionally, you can filter the report by one or more groups. Only students who are members of the selected groups are included in report results. Again this information could be used to increase the course activities that are most popular with the students.

- Display data on course items that have been aligned to goals. This is very important in discovering the course coverage by determining which course activities are more within the learning outcomes of the course and which learning outcomes were never covered or were covered very little by the different course activities.

- Display how a single course performs against a selected set of goals. One can use this information either to change the course activities or the course goals.

- Display the overall summary of user activity for all areas of your course, as well as activity dates, times, and days of the week. One can use this report to view student access as well as how often course activities are performed.

- Displays the number of user submissions in your course for assignments, tests, discussions, blogs, and journals within the chosen time frame. If no activity exists for an item type, no column appears. If no students submitted an assignment in the chosen time frame, no assignment column appears in the report.

- Display an individual student's activity within your course, sorted by date. Data includes the total overall time a student spent in your course. You can view detailed information about a student's activity, such as which items and content areas a student accessed and the time spent on each. Use this report to check a certain student's course activity.

- Display a summary of user activity in discussion forums in your course.

- Display a summary of user activity in groups for your course.

ISBN: 1-60132-454-5, CSREA Press ©

Retention Center

The Retention Center provides an easy way for the educator to discover which students in the course are at risk. One can also keep track of patterns over time. The patters include Missed deadlines, Grade alerts, Activity alert, Access Alert. By clicking on one of the patterns for a particular student, you get more information about student behavior in that pattern. This allows you to take the necessary actions to remedy the student risk. If you click on the name of a student at risk, it gives you more information about him. You can choose to monitor him by clicking on the monitor button or notify him by sending a message like "Your activity and performance levels have triggered an alert from this course. Please contact your instructor for details." The retention center can be customized by choosing the activities you want to monitor. These activities are included in this table.

Name of Activity	Type of Activity	Criteria of Activity
Default Activity Rule	Course Activity	Activity in the last 1 week(s) is 20% below course average
Default Course Access Rule	Course Access	Last access more than 5 day(s) ago
Default Grade Rule	Grade	External Grade is 25% below class average
Default Missed Deadline Rule	Missed Deadline	1 deadline(s) have been missed by more than 0 days

5. Conclusions

In this short study, we explained why knowledge discovery is important in higher education and tried to show how the Blackboard could be used for knowledge discovery. We showed that the objective of such use is twofold. First the knowledge discovery system of the blackboard allows monitoring student progress and predicting their performance in the course to identify at an earlier stage the students in need of the right advising or counseling before they drop out of the course. Second, the Blackboard knowledge discovery system allows educators to retrieve information about course usage and activity as well as data on course items that have been aligned to goals. This is very important as it allows educators to build better courses and better course assessments. In the future, we will show how this system can be integrated with educator intranets to visually display student performance so as to have a more sophisticated performance dashboard or even better a balanced score board to allow for visual analysis of student performance and the alignment of course activities with the course learning outcomes. We will also how this integration with educator intranets can provide the institute with a knowledge management system that provides knowledge capturing, sharing, and application processes in addition to the knowledge discovery process. This whole system will be an essential part of the Educational Computing System (ECS).

5. References

[1] B. K Baradwaj, S. Pal. Mining Educational Data to Analyze Students' Performance, (IJACSA) International Journal of Advanced Computer Science and Applications(Vol. 2, No. 6), 2011.

[2] Farzana Shafique. Knowledge Management In Higher Education : Applicability of LKMC Model in Saudi Universities, Computer Science & Information Technology (CS & IT),(pp. 175–181)., 2015.

[3] E. M Awad and H. M. Ghaziri.. Knowledge Management; Third Edition, Prentice-Hall, Inc.,2004

[4] Jehad Al-Sadi. The LMS: A Knowledge Management Base to Extract Information, Journal of Communication and Computer 9 (Pp376-383.\0, 2012.

[5] I. Becerra-Fernandez and R. Sabherwal.. Knowledge Management Systems and Processes, Second Edition, Routledge, 2015..

[6] Eric C. K. Cheng, Knowledge Management in School Education, SpringerBriefs in Education.

[7] J. Blackwell and P. Gamble.. Knowledge Management, Kogan Page Business Books, 2002.

[8] K. W. Chu, M. Wang, A. H.K. Yuen.. Implementing Knowledge Management in School Environment: Teachers' Perception, Knowledge Management & Learning: An International Journal, (Vol.3, No.2.pp.139-152)., 2011.

[9] L. Ali and al. Factors influencing beliefs for adoption of a learning analytics tool: An empirical study. Computers & Education. (Vol. 62. Pp. 130–148).,2013.

[10] L. A. Petuides and T. R. Nodine. Knowledge Management In Education: Defining The Landscape. The Institute For The Study Of Knowledge Management In Education, Ca, USA., 2003.

[11] Mamta Bhusry, Jayanti Ranjan, Implementing Knowledge Management in Higher Educational Institutions in India : A Conceptual Framework, International Journal of Computer Applications (Pp0975 – 8887, Volume 29– No.1)., 2011

[12] Raman, Murali;Ryan, Terry;Olfman.. Lorne, Designing Knowledge Management Systems for Teaching and Learning with Wiki Technology, Journal of Information Systems Education; (16, 3; pg. 311), 2005.

[13] Sangeeta Namdev Dhamdhere. Importance of Knowledge Management in the Higher Educational Institutes, Turkish Online Journal Of Distance Education-Tojde (Issn 1302-6488 Volume: 16 Number: 1 Article 11), 2015.

[14] Walid Qassim Qwaider Integrated of Knowledge Management and E- Learning System, International Journal of Hybrid Information Technology (Vol. 4 No. 4), 2011.

[15] Item Analysis at http://www. sites.psu.edu.itemanlysis/ discrimination.

Design of a Learning Management System for Small and Medium Sized Universities and Colleges

M. Beránek[1], V. Kovář[1], and V. Vacek[1]
[1]Information Technology Department, Unicorn College, Prague, Czech Republic

Abstract - *There has been recent trend towards the adoption of cloud-based Learning Management Systems (LMS). The benefits of cloud-based LMS systems include reduced costs and increased productivity resulting from sophisticated course development features, online course delivery, and anytime and anywhere availability of courses. Following the evaluation of a range of commercially available LMS platforms and their compatibility with our university information system, we have decided to develop our own LMS platform. This paper describes the design principles of the Parrot LMS platform and the main functions it supports.*

Keywords: Information System Architecture, Cloud computing, e-Learning managements system, Education system

1   Introduction

Unicorn College (UC) is leading private university based in Prague, Czech Republic that offers Information Technology (IT) and Business Administration (BA) courses both to local and international students. For more than ten years we have been developing and improving our Unicorn College Information System (UCIS) that is based on the Unicorn Universe cloud platform and supports all business processes that are required for the day-to-day running of the college [1, 2]. The Unicorn Universe platform is a tool that supports the construction of applications from reusable components. All student related information, including student results, teaching materials, research projects and international internships is available online. Our students can access learning materials online, view their results, communicate with their classmates and lecturers, submit their assignments, and perform various other activities using the UCIS on a 24/7 basis. As the new generation of Internet savvy students enters the higher education system, they often find traditional methods of delivery of courses using lectures with a heavy assignment load difficult to adjust to. We have analyzed changes in the pattern of social behavior of our students over the last decade and our results indicate that while the students are spending increasing amounts of time online, they are devoting less time to university related activities [3, 4]. It can be also argued that as more student activities take place online, university education must follow this trend to remain attractive and relevant.

Using the UCIS as a platform for our courses we have been experimenting with various types of learning tools, including Interactive Textbooks, Podcasts, Nearpod, etc. for a number of years [3]. While our experience with using interactive learning platforms is still relatively short, it is evident that interactive classroom environment can make the learning experience more rewarding for the students and at the same time lead to improved learning outcomes. Our results indicate that the effectiveness of using an interactive learning platform varies depending on the type of course and on the attendance pattern (i.e. full-time vs. part-time) [5, 6].

We have been using various multimedia learning tools as standalone components; our plan is to integrate the LMS into most of our courses and at the same time to evaluate the effectiveness of interactive learning processes. We have been looking for a suitable LMS that is consistent with our strategy and objectives, and that adds value to our existing UCIS. We have evaluated several LMS products, including TalentLMS, WizIQ LMS, Adobe Captive Prime, Training-Online.eu, Blackboard, Moodle, and Haiku Learning [7, 8 and 9], but we could not find any system that matches our requirements, and consequently, we have decided to develop our own platform for creating and delivering courses for our students and external collaborators.

Our LMS platform called Parrot is designed to have enhanced security features and to be fully integrated with the UCIS system. As a cloud-based LMS solution, the advantages of the Parrot system include low start-up costs, accessibility, fast deployment, cost predictability, easy maintenance, scalability and customizability. The Parrot LMS will be initially aimed at small and medium sized universities and training organizations. New versions of the system will be designed to support a range of popular mobile devices, integrating the features of educational and training systems, and supporting the requirements of universities and other types of organizations involved courses delivery. In this paper we describe the Parrot LMS platform in sections 2, and give our conclusions and plans for future development of our LMS platform in section 3.

2   Parrot LMS Platform

Parrot LMS is a Course as a Service platform – a special type of a PaaS (Platform as a Service) for developing and delivery courses. The main design goal of the Parrot LMS is to create a cloud-based educational system that supports the development of a variety of courses that can be accessed by students and external participants. We have defined the following key requirements for the Parrot LMS platform.

1. Individual courses determine the structure of the learning blocks, topics and lessons. Lessons consist of explanations and prepared tests.

2. Students' progress through individual lessons, answering questions and passing tests at the end of the lesson is managed by the system. Failure of the test indicates that the students do not fully understand the topic and results in repeating the study block or course.

3. Prior to taking the course, students may need to complete an entrance test.

4. During the course students may need to pass checkpoints.

5. At the end of the course students complete the final examination.

2.1 Parrot Application Structure

The Parrot platform is composed of two separate sub-applications: Parrot Business Environment Management (BEM) and Parrot Course (Figure 1). The Parrot BEM sub-application supports the central register of students, teachers, and other stakeholders and includes the accounting module; this sub-application will be implemented during the second phase of the Parrot platform development. Currently, we are focusing on the Parrot Course sub-application.

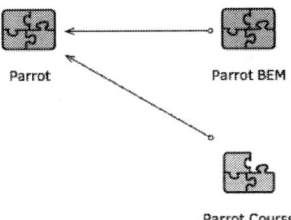

Figure 1: The structure of the Parrot platform

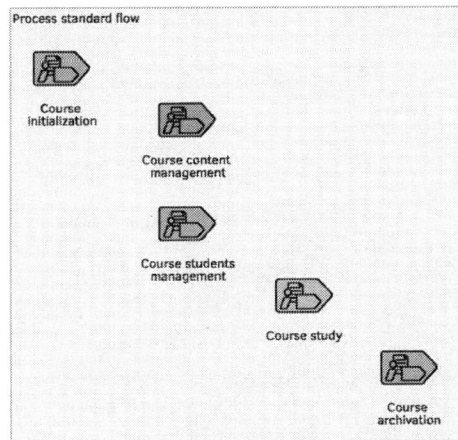

Figure 2: Process decomposition of the Parrot Course sub-application

The sub-application Parrot Course is used to implement individual courses and allows teachers and course authors to create courses, and students to study the courses.

Figure 2 illustrates process decomposition of the Parrot course sub-application depicting the standard process flow.

Course initialization process creates a new instance of the course that is prepared for content creation, but is not yet available to students.

Course content management process supports the creation and maintenance of course content (for example, by adding lessons, questions, tests, etc.).

Course participant management process performs student enrollment, withdrawal, suspension, etc.

Course study process allows enrolled students to browse through the course structure and content and to perform various course activities (i.e. lessons, exercises, tests, etc.), manage their profile and track their progress.

Course archiving process terminates the course, archiving and deleting the course instance.

2.2 Parrot LMS Terminology

Table 1 defines the Parrot LMS terminology used in this paper.

Table 1: List of basic Parrot terms and definitions

Term/ Definition	Description
Course	Course is a comprehensive unit of teaching (e.g. English 1st Year, Basic Physics for IT, etc.).
Block	Courses consist of Blocks; courses have between 1 and 9 blocks. Blocks are ordered units of teaching within the course.
Topic	Blocks consist of between 1 and 9 topics. Topics are ordered units of teaching within the block.
Lesson	Topics consist of between 1 and 9 lessons. Lessons are ordered units of teaching within the topic. Lessons include Questions.
Explanation	Teaching material for a lesson.
Question	Questions are clearly stated so that the corresponding answers can be automatically evaluated for correctness. Questions are of various predefined types.
Tutorial	Incorrectly answered questions from various activities are used to randomly generate Tutorials. Tutorials also contain about 30% of correctly answered questions.
Test	Tests consists from randomly generated questions from a particular component of the course. Test is set for the first or final lesson.

Checkpoint	Checkpoint is a special test that is set for each block. It generates questions from all lessons in the course up to the last lesson of the block, i.e. from the beginning to the end of the selected block. The last checkpoint is naturally the final test of the course.
Entrance Test	Entrance test is a special test that is set at the very beginning of the course (before attempting the first lesson) to assess the level of knowledge and skills of the student. Entrance test contains questions from the entire course (i.e. from the first to the last lesson of the course). The results of the entrance test are recorded and can be compared with the current results at various checkpoints or with the final test.
Prerequisite Test	Prerequisite Test assesses the minimal knowledge required for studying the course. Students that do not pass this test are very unlikely complete the course successfully. The test is generated from a special set of questions that are not covered in the course.
Student	A student or participant studying the course.
Educational activity	Educational activity is one of the following activities: Lesson, Tutorial and Test activity.

2.3 Business roles and Processes

There are five principal roles defined in the Parrot LMS platform. The *SysOwner* role allow users to create and initialize new instances of courses, and to delete existing course instances. The *Authorities* role is assigned to course owners. The *Executives-content* role allows users to manage (i.e. create, update, delete) course content. Courses can be managed using bulk administration (i.e. exporting or importing the entire course) or by administering individual parts of the course (editing lessons and questions). The *Executives-student* role allows users to assign students to a course. The *Student* role allows users to study the course, browse and view the course content, perform tests, carry out other activities such as manage their profile and track their progress.

2.4 Business Use Cases

We have identified set of business use cases (BUCs) within the processes of the Parrot Course sub-application. A sub-set of business use cases related to course content management process and to students is shown in Figure 3.

Identified BUCs allows course authors to import / export courses, define the course structure and to perform management of lessons, tests and questions. Test BUC involves configuration of tests (i.e. define the rules for question selection including number of question, range of topics, time limits, etc.). Students access courses through Course Portals; the Study Lessons BUC guides the students through the lessons, tests, exercises and checkpoints. A course or lesson

can be rated by the students (Rate course and Rate lesson BUCs).

The final version of the Parrot Course sub-application will provide additional BUCs for course initialization, adding, removing and suspending students, and course activation.

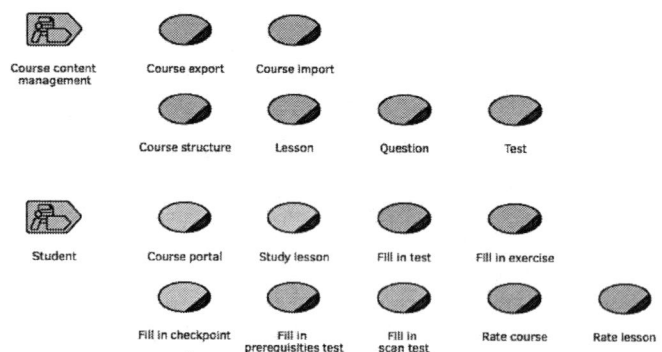

Figure 3: A sub-set of business use cases of the Parrot Course sub-application

2.5 Technical Consideration

We chose Unicorn Application Framework (UAF) as the platform for the development of the Parrot LMS. Unicorn has recently released the UAF - a cloud-based, mobile-first IoT ready architecture that incorporates standard infrastructure services and allows application developers to focus on use cases that support business functionality [10]. UAF provides the environment for the implementation and deployment of uuApp (Unicorn Universe Application) – a component that implements a cohesive set of application functions designed to solve a specific user requirement.

The Parrot platform will be implemented as a uuApp. Based on the uuApp concept, each sub-application called uuSubApp will have its own application server (uuAppServer) and structured data store (uuAppObjectStore). The Parrot BEM sub-application is planned to be a single-instance application, so that one instance of the sub-application will be shared within the platform. The Parrot Course sub-application is planned to be a multi-instance application with each course implemented as a sub-application instance, using a multi-tenant architecture and micro-services.

3 Conclusions

Following the evaluation of a range of commercially available LMS platforms and their compatibility with Unicorn College Information System, we have decided to develop our own LMS platform. This paper describes the design of the Parrot LMS platform and the main functions it supports.

The expected benefits of the Parrot platform include reduced costs and increased productivity resulting from online course delivery for students and employees, anytime and anywhere availability of courses (ability to study the courses from the comfort of your home, or on your mobile device), and ability to replay any part of the course multiple times. Courses can be created on any topic delivering professionally developed and enjoyable content. Another important benefit of the Parrot platform will be its close integration with the Unicorn College Information System.

Testing the various functions of the Parrot LMS platform within our university environment with the active participation of students and lecturers will undoubtedly accelerate the development of the platform, and give us confidence that the anticipated benefits of the cloud-based LMS solutions will be attained. We are currently working on detailed technical specification of the Parrot LMS platform and the first development phase which covers the Parrot Course sub-application.

4   References

[1]   Unicorn. (2017) Unicorn Universe Operating System. [Online] Available: https://unicornuniverse.eu/en/uuos.html

[2]   Unicorn. (2017) Unicorn Universe Process. [Online] Available: https://unicornuniverse.eu/en/uup.html

[3]   Beránek M., "Prospects of education process virtualization at an IT university", Dissertation thesis, University of Hradec Kralove, 2011.

[4]   Beránek M., Bory P., Vacek V. "Platform for Supporting Student Learning at Unicorn College," *International Journal of Education and Learning Systems*, 2016, vol. 1, p. 61-67.

[5]   Beránek M., Feuerlicht G., Kovář V., Petkovová L., Vacek V., "Evaluating the Impact of an Interactive Classroom Application on Student Learning Outcomes," In *Proceedings of the 15th International Conference on e-Learning, e-Business, Enterprise Information Systems, and e-Government (EEE'16)*, Las Vegas, 2016, p. 35-40.

[6]   Beránek M., Bory P., Kovář V., Vacek V., "Methods used for Effectivity Improvement of Learning at Unicorn College," *International Journal of Education and information technology*, 2016, vol. 10, p. 168-17.

[7]   Pappas Ch. (2015) Top 10 Cloud Based Learning Management Systems for Corporate Training. [Online]. Available: https://elearningindustry.com/top-10-cloud-based-learning-management-systems-for-corporate-training

[8]   Bora U. J., Ahmed M., "E-Learning using Cloud Computing," *International Journal of Science and Modern Engineering*, 2013, Vol. 1, Issue 2.

[9]   Riahi G., "E-learning Systems based on Cloud Computing: A Review", *Procedia Computer Science*, 2015, vol. 62, p. 352-359.

[10]   Unicorn. (2017) Unicorn Application Framework Documentation. [Online]. Available: https://uuos9.plus4u.net/uu-uu5doc/84723967990073193/public/

ISBN: 1-60132-454-5, CSREA Press ©

THE CYBERSECURITY ENHANCED LEARNING MODEL

(ELM)

Dr. Loyce Best Pailen, CISSP
Collegiate Professor
Director, Center for Security Studies
University of Maryland University College
240-684-2766
loyce.pailen@umuc.edu

ABSTRACT

In order to share a cybersecurity curriculum model for today's public- and private-sector managers, this paper emphasizes two very important subjects for ensuring continuous improvement and innovation in teaching. First, the author offers foundational background about the increasingly important field of cybersecurity. This subject area is constantly changing as a result of new cyber threats to the global public and private sectors. Because new threats appear daily, higher education programs and courses in this discipline are difficult to keep current and need to be continually updated in order to be relevant to technologists, policy-makers, managers and strategists. Second, with this basic knowledge about the cybersecurity field, a competency-based model of curriculum development is then discussed to provide the reader with a framework for designing and redesigning curriculum in this shifting cybersecurity environment.

Categories and Subject Descriptors

Cybersecurity professionals, IT and Cybersecurity Hiring Managers, Instructional Designers, graduate school-level Program Managers and Directors, Cyber Subject Matter Experts

General Terms

Management, Measurement, Documentation, Performance, Design, Experimentation, Security, Human Factors, Cybersecurity, Curriculum Development

Keywords

Cybersecurity curriculum, enhanced learning model, competency-based model, multi-disciplinary curriculum approaches, Open University

1. INTRODUCTION

UMUC is working on a comprehensive program review/revision project for its transformation to competency-based learning models. UMUC continues to invest in the capacity to have the best and most compelling programs in the world. Most recently, they started the curriculum development conversation with a clean slate, asking the question: "What should students know and be able to do in their area of expertise when they graduate from the best program in the world?" This freed the University to think outside of the boundaries of what they currently do, and literally "whiteboard" the best cybersecurity and information assurance programs in the world. The University looked to the professional organizations and/or accrediting bodies for expert input into their programs and received overwhelming guidance about what students should know and be able to do upon graduation. As well, the University scanned the environments of a few aspirant schools to see what they offered. Most importantly, using its cadre of public- and private- sector cybersecurity scholar practitioners, UMUC identified the student competencies that are critically important. This paper reviews what the University has done to assemble the fundamental list of all competencies, learning demonstrations, assessments and the like, thinking about the cybersecurity professions of today and tomorrow (i.e., what would students need to know and be able to do five years from now in various cyber roles)[4].

Summarizing why the University embarked on this mission, Kraus states, *"Adult learners have a 'career problem,' and they are looking for an educational institution partner to help them solve that problem. They want a better job, a different career, to achieve something. Their aspiration drives them to seek education that empowers them to achieve that aspiration - and the institution that does that better than anyone else will get their enrollment -- beyond what is said in marketing ads.*" [7]

To lay the foundation for this paper on curriculum redesign, the author begins by putting forth an understanding of the need for up-to-date and relevant courses in cybersecurity for the adult professional. The need is for not only those in the information technology and digital forensics arenas, but those in traditional, interdependent fields such as human resources, finance and accounting, law, public policy, and supply chain management.

2. MULTI-DISCIPLINARY APPROACH

2.1 Traditional Cross-Disciplines

Today, the requirement to understand and apply the concepts of cybersecurity such as technology, risk, policy, law, privacy, regulation and compliance, in one's managerial career has grown far beyond the needs and perceptions from only a few years ago. Why? Because on a daily basis, the news reports are strewn with stories about security breaches, privacy issues, hackers, insider threats, intellectual property concerns, hacktivism, anonymity, social media, ransomware and cyber warfare/threats.

College programs, training and development boot camps, and seminars exist but mainly teach students about information technology systems associated with network and applications software security, and digital forensics tools and technologies. Most university and training programs touch on the managerial, regulatory and policy arenas. The operative words though are "touch on" as they do so without providing the depth — neither needed for today's professionals, nor for maintaining the attention of the purely technical audience looking for career advancement along with the need to provide managerial and policy support for vulnerable organizations[2].

In addition, academic courses of studies versus training is significant because employers are looking for graduates who, in the context of their cybersecurity specialties, can do all of the following foundational skills. With much consideration, UMUC built the enhanced learning model based on these skills.[8]

- ✓ Think critically, creatively and strategically
- ✓ Communicate effectively through writing and speaking
- ✓ Synthesize information
- ✓ Analyze data, problems, information and issues
- ✓ Make sound decisions
- ✓ Lead AND follow

Research shows that the issues associated with managing in a world where cybersecurity matters reach into many disciplines. There is a lack of adequate training, professional development, and graduate level programs that meet the needs. This is true for non-technical managers in the public and private sectors, as well as technical managers in upper level, decision-making and strategy development positions.[6]

2.2 Critical Infrastructure Sector Workforce Needs

As important, cybersecurity management and policy programs geared toward the advanced professional who may work somewhere in the list of Department of Homeland Security (DHS) 16 critical infrastructure areas are desperately needed. These industry-specific managers must be prepared to address current and future cybersecurity issues and threats "from their perspectives." Supporting this need is the latest 2015 (ISC)^2 Global Information Security Workforce Study — a profile of over 14K respondents and the 2013 (ISC)^2 Global Information Security Workforce Study — a profile of over 12K -- who said that "a broad understanding of the security field" was the #2 or #1 factor, respectively, in contributing to career success.

An associated concern is the significant growth in data breaches within all industries requiring the attention of every manager in the financial, electronic medical records, and mobile technology fields — fields that the U.S. Department of Labor, Bureau of Labor Statistics have predicted to have unprecedented workforce growth.

3. CURRICULUM DEVELOPMENT

3.1 Cybersecurity Curriculum

Therefore, given projected traditional and future workforce demands, teaching courses that require rapidly changing content in the 21st century is a challenging task for any institution. Most progressive institutions update their course content at least annually for traditional disciplines, which is usually sufficient. What about those disciplines that are dynamic with change due to the introduction of advanced technologies, new public and private organizational tensions, new local, national and international threats, and the ever-changing nature of global enterprises and politics? Cybersecurity is greatly affected by these pressures, which require nearly constant

ISBN: 1-60132-454-5, CSREA Press ©

attention to keep courseware current, relevant, and useful to IT and non-IT cybersecurity professionals.

3.2 Overall Redesign Approach

In order to offer the highest quality career-relevant programs to adult learners, UMUC's Graduate School embarked on a total redesign of their programs, the success of which can be measured by the academic and professional accomplishments of its graduates. An overarching goal was to be the leading provider of high-quality workforce-relevant education to busy professionals.

Rejecting the traditional way of developing courses with a textbook, standard syllabus, research papers and tests, the course redesign mandated an approach that would make students, upon graduation, capable of "doing" the work using theoretical and practical foundations. High-functioning graduates would result —ready to immediately contribute to his or her employer's business goals and to society.

3.3 Competency-Based Approaches

3.3.1 American Council on Education, in its September 2014 publication entitled, "Clarifying Competency-Based Education Terms," defined CBE as:

"Competency based education (CBE) is an alternative to the credit hour-based system of credentialing. Student progress is based on demonstration of proficiency and/or mastery as measured through assessments and/or through application of credit for prior learning. In competency based education programs, time is the variable and student competency mastery is the focus, rather than a fixed-time model where students achieve varying results. In competency-based education, as distinct from competency-based learning, the focus is on academic programs, practices, and policies."[12]

3.3.2 Learning science has evolved rapidly over the past 20 years and the University has garnered a great deal about how to create experiences that help students learn best. The University used that research to put together the best student experience possible. UMUC did not need to reinvent the wheel, but brought together all of the best practices. This student learning experience is unique to UMUC and unmatched when looked at in its entirety, and that will differentiate UMUC students from competitors[3].

3.3.3 Many universities are looking at ways to modify curricula and academic models to ensure they are providing an education that enables students to be career-ready. Noted researcher, Dr. Tony Carnevale, Director of the Center on Education and the Workforce at Georgetown University, argues that higher education has to meet the needs of students who want to be career-ready. He has done considerable research on what training and education the workforce must have to receive the necessary skills to be successful in the labor market[3].

3.4 ELM Development

Enhancing the Learning Model (ELM) is the project through which UMUC reviews and revises its undergraduate and graduate programs. More specifically, the ELM model includes the development of learning goals that depict what students should be able to do and breaks them down into competencies, or discrete skills students will need to demonstrate mastery of the learning goals. In order to gain the competencies, learning demonstrations, authentic assessments and rubrics are used. (See Figure 3.1) The foundational thinking for learning goals and competencies is this: they are measurable, observable and define the behavior that, again, would signal mastery of a student's competency. It is also important to point out at this time that assessments are not tests in the traditional sense. They are planned, choreographed activities used by student to learn, demonstrate, and master. Modularized learning demonstrations allow for shifting and replacements as current events dictate.

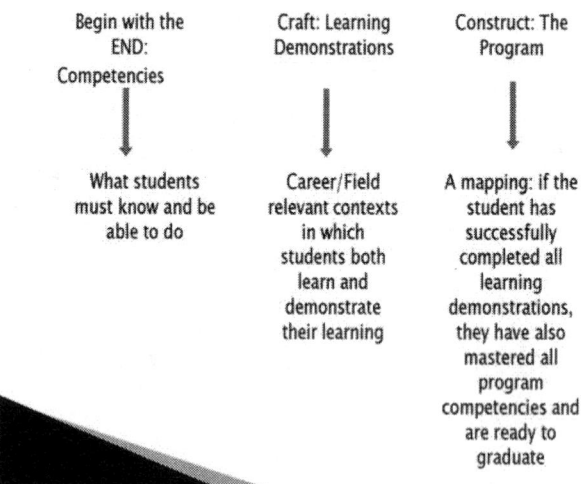

Figure 3.1 – ELM Process

3.4.1 Graduate School Cybersecurity ELM process

The "competency-based" approach was practical and pragmatic for the entire graduate school. Program Directors developed an approach to programs that focused on the capabilities of students in competency/ability and disposition in their profession. Career relevance and career connectedness were critical considerations in every step of the design process.

As noted in Figure 3.2, the University enlisted an ecosystem of experts to validate the new curriculum. Concepts from the NIST National Initiative for Cybersecurity Education (NICE) framework, ISACA, (ISC)² and their associated components were incorporated in the planning and development. Advisory councils and focus groups consisting of industry, government and military subject matter experts provided input to support the design, as well.

Employers and students were, and continue to be part of the "ecosystem," making sure programs are up-to-date and students are prepared to be successful in their profession. Programs are thoughtfully built on an appropriately sequenced series of profession-relevant learning demonstrations that help students build increasing levels of ability. Programs are built on "doing."

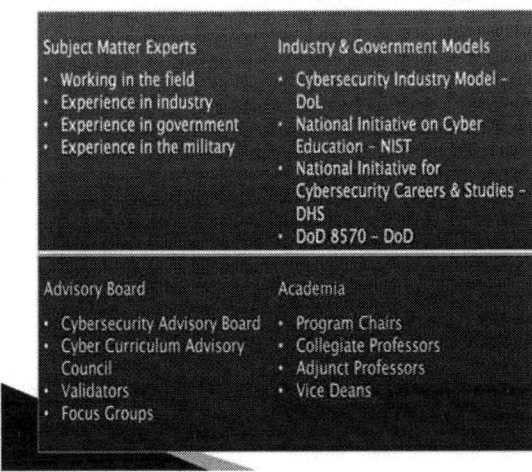

Figure 3.2. How We Validate the Program

Again, while this competency-based approach to curriculum development applied to the entire graduate school, it was especially relevant to the area of cybersecurity. Employers and employees who have policy-related skills are relevant today and tomorrow. Such graduates must be prepared to meet daily challenges immediately rather than go through an extended apprenticeship. The outcome of ELM has been curriculum and learning experiences that employers value because the programs are up-to-date and focus on abilities that do not become obsolete.

Throughout the graduate program, the students develop a portfolio of learning opportunities and paths that facilitate their entry into and/or update their skillset in the career they desire. For example, a learning opportunity may include an employer's requirement to develop an Internet Acceptable Use Policy. In the redesigned competency-based programs, graduates would have created one in their coursework and studies; so in the real world they have already mastered the competency, thus reducing learning curves "on the job." The model gives students the opportunity to get personalized feedback from the professors for every graded deliverable until they master the project. This is powerful and different from traditional grading that only allowed students a single assignment submission and a single grade.

Figure 3.3 is an overall depiction of the learning cycles.

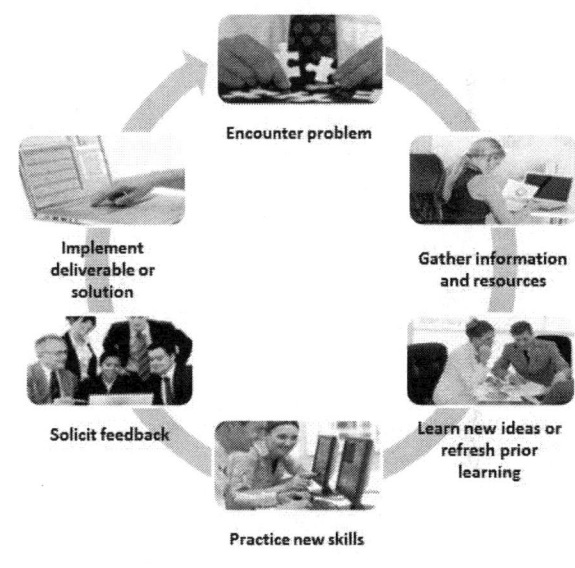

Figure 3.3 – ELM Learning Cycle

Source: ELM Workstreams Kickoff Design Criteria by Workstream

4. RESULTS

4.1 Results Planning

Early in the project, the University delineated clear definitions of what would be considered "done," or a completed effort. It was certain that with a competency-based learning model in place that focused on student learning achievement, leveraging learning science, and aligning with career/employer/professional needs, success could be attained.

ISBN: 1-60132-454-5, CSREA Press ©

Concerning supporting structures, the University would also have identified and implemented a new internal community with the appropriate resources, processes, policies, technology, culture, and communication mechanisms to deliver the desired student experience and support enhanced academic programs.

An example of an important supporting structure would be one that provides the means for selecting the appropriate instructors for this model and providing faculty with tools for teaching in a rapidly changing subject area and allocating ample time for professional development and curriculum guidance.

On the topic of the technology to support the desired student and faculty experiences in the new learning model, users would be fully trained and management of the model would be fully operationalized. Finally, feedback and analytics on the new learning model would be gathered and fed into a review process focused on continuous improvement.

4.2　Actual Results

Feedback from one semester of ELM courses exposed the following strengths, recommended improvements, features that worked and those that did not.

The new learning model requires repeated faculty-student interaction in a new way that allows both parties to focus on a task with frequent opportunities for feedback. Interaction and feedback with faculty was a very strong feature. With the repetitive feedback, the need for flexibility regarding due dates was a welcomed benefit for adult working students with "life issues" that influence their schedules. Parents, traveling professionals and active-duty military especially welcomed this flexibility.

Regarding the flow of the courses and the assignments' applicability to the program, students felt better connected to the real-life examples (not "busy-work") that they would likely encounter in the workplace.

In summary, the items in the new ELM designed courses that worked well were:

- Original design of the classroom – ease of navigation

- Teacher experience and interaction

- Course content relative to real-world examples

- Flexibility in due dates and ability to resubmit assignments for improvement for particularly motivated students

While the consensus about the course redesign was very positive, students and faculty also proffered recommended improvements. As the redesign effort is an ongoing, iterative process, the program administrators welcomed these recommendations:

Despite the fact that the layout of the class was good, students felt a bit overwhelmed with the number of steps in each of the graded projects. These required a significant level of effort to complete in the allotted period. While some students welcomed the aforementioned flexibility, others longed for deadlines, more rubrics and structured grades.

In addition, faculty feedback was well received by students but the timeliness of the feedback was reported as sometimes delayed. Faculty appreciated the opportunity to provide this feedback, but they initially felt overwhelmed with the number of feedback opportunities, (i.e. possibly, over the course of 15 project steps, **X** 4 projects **X** 25 students over the term). A missing link in the ELM model is the introduction of peer interaction and group projects. With students working on projects at their individual pace, peer interaction becomes difficult.

In summary, the items identified with the ELM project that did not work as planned were:

- Rubrics and the new grading model
- Project step length and timeframe
- Lack of deadlines/penalties
- Group projects and peer discussions
- Faculty workload

Therefore, with this project in motion, one can see that with motivated, active learners, you have a strong value proposition: a highly personalized, current, dynamic and relevant program. Upon completion, cybersecurity students who have aspired to different careers or higher levels in their careers can lay the foundation for success.

5.　CONCLUSION AND FUTURE RESEARCH

Cybersecurity concerns affect today's professionals in all disciplines and industries– personally and in the workplace. Failure to upgrade and maintain their knowledge and credentials will be detrimental to their careers, corporate interests, and society as a whole. Learning institutions are here to ensure success in this arena with focused, relevant, and up-to-date teaching and programs. The ELM project is a key step in support of these efforts.

Finally, the ELM project is part of a larger strategic goal for the University in its higher-level efforts to empower a cybersecurity workforce and to remove barriers to entry into a multitude of fields. The threefold strategic institutional approach includes: redesign of courses, open access, and linking learning with workforce needs that are beyond the technical environment.

ISBN: 1-60132-454-5, CSREA Press ©

This paper focuses on only one of the strategic approaches UMUC deploys to support the development of cybersecurity professionals for the workforce. However, the threefold approach to providing students with accessible, accelerated, and cyber-aligned curriculum include:

(1) As *the* Open University of the State of Maryland, the University focuses on the educational needs of nontraditional students which open the doors for diversity in academic and career backgrounds, scalability with customization, and alignment and acceleration of degree completion;

(2) Concern regarding the cybersecurity impact on traditional professions, the University works toward a more multi-disciplinary approach to including cyber in traditional curricula.

(3) As focused on in this paper, the University implemented a new style of cybersecurity education, offering a novel approach in grooming IT and non-IT executives as cybersecurity organizational leaders. [5]

Future research includes data analytics measuring the correlation between the threefold strategic efforts and the new curriculum development approach with ELM.

As previously stated, the overarching success of the efforts will be measured by the learning and professional accomplishments of the graduates and the University's efforts to be the leading provider of high-quality workforce-relevant cyber professionals.

6. ACKNOWLEDGMENTS

Thanks to the The Graduate School (TGS) at UMUC ELM project team under the leadership of Drs. Marie Cini and Aric Kraus for allowing the use of ELM documents and templates previously developed by the ELM Decision and Functional teams.

7. REFERENCES

[1] Kraus, A. (11/17/2015) "ELM Initiate Charter" University of Maryland University College. Engage Site.

[2] Pailen, L.B. and deGrazia, B. (2015). *A Multi-Discipline Cybersecurity Curriculum Model for Today's Public and Private Sector Managers*. AOM.

Academy-assigned submission number (17217). Presentation at the AOM conference 2015

[3] Kraus, A. (2014). ELM Workstream Kickoff Design Criteria by Workstream - Kimberly Underwood and Kathryn Klose Workstream Leads.

[4] Pailen, L.B. (March 15, 2015) . ELM Presentation, NIST. FISSEA Conference Presentation. *Conflict Changing Curriculum. New techniques for developing and conducting effective, meaningful training and education.*

[5] Pailen, L.B., deGrazia, B., and von Lehmen, G. 2016. NICE conference presentation. *Triple Threat Approach to Cybersecurity Learning and Workforce Development*

[6] McGettrick, A., *Toward Effective Cybersecurity Education*, University of Strathclyde. Co-published by the IEEE Computer and Reliability Societies. Education Journal. Nov/Dec 2013.

[7] Kraus, A. (2016). *Why are we doing Elm*? UMUC Engage Page

[8] Seferian, A. and Baltimore, D. 2014. Business and Management K12 Presentation. University of Maryland University College.

[9] Suby, M., 2013. *The 2013 (ISC)² Global Information Security Workforce Study*. Frost and Sullivan

[10] Suby, M. and Dickson, F., 2015. *The 2015 (ISC)² Global Information Security Workforce Study*. Frost and Sullivan

[11] Carnevale, A.P., Jayasundera, T., Gulish, A. *America's Divided Recovery College Haves and Have-Nots*, 2016 Georgetown University, Center on Education and the Workforce.

[12] Everhart, D., Sandeen, C., Seymour, D., Yoshino, K. Clarifying Competency Based Education Terms-A lexicon. Retrieved on March 12, 2017 from http://bbbb.blackboard.com/Competency-based-education-definitions

Unified Blended learning student ID allocation based on IPv6 and beyond 4G technologies

Ali M Alshahrani
Arab Open University
Riyadh ,KSA
a.shahrani@arabou.edu.sa

Abstract—the importance of blended learning in current time and the future is motivating researchers to enhance the services provided by this kind of educational systems. In this paper, we propose a new approach for presenting a unique and unified worldwide student identification number for students enrolled in educational institutions which are based on blended learning methodologies. The proposed approach depends on using two of most today's advanced technologies which are: IPv6 addressing system and the 4G mobile technologies. This approach aims to ensure the flexibility of transition (degrees upgrading or major changes) between different blended learning organizations within the organization itself or between different organizations.

Keywords— IPv6, 4G, Blended learning .

I. INTRODUCTION

Since a long age, people have been fascinated with virtual methods of communication apart from real communication that is done face to face. Communicating with someone by staying aloof creates an opportunity for the communicators to convey the message in a short process rather than travelling a long way. Communication through mobile is one of the most important factors in today's world that have been influential in the communication procedure of people. This report focuses on the review of 4G, which is known as the fourth generation of cellular telecommunications and wireless standards. The changes of Telecom industry with the development of standards, overcoming challenges, architectural and technological development along with the current trends like the 4th generation has been depicted in the review. The generation of future mobile brands has taken a step forward with the evolution of mobile standards and 4th generation communication through mobile. There exist three types of technologies that support the 4G technology, and they are LTE that is long term evolution, WiMax that is microwave access for worldwide interoperability and UMB. In the recent time, LTE and WiMax are the most common form of 4G Technologies deploying the networks all over the world. Evolution of Telecommunication services has been witnessed for years of developing the standard with every succeeding predecessor. History has been evident to show that existed many management initiatives for collaborating all the Global standards in a single unit. The formation of GSM's Phase 2+

had enabled the telecommunication services to introduce packet network switching for their customers innovatively. This was a parallel network to their existing network formation and enables the data consumption processes. Increasing data consumption factor is a burning issue that is affecting today's generation side of comparing it with the economic position. Wireless networking needs know what better solutions than 4G that will increase the efficiency of internet propagation are.

II. EVOLUTION OF MOBILE FROM ANALOGUE TO DIGITAL

The world has witnessed gradual evolution of Telecommunication services from first one 1G standard that was considered to be an analogue system supporting only voice system to develop networks like3G and4G which are having modern standards.

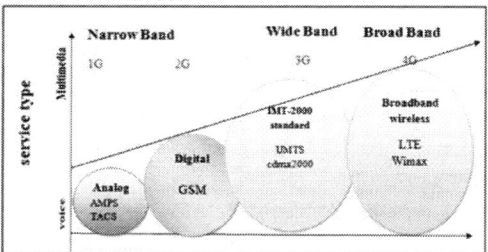

Figure 1:Evolution of mobile systems

The above figure shows the evolution of mobile systems and the networking standards from narrow to broadband. In between, it has the white band following up its limitations to 4G in the broadband system off mobile networking standards. 3G UMTS has been immediately succeeded by 4G that brought in advanced changes with faster connectivity speed and better services. 4G networking system is based on Internet protocol networks.

III. INTERNET PROTOCOL "IPv6" ADDRESSING

Until the recent time, the internet has been providing effective services for primary network applications like e-mail services and transfer of files. However, the existing protocol system of internet IPv4 does not support the upgraded formation of the networking applications. IPv6 has brought in new health for the generation of internet technology. A year of observation provides the report that an average of 4tpbs of network trafficking is seen every day. By analysing this, it has been easy to detect the trafficking of 4G. The decreasing supply of accessible IPv4 addresses has been comprehensively reported, as have the difficulties confronted by those wishing to move to IPv6.

Offering help for IPv6 on the planet is still transcendently IPv4 based. Additionally, it appears to be fascinating that there is no huge movement of clients from IPv4 to IPv6 according to the information. In any case, the noteworthy development of IPv4 movement suggests that the utilisation of IPv6 is additionally expanding, however at a similarly slower speed.

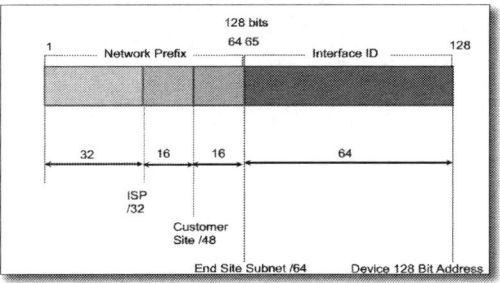

Figure 2:IPV6 Addressing Architecture

IV.   BLENDED LEARNING

Instructional procedures, for example, addressing, guided learning, discussion on exploratory matters, civil arguments and role-playing must be collaborated with web based learning apparatuses. For example, webcasts, podcasts, e-books and advanced video libraries, gigantic multiplayer web based diversions, wikis, and so forth to make a novel learning way of every learner. Mixed learning is making a blend of both disconnected and internet learning encounters in a way that they supplement each other. The web-based preparing condition empowers learners to attempt accessible time and place of tweaked preparing. Additionally, data innovation enables both mentors and learners to be decoupled as far as time, place, and space. In 2011-2012, multi-ethnic learners "still had the most astounding rate of culmination (73%). However, separate learners beat conventional classroom learners surprisingly (60% for customary classroom learners; 66% for principally online learners).

There are many educationalists and researchers who support the instructional design based on situations for models like blended theory approach. With application of this learning models and theories, the researchers have found five key ingredients that emerge as important element of the blended learning: L-O-C-A-R

- Life events: in this case, all the learners can participate equally that involves, in this case, all the learners can participate equally that involves as synchronous process.
- Online content: interactive sessions and learning procedure where a learner can complete their learning on time
- Collaboration: this refers to the environment of the ambience, but the learner communicate with each other

- Assessment: Assessing refers to examine your cross checking the learning adaptability of the learner and what he or she has learnt so far
- Reference materials: this refers to the online documentation procedures which help in on job reference material for enhancing the learning power of the learners
- Classes that are conducted for face to face interaction

Experiments have uncovered various key issues identified with the usage of separation instruction programs for learners. These incorporate:

- Distance instruction for the pilot action
- Setting a dream and building up objectives for the separation instruction program
- Organizing the separation instruction program
- Creating a situation that empowers experimentation
- Identifying and supporting separation instructors
- Monitoring accomplishment and assessment of the pilot remove instruction program
- Moving past the pilot and actualizing separation training into program administrations
- Connecting separation training with Workforce Innovation and Opportunity Act (WIOA) results.

V.   PROPOSED APPROACH

One of the main steps forwards is the using of available advanced technologies to enhance the education process; therefore, the next internet addressing system could be used along with beyond 4G systems of mobile communication.

Our idea here, to use the IPv6 address as a global and a unique student ID that can keep by student anywhere/ anytime, and always will be a reference for the particular student.

A. Proposed student ID format:

The proposed format for global student ID can be presented as the following:

Prefix	Global ID	Subnet & User ID

The explanation of a given student ID Format: Prefix is a fixed value that can be for example ED0C with the length of 16 bits as the following: 1110110100001100. IPv6 address with the given prefix will always refer to the global student ID system (should be reserved).

B. Global student ID system:

The global student Identification system is an integrated system with on the Internet (fig. 3), student unified domain name system (SUDNS). The SUDNS will contain specified IPv6 addresses along with students' names and some of the related data.

ISBN: 1-60132-454-5, CSREA Press ©

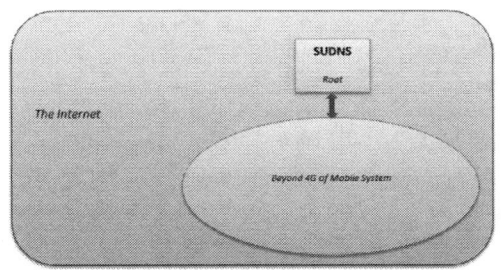

Figure 3:Student unified domain name system within the global network

Any new student has to receive an IPv6 when he/she is registered first time at any academic institution. The process of obtaining student ID will be illustrated by the following steps:

Step1: when a student will be registered at X University, for example, the X University will refer to Global Student ID System (GSIS, fig.1) using the well-known domain name that specified for this issue to receive the student ID for its newcomer student.

Step2: after reaching the GSIS, X University employee should request a given student ID (Student ID Request) by entering some related to student information e.g. Name, date of birth, level of education (1: Bachelor, 2: Master, 3:PhD) .

Step3: the SUDNS will check if this student is a new or already registered one, in the first case a student is a new one, student ID will be generated from the available IPv6 address in its addressing pool. A new student ID will be stored in SUDNS database for further use. The second case when a student is not new and already has its global student ID, the SUDNS will send a response containing a student ID to X University.

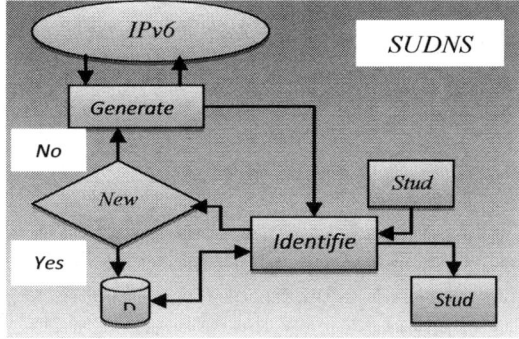

Figure 4:Proposed SUDNS algorithm

As known, the beyond 4G of mobile communication systems is based on IPv6 addressing system, and it will be a perfect environment that facilitates such proposals.

Finally, A global routings for this IPv6 student ID can be provided by using CIDR-like system specially developed for this issue. Conclusion

VI.   CONCLUTION

The SUDNS proposed system will overcome a problem, such as differentiation of student ID while transferring from one academic institution to another one, and from one specialization to another by providing a smooth handover of his personal data and records, furthermore, the proposed system can serve students and institutions from all countries over the world without any limitation taking into account the privacy of each country. As a future work, the proposed system could be enhanced to provide more functions related to this issue.

REFRENCES

1.   [1] Theodore S. Rappaport, Shu Sun , "Millimeter Wave Mobile Communications for 5G Cellular", May 2013.

2.   [2] Hamilton Setende, "4G and the future of mobile Telecommunications", Submitted in partial fulfilment of the Requirements for the BTECH degree in Information Technology, 2013

3.   [3] A Banupriya, T Suba, K Rajalakshmi and S Rajasri, "Milestone Of Wireless Communication 1g To 5G Technology", March 2015.

4.   [4] Hamilton Setende, "4G and the future of mobile Telecommunications", Submitted in partial fulfilment of the Requirements for the BTECH degree in Information Technology, 2013

5.   [5] Al-Fadhli, Salah Kuwait University, "Kuwait Instructor Perceptions of E-learning in an Arab Country: Kuwait University as a case study", e-Learning Volume 6. Number 2, ISSN 1741-8887, 2009

6.   [6] Dineva S., Nedeva V., "Development Interactive Courses of Education in Microbiology Based on E-Learning System Applying in Technical College of Yambol". The 4th International Conference on Virtual Learning ICVL, University of Bucharest & "Gh. Asachi" Tehnical University of Iasi, pp.231-238, 2009

7.   [7] Garrison, D. R.; H. Kanuka, "Blended learning: Uncovering its transformative potential in higher education", The Internet and Higher Education 7 (2): 95–105, 2004.

8.   [8] KHANDVE P. V.1 AND Dr. SHELKE M. E.2, "Blended Learning: The Future of Education Industry", 2002

9.   [9] Paliokas I., "Mapping the Spaces of Virtual Learning Environments". The 4th International Conference on Virtual Learning ICVL 2009, University of Bucharest and "Gh. Asachi" Tehnical University of Iasi, pp.83-90, 2009

10. [10] Margarita Pehlivanova1, Zlatoeli Ducheva1, Snejana Dineva, "Assessment of Blended Learning Education – Students' Opinion", 2010

ISBN: 1-60132-454-5, CSREA Press ©

SESSION

E-BUSINESS, E-COMMERCE, ENTERPRISE INFORMATION SYSTEMS, AND RELATED MANAGEMENT ISSUES

Chair(s)

TBA

ISBN: 1-60132-454-5, CSREA Press ©

Diffusion of Smart Grid in South Korea: The Relationship between Consumers' Awareness and Intention to Use

Jaehun Joo[1] and M. Minsuk Shin[2]

[1]Professor, Department of Management, College of Business and Economics, Dongguk University, 780-714, Sukjang-dong, Gyeongju-si, South Korea. Email: givej@dongguk.ac.kr

[2] Assistant Professor, Konkuk University, Department of International Trade, College of Commerce & Economics, Seoul South Korea. Email: shinm@konkuk.ac.kr

Abstract - *South Korea is one of the promising countries of smart grid technology and its diffusion. The study conducted in-depth interviews with users who participated into the Jeju testbed of smart grid, and the factors influencing consumers' awareness toward smart grid for its diffusion were identified. Three research hypotheses regarding the relationship between consumers' awareness and intention to use smart grid were proposed and tested. Consumers' positive awareness toward smart grid, and convenience and easiness of usage significantly influence intention to use it.*

Keywords: Smart grid; Diffusion; Consumer's awareness; Intention; Theory of planned behavior

1 Introduction

Smart grid is a typical example of emergent convergence technology integrating energy industry and information technology (IT) realizing the next generation of intelligent electric power grids. Smart grid enables both suppliers and consumers of electricity to engage in two-way communication by incorporating IT into existing power grids for the optimization of energy efficiency and utilization [1]. South Korea is one of the promising countries for implementing successful diffusion of smart grid technologies. South Korea, together with the U.S., the E.U., and Japan is one of the first-movers in the development of smart grid [1, 2].

Keeping the balance among the roles of government, firms, and consumers is a critical factor for smart grid to be successfully diffused in order to be reached to its ultimate goals such as optimization of energy utilization and a proper response to climate change. South Korea had been stressed the supply-side and technology perspectives for successful diffusion of the smart grid. It is necessary to reflect consumers' awareness and requirements on commercialization and diffusion of smart grid as well as technology development stage. However, there are a few studies on smart grid from the perspective of consumers. Thus, the purpose of the present study is to identify the relationship between consumers' awareness and intention to use the smart grid after reviewing the current trend and diffusing processes of smart grid in South Korea.

2. Diffusion of smart grid in South Korea

The Korean government suggested a master plan and roadmap for developing technology and business models of the smart grid, and its sequential implementation plans in 2009 as shown in Figure 1. The plan includes five areas as the platform for implementing smart grid projects such as smart power grid, smart electricity services, smart renewable energy, smart transportation, and smart consumers.

The Jeju smart grid testbed project was completed in 2013. A total of 12 consortia have been involved in the testbed project with government sponsorship. The reliability of 153 smart grid-related technologies in the five areas was tested in the Jeju testbed that a total of 6,000 households located in 12 small villages of Jeju island had participated from 2009 to 2013. The total investment to the Jeju testbed projects was 240M US dollars ($70 million from the Korean government and $170 million from consortia of firms) [1]. Then, Korean government and consortia involving smart grid-related firms have been conducting the plan to extend the smart grid projects including demand respond systems, vehicle to grid (V2G), microgrid, and building & factory management systems to eight metropolitans for achieving the goal by 2020. Unfortunately, users who participated into the Jeju testbed project had no more any supports from the consortia or government because the governmental budget had been reduced and the next projects had moved to metropolitans.

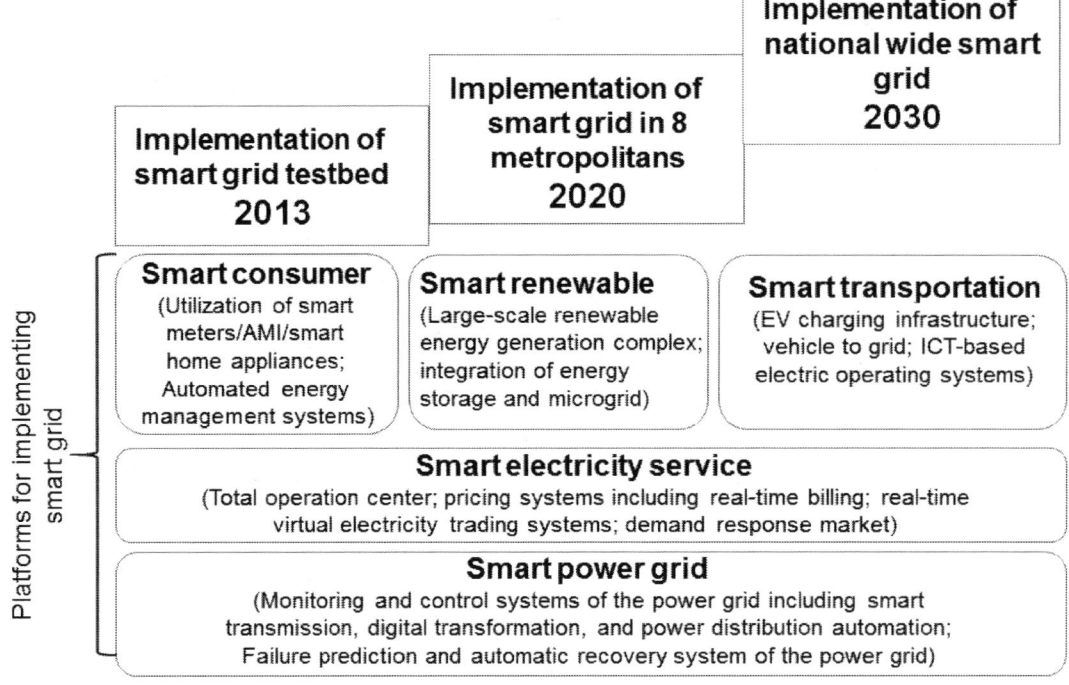

Sources: Ministry of Knowledge Economy and Korea Smart Grid Institute [7], Ministry of Trade, Industry and Energy [8].

Figure 1. Roadmap for implementing smart grid in South Korea

Most of all users disappointed, depressed, and felt some stresses. Supports or additional sponsors from suppliers were discontinued and some smart grid devices such as home appliances and smart meters except electric photovoltaic systems were withdrawn from the households. In-depth interviews with 29 users who had been participated into the Jeju testbed project and still have been using the electric photovoltaic systems were conducted. Although government-led projects for implementing the roadmap of smart grid in South Korea have some positive aspects, the technology push approach which is driven by suppliers jointed by both government and firms has some limitations to diffuse successfully the smart grid in national wide level. Table 1 shows the summary of comments from informants.

Table 1. Summary of interviews

Summary of comments	In-depth interview period
- No communication channels with suppliers - No contact points with suppliers - No after services of the smart grid devices - Difficulties in conducting maintenance and repairs - In particular, Users had experienced the effect of energy savings after adopting smart grid with solar photovoltaic systems. However, it was very difficult to introduce a new solar inverter because the extant suppliers did not any additional supports. - Too much cost was required to repair solar panels of replacing old chips of PV because supplier comes from Seoul away long distance. - No continuous monitoring for the testbed - Some suppliers ceased production of parts of PV including battery - Most of all users have been experiencing inconvenience and higher maintenance - No prompt response from suppliers	Oct. 27-31, Dec. 15-16, 2016

ISBN: 1-60132-454-5, CSREA Press ©

- Distrust in government has been accumulated since 2013
- Having feelings became a part of an experiment
- Just allowing our land and houses to do experiment of smart grid

3. Relationship between awareness and intention

3.1 Research hypothesis

According to the theory of planned behaviour (TPB) [3], consumers' attitude, subject norm, and perceived behavioural control influence their intention to use or purchase products or services. Consumers' awareness is a component of forming their attitude and has an impact on the social norm. Thus, three hypotheses based on TPB are proposed:

Hypothesis 1 (H1): Consumers' positive awareness toward smart grid positively influences intention to use it.

Hypothesis 2 (H2): Consumers' negative awareness toward smart grid usage negatively influences intention to use it.

Hypothesis 3 (H3): Consumers' negative awareness toward smart grid negatively influences intention to use it.

Table 2. Constructs and questionnaire items

Construct	Code	Question items
Positive awareness (POA)	POA1	I think that smart grid helps environmental protection
	POA2	I think that smart grid facilitates the diffusion of renewable energy
	POA3	I think that smart grid provides better quality of electricity power
	POA4	I think that smart grid facilitates the diffusion of electric vehicle
Negative awareness toward usage (NUA)	NUA1	I worry about difficulties to use smart grid
	NUA2	I have a feeling of uneasiness to use smart grid
Negative awareness toward security (NSA)	NSA1	I worry about my privacy
	NSA2	I worry about misuse of my personal information
	NSA3	I worry about attack to smart grid from hackers
	NSA4	I worry about some distribution of smart grid through hacking
Intention to use (INT)	INT1	I intend to use smart grid
	INT2	I will recommend smart grid to others

3.2 Analysis and hypothesis test

Data were collected from undergraduate students. 81 respondents who know smart grid out of 212 students were asked to answer the questionnaire (see Table 2). The ratio of junior and senior is about 89 percent as shown in Table 3. Demographic characteristics of respondents is provided in Table 3.

ISBN: 1-60132-454-5, CSREA Press ©

Table 3. Demographic characteristics

Variable	Categories	Frequency	Percent
Gender	Male	40	49.4
	Female	41	50.6
Grade	Freshman	1	1.2
	Sophomore	8	9.9
	Junior	20	24.7
	Senior	52	64.2

Exploratory factor analysis (EFA) was conducted using principal component analysis with Varimax rotation. The EFA identified four factors with eigenvalues over 1.0. All items had high loadings to their corresponding factors. Four factors jointly explained 74 percent of the total variance. In addition, Cronbach's alpha was calculated to assess the reliability of each factor. The reliability measures ranged from 0.659 to 0.843, indicating the satisfactory internal consistency of the extracted factors (Hair et al., 2010).

Table 4: Exploratory factor analysis and internal consistency

Rotated Component Matrix							
	Factor				Eigenvalue	Variance (%)	Cronbach's alpha
	1	2	3	4			
INT1	-.198	.143	-.086	.857	1.006	8.381	0.659
INT2	.119	.178	-.237	.768			
POA1	.131	.820	-.026	.219	2.994	24.949	0.838
POA2	.152	.780	-.051	.340			
POA3	-.082	.819	.025	.029			
POA4	-.079	.792	-.155	-.026			
NUA1	.015	-.104	.871	-.087	1.563	13.021	0.713
NUA2	.123	-.016	.836	-.210			
NSA1	.783	-.245	.210	-.042	3.318	27.646	0.843
NSA2	.856	-.022	.174	-.065			
NSA3	.864	.122	-.026	.096			
NSA4	.844	.170	-.144	-.074			

Confirmatory factor analysis (CFA) and path analysis were conducted using SmartPLS 3 [4]. The results of CFA were satisfactory. As shown in Table 5, CR measures for all constructs ranged from 0.853 to 0.924, exceeding 0.7 thresholds recommended by Fornel and Larcker [5]. AVE values exceed 0.5. Discriminant validity was examined by comparing the square root of the AVE for each construct with inter-construct correlation coefficients. The square root of the AVE on diagonal in Table 5 exceeded the inter-construct correlation coefficients, both suggesting sufficient discriminant validity [6].

Table 5. Convergent and discriminant validity

	CR	AVE	POA	NUA	NSA	INT
POA	0.891	0.672	**0.820**			
NUA	0.874	0.777	-0.166	**0.881**		
NSA	0.923	0.858	-0.113	0.246	**0.926**	
INT	0.854	0.746	0.358	-0.343	-0.155	**0.864**

CR composite reliability, AVE average variance explained

Table 6 shows path coefficients and results of the hypothesis test. Hypothesis 1 (H1), suggesting that consumers' positive awareness positively influences intention to use the smart grid is supported at the significance level of 0.01. Hypothesis 2 (H2), suggesting that consumers' negative awareness toward smart grid usage negatively influences intention to use smart grid is supported at the significance level of 0.01. Hypothesis 3 (H3), suggesting that consumers' negative awareness toward smart grid security negatively influences intention to use smart grid is not supported.

Table 6. Hypothesis test results

Hypothesis	Path	VIF	Path coefficient	SD	t	p	Result
H1	POA→INT	1.034	0.305	0.094	3.263	0.001	Supported
H2	NUA→INT	1.087	-0.280	0.109	2.573	0.010	Supported
H3	NSA→INT	1.071	-0.052	0.128	0.406	0.685	No Supported

VIF (Variance Inflation Factor) did not exceed 5.0. There are no collinearity problems.

4. Conclusion

In-depth interviews with users who participated into the Jeju testbed project show that government-led approach has some limitations to diffuse smart grid at national wide level. No follow-up supports after the testbed project resulted in psychological trauma to participants and they felt heavy mental stresses. Their experiences had an impact on a negative awareness toward smart grid. Thus, the present study tested three hypotheses regarding relationships between consumers' awareness and intention to use smart grid. Two hypotheses (H1 and H2) were supported, whereas H3 was not supported.

Promotion campaigns and education for citizens play an important role in the diffusion of smart grid because prior knowledge of smart grid helps them to understand and be aware of beneficial aspects of smart grid. Convenience and easiness to use smart grid devices also have a significant influence on intention to use them. Human-centred technology encourages users' active participation into the diffusion of smart grid at national wide level. Thus, smart grid with technology affordances should be designed and introduced. However, consumers' negative awareness toward the smart grid security had no a significant influence on their intention to use because privacy related to the smart grid is less susceptible.

5. References

[1] Joo, J. and Kim, L. (2016), "Strategic guidelines for the diffusion of smart grid technologies through a Korean testbed," *Information Technology for Development*, 22, 503-524.

[2] Mah, D.N., Vleuten, J.M.V.D., Jasper, C.M.I., and Peter, R.H. (2012), "Governing the transition of socio-technical systems: A case study of the development of smart grids in Korea," *Energy Policy*, 45, 133-141.

[3] Ajzen, I. (1991), "The theory of planned behaviour," *Organizational Behavior and Human Decision Processes*, 50(2), 179–211

[4] Ringle, C. M., Wende, S., and Becker, J.-M. 2015. "SmartPLS 3." Boenningstedt: SmartPLS GmbH, http://www.smartpls.com.

[5] Fornell, C. and Larcker, D.F. (1981), "Evaluating structural equation models with unobservable variables and measurement error." *Journal of Marketing Research*, 18(1), 39-50.

[6] Hair, Joseph F., Black, W.C., Babin, B.J., and Anderson, R.E. (2010), *Multivariate data analysis*, Pearson College Division.

[7] Ministry of Knowledge Economy and Korea Smart Grid Institute (2010), "Korea's smart grid roadmap 2030: Laying the foundation for low carbon, green growth by 2030".

[8] Ministry of Trade, Industry and Energy (2016), Implementation planning of smart grid, Available at https://www.smartgrid.or.kr/board.php?id=sub5_3&wr_id=194.

Financial Model for Pricing Decisions Support in SMEs of the Restaurant Sector in Mexico

Jorge Luis Fernandez[1], **Cynthia B. Pérez** [1], **Luis A. Castro**[1]

[1]Dept of Computing and Design, Sonora Institute of Technology (ITSON), Ciudad Obregon, Sonora, Mexico
(e-mail: jorgefdez@live.com; cynthia.perez@itson.edu.mx; luis.castro@acm.org)

Abstract - *Companies have always analyzed product prices. A good pricing strategy can help most businesses with profit margins. SMEs struggle with their pricing strategy, specially in Mexico where managers spent a lot of time deciding a product price. By taking advantage of sales and operational data, a SME could create a pricing strategy that helps it to maintain or improve customer sales along with the reduction of costs, time and improving profits. Hence, we propose a Financial Model based on input from small business owners which is included in a pricing decision support tool that analyzes costs, sales and production data, providing a vision of possible outcomes and also SMEs could visualize a What-if scenario helping managers in the decision-making process.*

Keywords: Pricing decision, SME, Financial Model

1   Introduction

One of the most important decisions of any company in terms of its sale and marketing strategy is the establishment of the price of the product or products offered, since it is one of the essential elements for the determination of profit. Within this decision, a price must be foreseen to ensure that production and sales numbers are in the same range as customer demand, as well as to what those customers are willing to pay for the good or service (Treviño Ayala, Villalpando Cadena, Treviño Ayala, & Lozano Treviño, 2013).

While making pricing decisions, one must keep in mind the concept of price and demand elasticity, thus considering the response of customers to the offered product in the face of a change in price (McConnell, C & Brue, S. 1997).

In many researches, it has been found that an increase in profits is based on an average price (O'Regan, Ghobadian, & Gallear, 2006, De la Garza, Ayub, Cheín, & Banda, 2009), as well as a competitive and fair price (Arslan & Kivrak, 2008) of any good or service. An ideal price level should therefore be considered to determine the positive response of customers at a price high enough to achieve a profit, having covered costs, considering that customers will only pay the price if they consider that the good or service is worth it (Zikmund, W. 1998).

Depending on the industry, the market and its size, each company can consider different factors to establish their prices. In supermarkets, for example, we consider product groups, wholesale costs, sales forecasts, promotions, market, sales strategies, among others, considering that these changes occur on a weekly basis (Montgomery, A. L. 2005). On the other hand, in the Hotel Industry, profit management systems are used to determine prices based on a forecast of supply and demand, as well as a comparison of characteristics, amenities, geographical position, between hotels, to mention but a few, (Kisilevich, Keim, Byshko, Tsibelman, & Rokach, 2011).

Although each industry may vary their price management processes, basic factors like fixed and variable costs are often the basis for pricing, especially in businesses such as Restaurants. Also, companies can use the information they generate in their sales systems to support decision making.

1.1.   SMEs in Mexico

In Mexico, small and medium-sized enterprises (SMEs) generally lack some essential elements for their growth, either from professional support or financial knowledge, and focus only on seeking a return on their investment (ROI). Business Intelligence (BI) can have a great impact on the growth of any company, but it is often omitted in the operation of SMEs, due to lack of knowledge or because the managers do not consider BI necessary for their growth in the medium or long term. It is common for SMEs not to achieve profits or cannot continue operating, and may end up even ignoring what went wrong, and this is how 52.5% of SMEs in Mexico tend to go out-of-business before their 2-year mark, mainly due to their inability to be profitable (Flores Kelly, 2016).

To comply with customer requirements and market challenges, SMEs must continuously improve their products, services and/or processes, and must also incorporate or develop technological assets that allow them to position themselves ahead of their competition. In fact, it has been reported that most SMEs that only make new investments once the competitors get good results are destined to fail (Rubio Bañón y Aragón Sánchez, 2006).

The information generated by a SME can serve as a starting point for good and solid decision-making, but the culture that prevails in small and medium-sized enterprises in any industry leaves out important information. As Legendre (2005) mentions, "Unlike what many might think, SMEs can use the benefits of systematizing their Business Intelligence."

ISBN: 1-60132-454-5, CSREA Press ©

Accessibility to information systems in recent years in SMEs has provided challenges and opportunities for both owners and managers. The most accessible data in PyMEs is transactional, which can be captured through barcode readers or, in the case of restaurants, when registering customer order in the system. Therefore, it is possible to track each of the sales movements of any item through the use of this data, providing a wealth of information on the reaction of customers related to prices and promotions. Hence, it is promising when this information is analyzed to improve any pricing strategy (Montgomery, A. L., 2005).

Price and product, as well as the service offered, provide a competitive advantage within the markets in which each SME can participate. Each company intends to provide a differentiated service in each product or service offered to create that competitive advantage, and at the same time an optimum price that attracts a greater number of customers. A pricing strategy for any differentiated service in a competitive market is highly important since, regardless of the quantity of products or services, the price needs to be the most appropriate, and at the same time it must be periodically revised (Cassaigne, N., & Singh, M. G., 2001).

1.2. Costs in the restaurant sector in Mexico

In restaurants, the prices are usually influenced by the competition and the target market. However, the basis of the unit cost of each product has its origin in the cost of the raw materials used, based on its yield and the its cost of preparation. Also, the fixed costs of operation must be considered when calculating the proportional cost of each product, and based on this and the desired profit we can generate a price in line to the ideal demand and the market, taking in consideration any applicable taxes. It is also important to consider any price adjustments in order to avoid a high difference between products that could cause a high flow of "cheap" products that affect the sales of "expensive" products, which usually provide that differentiation that is sought in the market in which we are competing (Cuevas, J. F., 2016).

Commonly, pricing decisions in SMEs in the restaurant industry in Mexico are carried out by hand, using only a calculator to sum up the average input costs per unit and operating costs based on the financial statements, as well as the desired profit without "punishing" the customer or the products profit margin. In addition, external factors such as the competition's quality and prices are taken into account, as well as changes in tax or fuel costs that directly impact the finances of the company. This situation is not uncommon among SMEs in this sector, so it is necessary to evaluate the way in which the analysis of information, generated and captured daily in a system, can be used to make pricing decisions at the managerial level (Legendre, 2005).

Carrying out a pricing decision can result in an exhaustive task that leads to consuming more time than necessary, because it can be interrupted at different times,

making it tedious, highly time consuming and prone to errors. Based on this, the following question arises:

How could the analysis of management-level information on the raw materials, product preparation and operation costs of a SME in the restaurant sector be enabled, to support pricing decisions?

The objective of this research is to design a Financial Model that allows the analysis of the cost costs related to the operation and production areas, whether a cost is fixed or variable. Thus, the aim is to carry out a price and profit valuation showing different options to the user, based on trends, that allow a more accurate and agile pricing decision within SMEs of the restaurant sector in Mexico.

2 Financial Model

One of the challenges of any company is the optimal management of financial resources, since all efforts and processes need to be expressed in a solid and structured way that reflects the performance attained. Likewise, it is extremely important to plan and implement said process (Pastor, 2009).

Based on the above, a need for a Financial Simulation Model to support the decisions of management in business processes was found, specifically for product pricing. This model is planned to be implemented in a business intelligence system so that the person in charge can visualize the information through dashboards. This business intelligence tool can be used online, providing a competitive advantage for the company as it will be able to visualize its information from any mobile device at any time, as long as it has internet access. Also, the proposed model can be easily replicated for different products, branches and even companies of the same industry.

2.1 Input and Output Analysis

A Financial Model would help to define and analyze the variability of the prices of the products. It would also be able to offer an optimum perspective on profit generation based of the price of each product and its sales, as well as the approximate cost by volume based on tendencies.

To carry out a financial model, it is necessary to identify the basic concepts that comprise it, such as the inputs or the elements on which it works, and the outputs or results that the model must produce. This stage is known as the generation of the Black Box of the model, according to Eppen (Eppen, Gould, Schmidt, Moore, & Weatherford, 2000). Initially the logical relations between each input and output element within the model are unknown. Despite its simplicity, this black box causes the following to be considered from the beginning of the process: what should be included, what should be excluded and the classification of the different factors that make it up.

Based on the above, the input data is defined, as well as the desired output and, from this, a Black Box diagram is generated, see Figure 1.

ISBN: 1-60132-454-5, CSREA Press ©

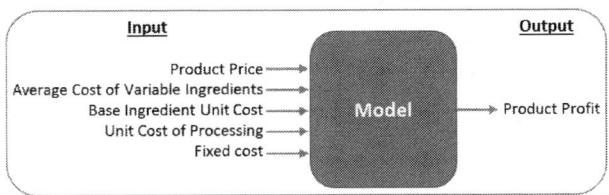

Figure 1.   Black Box of the Financial Model.

2.2   Graphic Model Design

According to Eppen, et al. (2000) to define the logical relations, a very useful technique of model construction from data can be used, in which the desired relationships must be illustrated and it is not necessary to begin with the final mathematical equation. However, the graph would help us to deduce an equation for the final model. In this regard, using the same graphic model design technique it is possible to perform a primary data analysis, useful for the estimation of parameter values.

In order to have a clear definition of the relationships between the input and output data, it is advisable to generate the model as a graphic. Initially, the performance measure is chosen, in this case the Profit is decomposed into Revenues and Total Costs, see Table 1, and these in turn are decomposed into each of their elements until they reach the originally defined input elements. There are no strict rules for detailing the graphic model variables, since their sole purpose is to assist in the construction of the model more easily, not in its final definition (Eppen, et al., 2000). Once the model is constructed graphically, the relationships between each basic element, such as price and costs, and its evolution to profit can be observed, see Figure 2. To identify the price as the data *manipulated* by the user, it is marked in a different way than the rest of the variables within the graph, since this is the initial input data of the model. This data can be changed by the user in order to obtain different results that allow a better view of the possible costs and profit that could result from the selected price.

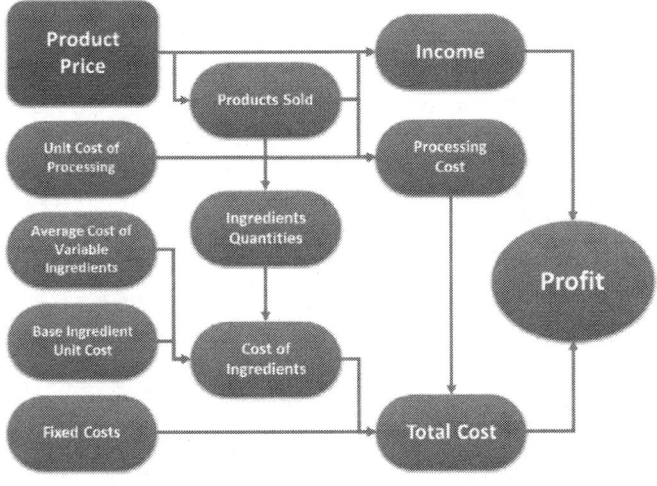

Figure 2.   Graphic Model with relationships.

2.3   Equations

Once the model is constructed, the basic equations that indicate the relationship between the variables can be defined for the calculation of Profit, see Table 1. These equations are the basis for building the Financial Model since the Profit is calculated using this information. Hence, each equation solves a variable and is placed in reverse order in the table starting with Profit (output) and ending with the input variables, see Table 1. This way, Figure 2 illustrates the relationships between the variables used for the profit calculation.

Table 1. Equations Table

Variable		Equation
Profit	=	Income – Total Cost
Income	=	Product Price x Products Sold
Total Cost	=	Processing Cost + Cost of Ingredients + Fixed Costs
Cost of Ingredients	=	(Variable Ingredients Quantity x Average Cost of Variable Ingredients) + (Base Ingredient Unit Cost x Base Ingredient Quantity)
Processing Cost	=	Products Sold x Unit Processing Cost

3   Case Study

3.1   General info

This case study is carried out in a SME of the restaurant sector in Mexico. This company has 4 branches in the same city with about 100 full time employees. The growth of the company over 11 years of operation has been carried out informally, finances have historically been handled on paper, and sometimes digitally through spreadsheets. After 6 years of operation, a Point of Sale (POS) software with several management features was implemented, but it is only used to accelerate the process of capturing customer orders. None of the remaining business processes are currently being managed through the existing system, despite having the functionalities to do so.

3.2   Price/Sales Limit Equation

In order to generate the proposed Financial Model, an equation was defined together with the business owners, where it is assumed that for each $10 pesos between prices, there would be a difference of 200 daily product sales, based on their experience. At higher prices, they have experienced less demand or fewer products sales. For this matter, it was defined by business owners that if the product costs $100 pesos, it would not sell. Thus, the data presented in Figures 3, 4 and 7 are test data for model elaboration purposes, this data was also provided by the business owners and managers. This equation is defined as follows:

$$Products\ Sold = 2000 - (20\ x\ Product\ Price) \qquad (1)$$

Once these parameters were defined, the base model was elaborated using a spreadsheet. Hence, the current price used in the base model was $75 pesos, see Figure 3.

ISBN: 1-60132-454-5, CSREA Press ©

Financial Model (Daily Sales)

Decision Variable

Product Price	$	75.00

Parameters

Average Cost of Variable Ingredients ($ per Product	$	20.00
Base Ingredient Unit Cost ($ per Product)	$	15.00
Unit Cost of Processing ($ per Product)	$	13.00
Fixed Costs	$	1,000.00

Sold Products Equation

Intersection	2000
Slope (linear coefficient)	-20

Cost Processing Equation

Linear Coefficient

Quadratic Coefficient

Physical Results

Products Sold	500

Financial Results

Income	$37,500.00
Processing Cost	$10,000.00
Cost of Ingredients	$14,000.00
General Costs	$ 1,000.00
Total cost	$25,000.00
Profit (before taxes)	$12,500.00

Figure 3.   Base Financial Model.

3.3   Processing Cost Trend

When analyzing processing costs, it was found that the sold products equation results matched with the branch's current numbers for the amount of products sold. However, when comparing different quantities of sold products, the branch's numbers did not match the ones showed by the equation. To adjust this mismatch, a comparison was made with current data on the cost of processing for different levels of production, see Figure 4.

Cost Data (Thousands of Pesos)

Product Quantity (00)	Processing Cost (Real)		Processing Cost (Model)	
2	$	6.00	$	7.00
3	$	8.00	$	9.00
4	$	10.00	$	11.00
5	$	12.00	$	13.00
6	$	15.00	$	15.00
7	$	18.00	$	17.00
8	$	21.00	$	18.00
9	$	24.00	$	20.00
10	$	27.00	$	22.00

Figure 4.   Comparison Chart of Processing Costs.

In order to obtain a Financial Model that is close to reality, the comparative chart was graphed, see Figure 4, and a trendline was applied to adjust the information to the current data. From this graph, a cost-processing equation was obtained. When applying the trend line between cost of processing and the number of products, a polynomial cost processing equation was chosen for use, which automatically appears on the same chart, see Figure 5.

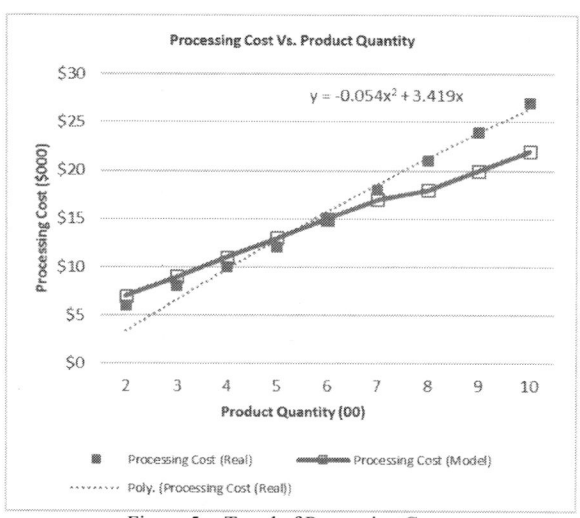

Figure 5.   Trend of Processing Costs.

From Figure 5 the polynomial cost processing equation was obtained, see Equation 2. From it, the Linear Coefficient (x) and Quadratic Coefficient (x^2) are extracted and are added to the proposed model in order to obtain a real trend of processing costs.

$$y = -0.054x^2 + 3.419x \qquad (2)$$

3.4   Linear and Quadratic Coefficients

Both coefficients are applied to the model, replacing the Processing Cost previously considered. This gives the financial model accuracy on price calculation, profits and products sold. This projection becomes closely similar to the current numbers generated at the case study branch, since the calculations are based on the actual cost trend, calculated from the linear coefficient and the quadratic coefficient, see Figure 6.

Financial Model (Daily Sales)

Decision Variable

Product Price	$	75.00

Parameters

Average Cost of Variable Ingredients ($ per Product	$	15.00
Base Ingredient Unit Cost ($ per Product)	$	10.00
Fixed Costs	$	1,000.00

Equation Coefficients

Sold Products Equation

Intersection	2000
Slope (linear coefficient)	-20

Cost Processing Equation

Linear Coefficient	3.419
Quadratic Coefficient	0.054

Physical Results

Products Sold	500

Financial Results

Income	$ 37,500.00
Processing Cost	$ 15,209.50
Cost of Ingredients	$ 12,500.00
General Costs	$ 1,000.00
Total cost	$ 28,709.50
Profit (before taxes)	$ 8,790.50

Figure 6.   Financial Model adding Coefficients.

ISBN: 1-60132-454-5, CSREA Press ©

Financial Model (Daily Sales)

Decision Variable							
Product Price	$ 65.00	$ 70.00	$ 75.00	$ 80.00	$ 85.00	$ 90.00	$ 95.00
Parameters							
Average Cost of Variable Ingredients ($ per Product	$ 15.00	$ 15.00	$ 15.00	$ 15.00	$ 15.00	$ 15.00	$ 15.00
Base Ingredient Unit Cost ($ per Product)	$ 10.00	$ 10.00	$ 10.00	$ 10.00	$ 10.00	$ 10.00	$ 10.00
Fixed Costs	$ 1,000.00	$ 1,000.00	$ 1,000.00	$ 1,000.00	$ 1,000.00	$ 1,000.00	$ 1,000.00
Equation Coefficients							
Sold Products Equation							
Intersection	2000	2000	2000	2000	2000	2000	2000
Slope (linear coefficient)	-20	-20	-20	-20	-20	-20	-20
Cost Processing Equation							
Linear Coefficient	3.419	3.419	3.419	3.419	3.419	3.419	3.419
Quadratic Coefficient	0.054	0.054	0.054	0.054	0.054	0.054	0.054
Physical Results							
Products Sold	700	600	500	400	300	200	100
Financial Results							
Income	$ 45,500.00	$ 42,000.00	$ 37,500.00	$ 32,000.00	$ 25,500.00	$ 18,000.00	$ 9,500.00
Processing Cost	$ 28,853.30	$ 21,491.40	$ 15,209.50	$ 10,007.60	$ 5,885.70	$ 2,843.80	$ 881.90
Cost of Ingredients	$ 17,500.00	$ 15,000.00	$ 12,500.00	$ 10,000.00	$ 7,500.00	$ 5,000.00	$ 2,500.00
General Costs	$ 1,000.00	$ 1,000.00	$ 1,000.00	$ 1,000.00	$ 1,000.00	$ 1,000.00	$ 1,000.00
Total cost	$ 47,353.30	$ 37,491.40	$ 28,709.50	$ 21,007.60	$ 14,385.70	$ 8,843.80	$ 4,381.90
Profit (before taxes)	$ (1,853.30)	$ 4,508.60	$ 8,790.50	$ 10,992.40	$ 11,114.30	$ 9,156.20	$ 5,118.10

Figure 7. "What-If" Analysis

With these adjustments applied to the model, it is possible to observe a profit more in line with current financial statements from the branch, based on the product price provided by the business owners.

4 Results

Once the model is elaborated, an analysis of different prices can be carried out by means of a projection with "What-If" scenarios, which provide a framework for comparing the possibilities of profits, based on a price range, see Figure 7.

Thanks to this analysis, business owners can compare the behavior of each of the possible prices, including the current price ($ 70.00 pesos). Each option shows every parameter considered, fixed and variable, and the financial impact they

have on the results, including the assumption that a higher price would represent a smaller number of products sold. This analysis also shows the sales income behavior and the fluctuation in the costs for the preparation of each sold product. With this, the entrepreneur can quickly observe that the optimal profit range is between $80 and $85 pesos, by showing the projected profit for each of these prices.

Finally, a graph is generated showing the behavior of each element analyzed by the business owners. Here, the "What-If" analysis shows the break-even point at the intersection of the Profit line with the X-axis of prices, which is an approximate price of $ 66.30 pesos, and the optimum price predicted at the highest point of the same graphed profit line, which again can be considered between $80 and $85 pesos per product, see Figure 8.

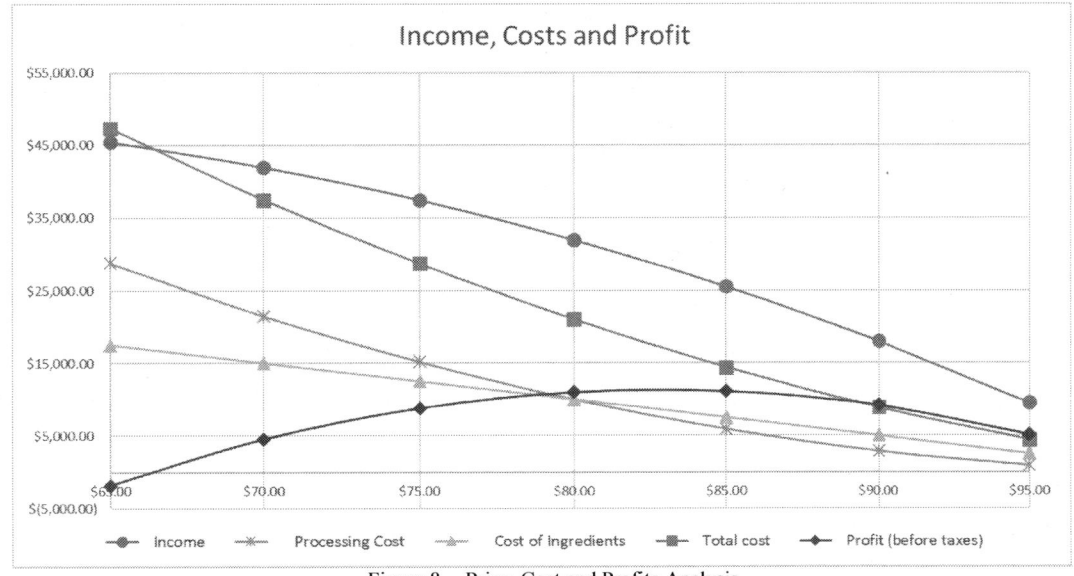

Figure 8. Price, Cost and Profits Analysis.

ISBN: 1-60132-454-5, CSREA Press ©

5 Conclusions

In this contribution, we have presented a Financial Model that offers a clear and concise view of the possible scenarios to which a SME may be exposed by making changes in the prices of its products. This model was applied in a case study related to a restaurant in Mexico showing a "What-if" scenario using a spreadsheet, helping business owners in the decision-making process and also saving time while reducing uncertainty. Thanks to the model provided, business owners were able to create pricing and promotion strategies faster and easier. Having different pricing and profit scenarios helped them save time when deciding new prices, and also to evaluate the current ones.

The Financial Model can be modified to suit different SMEs. Easy-input controls should be added to avoid undesired manipulation of the data within the spreadsheet. Thus, we are working on the development of a business intelligence system where the proposed Financial Model will be integrated, helping business owners in the decision-making process anywhere, anytime as long as they are connected to the internet. The idea is to provide through this system not only the ability to perform a constant analysis of profit behavior but also allowing business owners to make price adjustments without having to wait for monthly or quarterly results in order to make a decision.

6 References

[1] Kelly, J. F. (2013, March 20). México necesita menos Pymes. Retrieved July 13, 2016, from http://www.forbes.com.mx/mexico-necesita-menos-pymes/

[2] Rubio Bañón, A., & Aragón Sánchez, A. (2006). Competitividad y recursos estratégicos en las pymes. (Spanish). Revista De Empresa, (17), 32-47.

[3] Legendre, R. (2005). ¿Es la Inteligencia de Negocio aplicable a las PYMEs? PUZZLE, Año 4, Edición No 17(Mayo-Junio), 4–9.

[4] Montgomery, A. L. (2005). The implementation challenge of pricing decision support systems for retail managers. Applied Stochastic Models in Business and Industry, 21(4–5), 367–378. http://doi.org/10.1002/asmb.572

[5] Cassaigne, N., & Singh, M. G. (2001). Intelligent decision support for the pricing of products and services in competitive consumer markets. IEEE Transactions on Systems, Man and Cybernetics Part C: Applications and Reviews, 31(1), 96–106. http://doi.org/10.1109/5326.923272

[6] Cuevas, J. F. (2016). Control de Costos y Gastos en los Restaurantes. México D.F., México Limusa

[7] Treviño Ayala, M. E., Villalpando Cadena, P., Treviño Ayala, R. A., & Lozano Treviño, D. F. (2013). La mercadotecnia en las PYMES y su influencia en el crecimiento de utilidades. Innovaciones de Negocios, 19(10), 125–144.

[8] Zikmund, W. (1998). Investigación de mercados. México, D.F: Pearson Educación.

[9] McConnell, C & Brue, S. (1997). Economía. México, D.F McGrawHill.

[10] O'Regan, N., Ghobadian, A., & Gallear, D. (2006). In search of the drivers of high growth in manufacturing SMEs. Technovation, 26(1), 30-41.

[11] Arslan, G., & Kivrak, S. (2008). Critical factors to company success in the construction industry. Proceedings of World Academy of Science, 35, 405-408.

[12] Kisilevich, S., Keim, D., Byshko, R., Tsibelman, M., & Rokach, L. (2011). Developing a price management decision support system for hotel brokers using free and open source tools. In ICEIS (pp. 147-156).

[13] Pastor, R. A. T. (2009). Modelo de gestión financiera para una organización. Perspectivas, (23), 55–72.

[14] Eppen, G. D., Gould, F. J., Schmidt, C. D., Moore, J. H., & Weatherford, L. R. (2000). Investigación de operaciones en la ciencia administrativa: construcción de modelos para la toma de decisiones con hojas de cálculo electrónicas. México; Prentice Hall Hispanoamericana.

SESSION

E-GOVERNMENT, ETHICAL ISSUES AND POLICIES

Chair(s)

TBA

ISBN: 1-60132-454-5, CSREA Press ©

Analysis of the development phases of the e - government local: case of Mexico

Israel Patiño Galván [1]

[1] Research Division of the Innovation Park - University La Salle Northwest, Obregon City, Sonora, Mexico

Abstract - *The Communication and Information Technologies, they have potentiated and optimized human activities about from industrial, educational, social, governmental sectors among others. In this last one, the government called e-government has been forced to make changes to its regulatory framework, as well as the modernization of technology infrastructure to support the incorporation of ICT. However, it is important that strategies and mechanisms are configured for local governments. Therefore, it should identify a set of indicators on local governments to determine the decrease of process and through they, identify and increase efforts to ensure its successful implementation. Due to the above, are suggested a series of indicators based for the UN suggested.*

Keywords: Indicators; local e-government; strategies, Communication Information Technologies

1   Introduction

Governments are responsible for providing public services to its citizens as stipulated by the regulatory framework for each region, for it must have the necessary resources to cover them permanently and achieve participation, transparency and access to information. However, as the population grows, they demand better public services, so the leaders are forced to implement strategies to fulfill their responsibilities. In this sense, in seeking strategies, The Information Communication Technologies provide a comprehensive solution in the short, medium and long term, to resolve these responsibilities. However, it is not enough the incorporate information technology, but must also generate the enabling environment for proper incorporation, and would take advantage the benefits and capabilities of this tool. This brings as advantages better service in terms of attention span, doing the activities more efficient and effective of the local governments. In addition, costs to provide services may be lower and the government services to be accessible.

Due to the above, some governments have begun the process of implementing, too known as e-government, trying of take the Information Technologies for optimizing their activities, ranging from the use of word processors, spreadsheets, presentations, web development, interaction with social networks, as well as information systems to provide to public services care. However, this is not enough as they must generate comprehensive strategies for solutions to be long term, but it is understood to be a process in which local and regional governments must realize that you can only get satisfactory results if the use of it is planned long term. That is, although used websites and social networks, if the population does not have Internet access or if not given to requests

2   Theoretical Framework

This section describes the concepts of this proposal. The e-government. It refers to the use of information and communications technology by the public sector with the aim of improving the provision of information and public service provided. In this sense, it is encouraging citizen participation in the decision-making process, making the government more accountable, transparent and efficient [1]. Moreover, it is important to identify the stages for the cross the governments, in the scanning process and implementation of information technologies and communication, for it then presented the evolution of an e-government. Evolution and stages of e-government ONU [2]. These stages are nonhierarchical, that is, it is not necessary that one end to another begins, if they evolution, in the measure that increases the complexity of systems, where it is associated with technological developments and (ICT) tools are incorporated for governance, where the whole society are benefited [3], the levels are:

- Stage 1. Emergent or basic, Stage 2. Interaction, Stage 3. Transaction, Stage 4. Connected or processing, Stage 5. Integrated Process

To identify the stage, briefly describes each [2]

- Stage 1. Emerging information services, Stage 2. Enhanced information services, Stage 3. Transactional services, Stage 4. Connected services

3   State of art

To perform this research, and analyze the development in the implementation of e-government, it did a documentary study about the indicators suggested by the UN [2], besides indicators suggested by the Nasser [4], to identify as they help assess progress in the implementation of information technology in government, however these are not apparent in local level (local governments), which it gave rise to these research and proposal.

In the Illustration 1, it shows the components of the indicators suggest by UN for the e - government

Illustration 1. *Components of the development index of e-government*

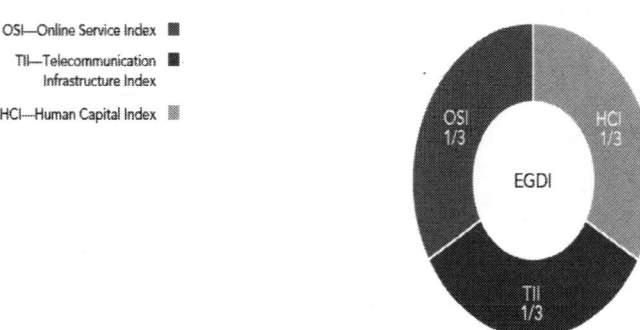

Source: United Nations e-government Survey 2014, UN, 2014, p. 14

As can be evidenced are 3 major components: the index of online services, telecommunications infrastructure and finally the index of human capital. What makes e-government index is integral. Moreover, in Illustrations 2, 3 and 4 it shows the indicators of each component to identify in detail the areas that give rise to e-government Index:

Illustration 2 *Telecommunications infrastructure index*

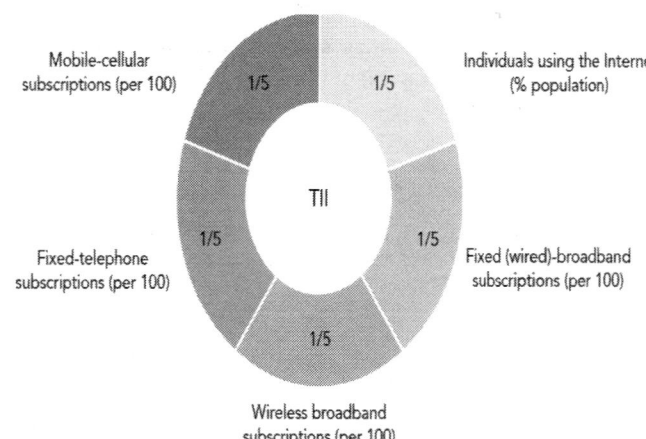

Source: United Nations e-government Survey 2014, UN, p. 188

Illustration 3 *Human capital index*

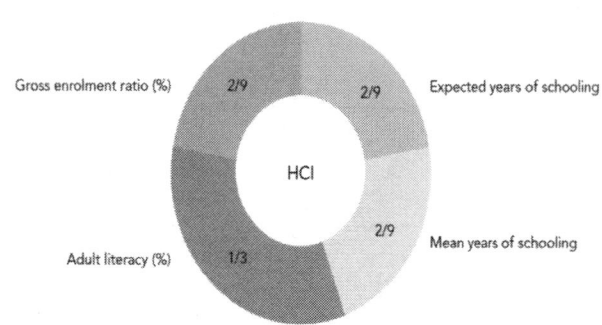

Source: United Nations e-government Survey 2014, UN, p. 188

Illustration 4 *Online Services Index*

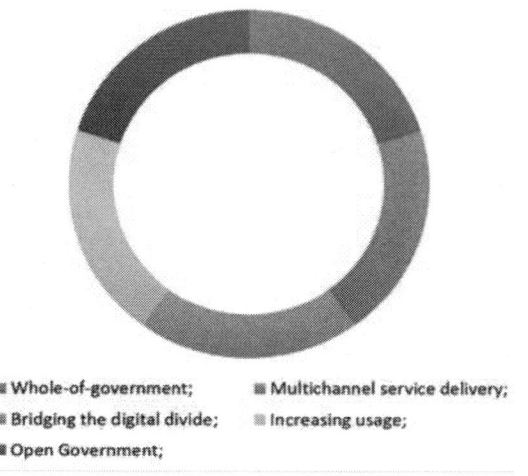

Source: United Nations e-government Survey 2014, UN, p. 192

It is important to note that the Human Capital Index (Illustration 4), consider the Survey questionnaire is organized in specific thematic (Subthemes) structured in four topics, Corresponding to the four stages of e - government development. the thematic subthemes are identified by UN [2]: Moreover, Naser [4], makes a proposal of 10 indicators plus 6 extended, to the evaluation of e-government. it should be noted that there are still no known data of these indicators, however, it is important to publicize, since in some future could work to obtain information.

The key indicators are [4]:

1. CEG1 Percentage of employed in government institutions routinely using computers for their work
2. CEG2 Percentage of employees in government institutions routinely use the Internet for their work
3. CEG3 Percentage of employees in government institutions routinely use e-mail for your work
4. CEG4 Percentage of government institutions with Internet presence in your own website or the website of another entity
5. CEG5 Percentage of government institutions with corporate networks (LAN, WAN, Intranet)
6. CEG6 Percentage of government institutions with interoperability standards
7. CEG7 Percentage of government institutions with Internet access by type of access (narrowband, fixed broadband and mobile broadband)
8. CEG8 Percentage of government organizations offering services platforms users, according with this type of platform available: web, phone, fax and mobile phone
9. CEG9 Percentage of government institutions offering online services by type of activity
10. CEG10 Percentage of government institutions offering online services by type of service

Extended Indicators
1. EEG11 Percentage of ICT expenditure in the total expenditure, government organizations

ISBN: 1-60132-454-5, CSREA Press ©

2. EEG12 Percentage of employees in ICT in government organizations
3. EEG13 Percentage of employees in government institutions with computer skills
4. EEG14 Percentage of employees in government institutions with skills in using internet
5. EEG15 Percentage of government organizations that provide ICT training to their employees
6. EEG16 Percentage of ICT budget spent on ICT training

4 International context of the e-government

It is important to highlight the effort made by the countries around the world to implement and improve the rate of development of e-government. To do this, are presented below in Table 1, world leaders in this area, grouped by continent, as well as a comparative growth between 2012 and 2014 [2]

Table 1. *world leaders in e-government*

World e-government leaders	Regional e-government leaders	
Republic of Korea	AFRICA	Tunisia
Australia		Mauritius
Singapore	AMERICAS	United States of America
France		Canada
Netherlands	ASIA	Republic of Korea
Japan		Singapore
United States of America	EUROPE	France
United Kingdom		Netherlands
New Zealand	OCEANIA	Australia
Finland		New Zealand

Source: United Nations e-government Survey 2014, UN, 2014, p. 5

On the other hand, are shown in Table 2, the ranking of countries in Africa, in they the more meaningful advances are 20 and up to 70 among of 2012 vs 2014 positions on the top-ranked 2014 where Tunisia at position 75 are displayed.

Table 2. *Ranking e-government of the African countries*

Country	Level of Income	EGDI	2014 Rank	2012 Rank	Change in Rank
High EGDI					
Tunisia	Upper Middle	0.5390	75	103	↑ 28
Mauritius	Upper Middle	0.5338	76	93	↑ 17
Egypt	Lower Middle	0.5129	80	107	↑ 27
Seychelles	Upper Middle	0.5113	81	84	↑ 3
Morocco	Lower Middle	0.5060	82	120	↑ 38
Middle EGDI					
South Africa	Upper Middle	0.4869	93	101	↑ 8
Botswana	Upper Middle	0.4198	112	121	↑ 9
Namibia	Upper Middle	0.3880	117	123	↑ 6
Kenya	Low	0.3805	119	119	-
Libya	Upper Middle	0.3753	121	191	↑ 70
Ghana	Lower Middle	0.3735	123	145	↑ 22
Rwanda	Low	0.3589	125	140	↑ 15
Zimbabwe	Low	0.3585	126	133	↑ 7
Cape Verde	Lower Middle	0.3551	127	118	↓ 9
Gabon	Upper Middle	0.3294	131	129	↓ 2
Algeria	Upper Middle	0.3106	136	132	↓ 4
Swaziland	Lower Middle	0.3056	138	144	↑ 6
Angola	Upper Middle	0.2970	140	142	↑ 2
Nigeria	Lower Middle	0.2929	141	162	↑ 21
Cameroon	Lower Middle	0.2782	144	147	↑ 3
Regional Average		0.2661			
World Average		0.4712			

Source: United Nations e-government Survey 2014, UN, 2014, p. 22

Table 3. *Ranking e-government of the American Countries*

Country	Level of Income	EGDI	2014 Rank	2012 Rank	Change in Rank
Very High EGDI					
United States of America	High	0.8748	7	5	↓ 2
Canada	High	0.8418	11	11	-
High EGDI					
Uruguay	High	0.7420	26	50	↑ 24
Chile	High	0.7122	33	39	↑ 6
Argentina	Upper Middle	0.6306	46	56	↑ 10
Colombia	Upper Middle	0.6173	50	43	↓ 7
Costa Rica	Upper Middle	0.6061	54	77	↑ 23
Brazil	Upper Middle	0.6008	57	59	↑ 2
Barbados	High	0.5933	59	44	↓ 15
Antigua and Barbuda	High	0.5927	60	49	↓ 11
Mexico	Upper Middle	0.5733	63	55	↓ 8
Venezuela (Bolivarian Republic of)	Upper Middle	0.5564	67	71	↑ 4
Peru	Upper Middle	0.5435	72	82	↑ 10
Panama	Upper Middle	0.5242	77	66	↓ 11
Grenada	Upper Middle	0.5220	78	75	↑ 3
Ecuador	Upper Middle	0.5053	83	102	↑ 19
Middle EGDI					
El Salvador	Lower Middle	0.4989	88	74	↓ 14
Saint Kitts and Nevis	High	0.4980	90	81	↓ 9
Trinidad and Tobago	High	0.4932	91	67	↓ 24
Bahamas	High	0.4900	92	65	↓ 27
Regional Average		0.5074			
World Average		0.4712			

Source: United Nations e-government Survey 2014, UN, 2014, p. 24

In the case of America (see Table 3) the countries that have experienced a significant increase in the index e-government are Uruguay, Chile, Argentina, Costa Rica and Brazil. In the case of Mexico, it fell 8 positions in relation 2014 vs 2012.

Table 4. *Ranking e-government of the Asian Countries*

Country	Level of Income	EGDI	2014 Rank	2012 Rank	Change in Rank
Very High EGDI					
Republic of Korea	High	0.9462	1	1	-
Singapore	High	0.9076	3	10	↑ 7
Japan	High	0.8874	6	18	↑ 12
Israel	High	0.8162	17	16	↓ 1
Bahrain	High	0.8089	18	36	↑ 18
High EGDI					
Kazakhstan	Upper Middle	0.7283	28	38	↑ 10
United Arab Emirates	High	0.7136	32	28	↓ 4
Saudi Arabia	High	0.6900	36	41	↑ 5
Qatar	High	0.6362	44	48	↑ 4
Oman	High	0.6273	48	64	↑ 16
Kuwait	High	0.6268	49	63	↑ 14
Malaysia	Upper Middle	0.6115	52	40	↓ 12
Georgia	Lower Middle	0.6047	56	72	↑ 16
Cyprus	High	0.5958	58	45	↓ 13
Armenia	Lower Middle	0.5897	61	94	↑ 33
Mongolia	Lower Middle	0.5581	65	76	↑ 11
Azerbaijan	Upper Middle	0.5472	68	96	↑ 28
China	Upper Middle	0.5450	70	78	↑ 8
Turkey	Upper Middle	0.5443	71	80	↑ 9
Sri Lanka	Lower Middle	0.5418	74	115	↑ 41
Regional Average		0.4951			
World Average		0.4712			

Source: United Nations e-government Survey 2014, UN, 2014, p. 28

In the case of the countries of Asia (see Table 4) are led by Republic of Korea, Singapore, Japan and Israel, in some cases increased over 12 positions in the top 20 worldwide. It is important to note that countries like Armenia rose Azerbaijan and 28 and 33posiciones of 2012 to 2014.

ISBN: 1-60132-454-5, CSREA Press ©

Table 5. Ranking e-government of the Europe countries

Country	Level of Income	EGDI	2014 Rank	2012 Rank	Change in Rank
Very High EGDI					
France	High	0.8938	4	6	↑ 2
Netherlands	High	0.8897	5	2	↓ 3
United Kingdom	High	0.8695	8	3	↓ 5
Finland	High	0.8449	10	9	↓ 1
Spain	High	0.8410	12	23	↑ 11
Norway	High	0.8357	13	8	↓ 5
Sweden	High	0.8225	14	7	↓ 7
Estonia	High	0.8180	15	20	↑ 5
Denmark	High	0.8162	16	4	↓ 12
Iceland	High	0.7970	19	22	↑ 3
Austria	High	0.7912	20	21	↑ 1
Germany	High	0.7864	21	17	↓ 4
Ireland	High	0.7810	22	34	↑ 12
Italy	High	0.7593	23	32	↑ 9
Luxembourg	High	0.7591	24	19	↓ 5
Belgium	High	0.7564	25	24	↓ 1
High EGDI					
Russian Federation	High	0.7296	27	27	-
Lithuania	High	0.7271	29	29	-
Switzerland	High	0.7267	30	15	↓ 15
Latvia	High	0.7178	31	42	↑ 11
Regional Average		0.6936			
World Average		0.4712			

Source: United Nations e-government Survey 2014, UN, 2014, p. 31

In the case of countries of European (See Table 5) increases between 2012 and 2014. are displayed increase to 12 positions for Denmark and decrements of 15 positions for Switzerland, Nonetheless the countries shown are within the top 35 worldwide.

Table 6. Ranking e-government of the Oceania Countries

Country	Level of Income	EGDI	2014 Rank	2012 Rank	Change in Rank
Very High EGDI					
Australia	High	0.9103	2	12	↑ 10
New Zealand	High	0.8644	9	13	↑ 4
High EGDI					
Fiji	Upper Middle	0.5044	85	105	↑ 20
Middle EGDI					
Tonga	Upper Middle	0.4706	98	111	↑ 13
Palau	Upper Middle	0.4415	108	113	↑ 5
Samoa	Upper Middle	0.4204	111	114	↑ 3
Micronesia (Federated States of)	Upper Middle	0.3337	130	127	↓ 3
Kiribati	Upper Middle	0.3201	132	149	↑ 17
Tuvalu	Upper Middle	0.3059	137	134	↓ 3
Marshall Islands	Upper Middle	0.2851	142	146	↑ 4
Nauru	Upper Middle	0.2776	145	141	↓ 4
Vanuatu	Lower Middle	0.2571	159	135	↓ 24
Low EGDI					
Solomon Islands	Lower Middle	0.2087	170	168	↓ 2
Papua New Guinea	Lower Middle	0.1203	188	177	↓ 11
Regional Average		0.4086			
World Average		0.4712			

Source: United Nations e-government Survey 2014, UN, 2014, p. 36

Finally, the continent of Oceania, showing two of its top 10 leaders in the world, which have experienced increases in positions 10 and 4 (Australia and New Zealand respectively).

Moreover, countries like Vanuatu reflect a decrease of 24 positions, while Kiribati increased by 17 positions of this index among 2012 to 2014 (See Table 6)

5   Local context of the e-government in Mexico

In the case of Mexico, although it has tried to stay above the world average, it takes further efforts to improve the index e-government, and likewise that not only the federal government evidencing progress on these indicators, the state governments and even local governments could make the effort to incorporate the indicators suggested by the UN, to standardize efforts and generate synergy in the solutions in the three levels of government as well as sharing knowledge and skills. I suggest a uniform growth in the nation or even region of Latin America. However, this does not happen in the case of local governments, not generate their own indicators, that result confuse the objective pursued with the Information Technology and Communication, as is the use of social networks as a channel only communication for contact with citizens, or generate web portals that not receive attention causing loss credibility. In this *sense,* it is presented in Table 7, a perspective of local e-government in Mexico, which is to identify the degree of maturity of e local *government,* but they do not consider all the indicators identified by the UN to validate the level of progress. However, they support to give us an idea of which areas needed to develop.

Table 7. Maturity of e-government in Mexico in 2009

Topic	Weighing
ICT infrastructure	27%
Organizational structure	22%
Regulatory framework	8%
Impulse to digital government	18%
Digital service maturity	17%
Security and privacy of information	8%
Total	100%

Source: Secretary of the public function, cited in Ruiz Morales Contreras (2014) "Perspectives local e-government in Mexico," Toluca, Autonomous University of the State of Mexico, p. 79.

In this line of ideas, as mentioned above, local governments generate their own indicators such as the use of social networks, possession and creating web pages, interaction with mobile devices and digital communication, that serving to measure the use of information technologies, they do not use the indicators suggested by the UN [2], which that can disperse the real goal with the of e-government, where local governments are more concerned about the use of these digital media, that by all the context surrounding the use and successful implementation of ICT. In this sense, it shown the digital government index, which takes as indicators [5]:

- Use social networking
- Tenure and website creation
- Interaction with Mobile Devices

ISBN: 1-60132-454-5, CSREA Press ©

- Digital communication

Due to the above, below it shows the ranking of the top ten municipalities in Mexico in digital government (see Table 8)

Table 8. *Ranking of the first 10 municipalities in the digital government index in Mexico*

No.	Municipality	State
1	Culiacán	Sinaloa
2	Celaya	Guanajuato
3	Tlajomulco de Zúñiga	Jalisco
4	Torreón	Coahuila
5	Miguel Hidalgo	Distrito Federal
6	Colima	Colima
7	Cuautitlán Izcalli	Estado de México
8	León	Guanajuato
9	Irapuato	Guanajuato
10	Guanajuato	Guanajuato

Source: Digital Municipality government (2014), http://indicemunicipal.mx/ recovered 06/01/2016

On the other hand, are shown in Table 9, the ranking of the last 10 places of 500 registered in the study [5].

Table 9. *Ranking of the last 10 municipalities in the index of digital government in Mexico*

No.	Municipality	State
490	Palmar de Bravo	Puebla
491	Pijijiapan	Chiapas
492	Pinotepa Nacional	Oaxaca
493	Reforma	Chiapas
494	Salto de Agua	Chiapas
495	San Pedro	Coahuila
496	Santa María del Río	San Luis Potosí
497	Santo Domingo Tehuantepec	Oaxaca
498	Tres Valles	Veracruz
499	Zinapécuaro	Michoacán
500	Zongolica	Veracruz

Source: Digital Municipality Government (2014), http://indicemunicipal.mx/ recovered 06/01/2016.

Within the index Digital Municipal Government, several problems that have been identified are presented, and generate miscalculation and uncertainty in its application, as listed below:

A. Portal web and formalities online
- 16% of the 500 most populated municipalities of Mexico does not yet have its own website
- Only 17% of municipalities offers transactional procedures on its website; that is, you can start and conclude online
- Half of the municipalities do not have an email account contact your website

- Only 4.4% of municipalities with web site has a chat and 5.2% with a blog. 28.2% have a newsletter
- Only half of municipalities use video as a communication tool, either via web or via YouTube
- The news section is the content that is found more often in municipal websites (84%)

B. Social Networks
- 25% of municipalities do not use social networks
- Of the municipalities that use social networks, only 33% responded to the public in the last month
- Facebook is the most used social network by municipalities; 60% have an account
- 52% of municipalities have a Twitter account, 42% have a YouTube channel and only 23% have a Google+ account
- A minority of 12% of the municipalities has four major social networks:
- Facebook, Twitter, YouTube, Google+

C. Mobile
- Only a quarter of municipalities have website for mobile phones
- Only 3% of the municipalities has a native application for smartphones
- Only 20 of 500 municipalities have SMS service to receive complaints or questions of citizenship
- 11% of the municipalities that have formats to send data or a search engine on your site, but, do not have in their mobile version

6   Discussion

This research was based on the number of households with access to internet as a basis for the proposed of additional indicators that suggest the UN, within this were conducted comparative of indicators as the "per capita income", "economically active population "to generate relationships and analysis and interpretation.

This analysis was conducted with a sample of 50 municipalities with 2554, of which the first places were taken with internet access; this information is found available in the INEGI [6].

At the beginning of the investigation, they suggest include two indicators in the index of human capital, however, the end of the analysis and comparison between indicators was noted that the only indicator that was related to internet access was the per capita income. The results were that 62% of the municipalities that were in the top 50, remained at the top in relation to housing with internet and with the best per capita income. Moreover, by mixing the third indicator related to the economically active population, only 38% of municipalities were retained in the top 50. From the above, it is suggested to include only the indicator of per capita income indicators to human capital as suggested by the UN. Moreover, it is worth commenting that the exercise includes the number of school years by municipality and this indicator remained in the top 50 in all three indicators studied, this indicator is already included in suggested by the United Nations. It should be noted that the indicator is suggested to include the rest of the already suggested by the UN, must collaborate with the other indicators

ISBN: 1-60132-454-5, CSREA Press ©

and not be treated independently. It would have been worth a complete exercise where all indicators will be analyzed and proposed be added, however, the information not exist for these indicators at the municipal level. Moreover, it is well imperative to mention that all indicators suggesting the UN should be included by municipal governments, to perform a comprehensive study, which would make local governments on the one hand implement all indicators, and on the other hand, could identify their weaknesses, develop strategies to reduce and expand their strengths, and gradually increase their indicators of e-government. From the above, it is presented in Table 10 a comparative performed and the results, analysis and interpretation resulted in the proposal of the indicator.

Table 10. *Relation and analysis of indicators of Households with internet, per capita income and Economically Active Population.*

Municipally	State	VCI*	IPer	EAP
San Pedro Garza García	Nuevo León	1	3	163
Benito Juárez	Ciudad de México	2	4	2
Coyoacán	Ciudad de México	3	10	26
Miguel Hidalgo	Ciudad de México	4	7	11
San Nicolás de los Garza	Nuevo León	5	13	57
Álvaro Obregón	Ciudad de México	6	67	15
Tlalpan	Ciudad de México	7	39	37
Cuajimalpa de Morelos	Ciudad de México	8	6	34
Zapopan	Jalisco	9	28	40
Metepec	Estado de México	10	20	136
Azcapotzalco	Ciudad de México	11	42	41
Cuauhtémoc	Ciudad de México	12	41	7

Corregidora	Querétaro	13	11	58
Huixquilucan	Estado de México	14	16	160
San Sebastián Tutla	Oaxaca	15	25	12
Atizapán de Zaragoza	Estado de México	16	43	71
La Magdalena Contreras	Ciudad de México	17	121	42
Guadalajara	Jalisco	18	57	29
Iztacalco	Ciudad de México	19	87	32
Monterrey	Nuevo León	20	21	122
Cuautitlán Izcalli	Estado de México	21	29	106
Ciudad Madero	Tamaulipas	22	18	313
Guadalupe	Nuevo León	23	50	90
La Paz	Baja California Sur	24	12	36
Hermosillo	Sonora	25	40	76
Cuernavaca	Morelos	26	14	53
Tlalnepantla de Baz	Estado de México	27	48	143
Venustiano Carranza	Ciudad de México	28	91	30
San Andrés Cholula	Puebla	29	76	229

Chihuahua	Chihuahua	30	24	125
Coacalco de Berriozábal	Estado de México	31	63	117
Tampico	Tamaulipas	32	49	133
Gustavo A. Madero	Ciudad de México	33	89	61
Cananea	Sonora	34	62	1116
Querétaro	Querétaro	35	34	39
Naucalpan de Juárez	Estado de México	36	59	128
Boca del Río	Veracruz	37	17	131
Xochimilco	Ciudad de México	38	147	79
Xalapa	Veracruz	39	45	101
Zacatecas	Zacatecas	40	68	225
Victoria	Tamaulipas	41	102	132
Tijuana	Baja California	42	32	54
Mexicali	Baja California	43	101	110
San Luis Potosí	San Luis Potosí	44	22	154
Mérida	Yucatán	45	31	75
Monclova	Coahuila	46	136	496
Villa de Álvarez	Colima	47	38	20
Santa Catarina	Nuevo León	48	106	64
San Andrés Huayápam	Oaxaca	49	267	13
Cozumel	Quintana roo	50	33	25

* VCI. Households with Access to Internet, Ipre. Percapita income, PEA. Economically Active Population. **. per capita income y Economically Active Population was generated from all 2554 of 2005, as it was the most complete information, on the other hand, the number of households with internet access was obtained of 2010 of the INEGI (2010).

Source: Owner (2016), based on information from INEGI (2010)

7 Conclusions

We can conclude that it is not to include indicators irrationally, but rather to suggest indicators to those already proposed by the UN, to enrich and highlight the areas in which local, regional and national governments channel their efforts to raise the rate and e-government and with it successfully incorporate the Information Technology and Communication way, which potentiate and maximize the resources that municipal governments have besides generating transparent, economic, processes available and which collaborate with policy decisions to know what strengths and weaknesses are. In this case, it was confirmed that the indicator of per capita income could collaborate with other indicators which allow local governments to identify and progress that are in the process of e-government. Moreover, it is important to mention that municipal governments should understand that ICT have many dimensions of use, however, requires analysis and projections that exceed their mandates, however, must generate plans in which these technologies can continue to be implemented long term, so that (as) following leaders continue this process of incorporation and take advantage of the benefits associated with the use and implementation of information and communication technologies

ISBN: 1-60132-454-5, CSREA Press ©

8   References

[1] Ruiz, Morales, & Contreras. (2014). Perspectivas del gobierno electrónico local en México. Toluca: Universidad Autónoma del Estado de México.

[2] United Nations. (2014). United Nations e-government Survey. United States of America.

[3] Pérez, Camacho, Mena, & Arroyo. (2016). Análisis General del Gobierno Electrónico en México. Revista de Tecnología y Sociedad, 5(9). Obtenido de http://www.udgvirtual.udg.mx/paakat/index.php/paak at/article/view/253/376

[4] Naser. (05 de 01 de 2010). Indicadores de gobierno electrónico. Recuperado el 01 de 05 de 2016, de http://www.cepal.org/ilpes/noticias/paginas/1/43321/I ndicadores_sobre_GE.pdf

[5] Digital Municipal Government . (06 de 01 de 2014). Gobierno Digital. Recuperado el 01 de 05 de 2016, de http://indicemunicipal.mx/

[6] INEGI (2010) Censos economicos y poblacional, México

Ethical Concerns Regarding the use of Bioinformatics and Computational Genomics

Suhair Amer
Department of Computer Science, Southeast Missouri State University,
Cape Girardeau, MO, USA

Abstract *–Bioinformatics is an interdisciplinary field that develops methods and software tools for understanding biological data. Computational genomics refers to the use of computational and statistical analysis to decipher biology from genome sequences and related data. This paper will briefly discuss Bioinformatics, its uses, some of its advantages and disadvantages and the ethical concerns regarding the use of Bioinformatics.*

Keywords: bioinformatics, computational genomics, science, technology, genome, data.

1   Introduction/definition

The development of humans throughout history is associated with the development of their technology. Technology has gone from being simple tools used for hunting to highly cutting-edge technology of today. Among the developments are bioinformatics and computational genomics. These two concepts combine cyber technology with biological data and genetics. Bioinformatics is defined as *"the application of information technology to ... molecular biology ... now [through] the creation and development of databases, algorithms, computational and statistical techniques, and theory to solve formal and practical problems arising from the management and analysis of biological data"* [Marturano 2016].

Another definition of bioinformatics simply relates computer science, biology, and statistics. It refers to the application of computer science to biological issues or problems. It may refer to a variety of topics including *"epidemiology, the modeling of cell dynamics, to its now more common focus, the analysis of sequence data of various kinds"* [Lewis and Bartlett 2016]. Genomics is one example for a method of analysis of data sequences, which is the *"study of structure, content, and evolution of genomes"* [Gibson and Muse 2009]. The study of genomics includes research on both proteins and genes.

There are constantly new discoveries and advancements in the fields of cell science, which relies heavily on the utilization of computers, computational systems, and techniques. This has driven the development of bioinformatics and computational genomics that involve both the software engineering and science communities [Tavani 2013].

Bioinformatics, which is a branch of informatics that comprises the investigations, transmission, sharing, representation, and recreation of data on a computer. This exposes and improves quality based medication which was possible because of the openly accessible genomic data which was the consequence of the Human Genome Project [MscBio 2016].

Computational genomics uses electronic systems, apparatuses, and ways to obtain, store, compose, examine, incorporate, envision, and recreate information. The information is constrained to genomic data, rather than the more extensive, natural information [Tavani 2013].

Computational genomics can help break down tremendous amounts of DNA-sequencers-fragmentary proof. It can display organic data, allow us to make forecasts, allow us to consolidate information from unique datasets, and permit us to achieve new conclusions, stores substantial amounts of information financially and safely. This can be achieved by utilizing calculations, information structure, design coordinating, indexing pressure, data recovery, dispersed and parallel figuring, distributed computing, and machine learning [Langmead].

Cell biology has been researched and depends on the application of computers and computational techniques and methodologies. In general, Bioinformatics is a branch of informatics, which involves the acquisition, storage, manipulation, analyses, transmission, sharing, visualization, and simulation of information on a computer. Biological data consist of, biological systems, and medical and health data. Similarly, computational genomics uses computerized techniques, tools, and approaches to acquire, store, organize, analyze, synthesize, visualize, and simulate data. However, the analyzed data is limited to genetic/genomic information [Tavani 2013].

The Human Genome Project [OEK 2016] demonstrated the role that computer technology and computational tools can play in genetic research and providing information related to gene sequences.

The explosion of publicly available genomic information resulting in the Human Genome Project has precipitated the need for bioinformatics capabilities. The goal of the project was to determine the sequence of the entire human genome that would be reached by the year 2002. Bioinformatics is essential to the use of genomic information in understanding human diseases and in the identification of new molecular targets for drug recovery. [BioPanet 2016]

In the mid of 1990s, Bioinformatics grew rapidly as a field due to the increase of genetic and biochemical data and the demand for the ability to handle the large quantities of information. *"To understand the links between pieces of information from research areas such as molecular biology, structural biochemistry, enzymology, cell biology, physiology, and pathology, bioinformatics uses computational power to catalog. Organize, and structure these pieces into biologically meaningful entities"* [Rashidi and Lukas 2000]. Entities describe how genetic and biomedical data are organized based on its cellular characteristics which lead to determining ancestral-form-of-life from which all life evolved [Rashidi and Lukas 2000]. DNA is a common topic of study and research in bioinformatics which is used to determine and understand gene codes. Furthermore, comparative genomics studies the relationship of homologous genes and evolution in all species and utilizes bioinformatics [Rashidi and Lukas 2000].

2 Examples of Uses

Bioinformatics and computational genomics was utilized as a key part of the Human Genome Project. This significantly quickened the exploration done in the project and permitted researches to outline completely human genome in advance [Tavani 2013]. This project incorporated forms of technology used in molecular biology into the study of the human genetic code and the speeding up of gene processes. It allowed for the use and development of computer programs that can compare and predict the sequences and structures of DNA, RNA, and proteins for medical and experimental purposes [Marturano 2016].

Computational genomics was utilized as a part of the improvement of the BLAST succession arrangement program, which utilized instrument and installation to organic examination [Langmead]. It was used to anticipate new individuals from quality families, investigate developmental connections, sequence entire genomes, and utilize arrangement similarity to foresee the area and capacity of protein-coding regulation areas in genomic DNA [BLAST].

Bioinformatics is, also, used in *"Microbial genome applications, molecular medicine, personalized medicine, preventative medicine, gene therapy, drug development,* *antibiotic resistance, evolutionary studies, waste cleanup, biotechnology, climate change studies, alternative energy sources, crop improvement, forensic analysis bio-weapon creation, insect resistance, improve nutritional quality, development of drought resistant varieties, and veterinary science"* [Lappidus 2005] .

Bioinformatics is used in clinical testing and is a key component in next-generation sequencing (NGS) technologies that can be used to give patients more accurate genome test results. A patient's DNA is compared with genetic data stored in other databases using software programs, known as the "bioinformatics pipeline," in order to obtain results. *"This so-called bioinformatics pipeline uses algorithms to align multiple copies of overlapping raw sequences to a human reference sequence and then uses other algorithms to detect where the patient's DNA differs from the reference sequence"* [Yohe et al. 2015].

Another example is the use of bioinformatics and computational genomics in testing and experimenting with plants, animals, and bacteria. Many different plants and animals have been genetically modified for scientific and agricultural study. Bioinformatics and computational genomics have made it possible to model the genetic and biological makeup of these organisms, allowing scientists to analyze which portions of the DNA to manipulate for experiments [Gersbach 2014]. There have been fifty-five plant genomes sequenced and produced such as the *Arabidopsis thaliana* [Michael and Jackson 2013] . Using selective breeding strategies, there have been agricultural developments and the food quality or sustainability of crops has been optimized. For instance, scientists have *"genetically engineered frost-resistant plants with a gene from a cold water fish"* [Key et al. 2016] .

Computing related to bioinformatics utilizes algorithm analysis, data structures, information retrieval, and software engineering. Algorithms are used for searching and information retrieval. Data structures allows us to organize data, and create interfaces that are beneficial to the user. Software engineering build the complicated software [Lesk 2002]. Raw, scientific information and details including experimental results, annotations, or supplementary information are stored in a databank or a database. Databases and the World Wide Web allow bioinformatics to organize the genetic and biochemical data. Online websites can act as databases, such as the NHI website that contains both the GenBank database that contains genetic sequences and the PubMed database that houses a literature search engine [Gibson and Muse 2009].

By using bioinformatics, a complete microbial genome can be predicted, which allows us to determine the gene length of microbial species. For example, the gene length of a strain of *Escherichia coli (E. coli)* 4,288 predicted genes. Research of species-specific and developmental genes and eliminating pathogenic agents; facilitated the understanding of genes of

ISBN: 1-60132-454-5, CSREA Press ©

malaria, especially its transmission via mosquito that assisted in creating preventative or contingent measures for diseases [Gibson and Muse 2009].

3   Advantages and Disadvantages

3.1   Advantages

Bioinformatics and computational genomics has the capacity to take in unlimited measures of data, have precise confirmation, and time efficiency, have the capacity to store and distinguish attributes, and have open, vast databases readily available [MscBio 2016] .

Another advantage of bioinformatics and computational genomics involve healthcare and the use of genetic studies in diagnosis and treatment of diseases with the advances in computing technology. In addition, advanced concepts such as grid, pervasive, and universal computing offer computational power for the collaborative and on-demand services needed by bioinformatics [Kesh and Wullianallur 2016].

Computational analysis can make genome sequences much easier to read and understand [Koonin 2001] which provides the basis for the medical advances made concerning the human genome. Sequencing technology has become more broadly used and available. Doctors use this technology to test and treat patients. A person's genome sequencing data can be analyzed through many different software packages and then compared to a reference sequence in order to find any differences or abnormalities [Yohe et al. 2015]. If a patient has some type of defect, mutation, or vulnerability to a certain disease, the patient can undergo gene editing or gene therapy in order to alter or replace the defective or vulnerable genes [Gersbach 2014].

Genetic modifications to plants have been advantageous to multiple industries such as agriculture, food, and medical. Plants and crops are now engineered to sustain environmental stresses, such as drought, extreme temperature or salinity, insects and pathogens [Key et al. 2016]. The crop's nutritional content, for corn and soybean, for example, can also be boosted which is an advantage especially for developing worlds [Key et al. 2016]. Crops and plants are also being developed for "*recombinant medicines and industrial products, such as monoclonal antibodies, vaccines, plastics and biofuels*" [Key et al. 2016] .

Finally, bacteria such as *E. coli* can be treated or prevented through the study of microbial genomics; whereas, utilizing parasite genomics, tropical diseases such as malaria or yellow fever can be treated [Gibson and Muse 2009].

3.2   Disadvantages

To have access to the knowledge that would change our lives, more powerful and vigorous computing is needed to develop the tools for genetically based drug design, medical diagnosis and treatment, and agricultural application. This requires constant development of both software algorithms and hardware to deal with the enormous size of databases and efficient use of algorithms [Kesh and Wullianallur 2016].

Computing professionals, including developers, programmers, consultants, and vendors, are concerned with building and testing robust applications and dealing with performance issues such as correctness of data, reliability, and real-time processing, and integration and management of data deployed to serve multiple purposes simultaneously. This is because the public is concerned with the ethics, privacy, potential misuse of data, and public and social policies related to medical applications. This is because every citizen is involved in these issues, including social workers, legal and medical professionals, lawmakers, patients, and other participants, including pharmaceutical companies and healthcare providers [Kesh and Wullianallur 2016].

Bioinformatics and computational genomics provide the ability to potentially fix genome defects and prevent disease, but their long-term effects are still uncertain. They may fix specific problems now but could possibly lead to others later on. "*Such technologies imply new possibilities for improving health but, on the other hand, they are still at an experimental stage and therefore should be implemented under rigorous safety testing before going on general release*" [Marturano 2016] .

The use of technology in genome studies can be beneficial, but it is becoming dependent on it, which could lead to serious problems such as the possibility of having lack of human skill in those fields. Originally, genetics used to be thought of as a science that did not need computers, but the development of bioinformatics and computational genomics has made computer technology almost a requirement for further studies of the human genome [Marturano 2016].

Other disadvantages is related to the use of vulnerable tools and multiple bioinformatics software packages in analyzing a person's genome sequence. If the tools are improperly used or developed, they can influence the results. It has been noticed that different software packages are not all specific and sensitive to the same degree when looking for differences in DNA sequences and structures [Yohe et al. 2015].

The use of bioinformatics could lead to a "designer baby", where parents choose the physiological traits of their children or offspring [Singh 2012]. It could also negatively affect the gene pool including animals and plants. It can cause discomfort if it is related to animal breeding and can negatively affects the environment by the "*elimination of natural populations and the processes of natural selection*" [Perzigian 2016]. Hybridization of genetically modified plants is also a concern. Through the transfer of pollen, genetically modified plants will hybrid with non-modified plants, which will alter the genetics of the natural plant. Genetically modified plants may become invasive or pose a threat to consumers' health [Key et al. 2016]. Disadvantages within microbial or parasite genomics include having the strains of DNA of bacteria or disease may become tolerant to products used to treat them and therefore spread uncontrolled [Gibson and Muse 2009].

In summary, Bioinformatics and calculation genomics requires extensive processing power. There is the assumption that every new research must incorporate technology. Identifiable qualities can be lost without printed versions. Accessing inconceivable databases are resource and time consuming [MscBio 2016].

4   Ethical Concerns

Most new ideas are met with controversy, and bioinformatics and computational genomics have not been an exception. Some believe that using bioinformatics and computational genomics is not unethical because of the potential health benefits, such as gene therapy [Gersbach 2014]. Others see it as invasive and threatening to individual privacy and rights [Marturano 2016] [Howard et al. 2013].

The term "bioethics" was first used to deal with the application of moral philosophy to medical dilemmas. It emerged because there was a need to reflect philosophically on the problems related to modern medicine. Internet and the use of computers affected the lives of many people as it can alter societies similar to modern medicine. Biotechnology partnered with computer technology affects many aspects of our physical and social lives which lead to concerns regarding computer and applied ethics [Martensen 2001]

By arranging properties or qualities, data mining can distinguish an individual from a group or it can identify groups that have common characteristics. Such classification or profiling is questionable because it is utilizing characteristics that can identify individuals and sometimes is not correct. Bioinformatics and computational genomics can imply certain facts about individuals or groups, which makes them liable. One's personal genetic data can be used in making judgements about individuals, which can result in them being denied employment or insurance. In addition, data collected by bioinformatics and computational genomics is the result of educated assent and picking up consent from human subjects who are interested in the hereditary studies. Such data may not meet the required conditions for as substantial educated assent because some people will shield themselves from vulnerability [Tavani 2013].

Bioinformatics and computational genomics raised ethical concerns with regard to privacy. A person could potentially be identified through his or her genetic data in a bioinformatics computer system. This could lead to the exposure of confidential medical information or other materials that could potentially harm the person [Marturano 2016] .

Ethical issues can affect the methodology used by bioinformatics and computational genomics research that may have consequences with regard to the information clinicians deliver to patients. Contexts can be different according to the type of studies performed. The different study designs will require different ethical issues. The use of different types of biological samples, from DNA genotyping to proteomics, may provide results with varying consequences to individuals and the population [Elston, Olson and Palmer 2002] [Barnetche, Gourraud, and Cambon-Thomsen 2005].

Another ethical issue with the use of bioinformatics and computational genomics is concerned with the intellectual property and ownership of genetic data. Since participants in genetic studies donate samples of their DNA to databases, it is not clear if they forfeit all of their rights concerning the use of their genetic data. It is not clear if the database have total control of the data. It is not clear if the government have any say and who is the true owner of this genetic data. There are few laws that have been put in place to protect the privacy of and autonomy of participants in genetic research, but they do not say who technically owns the genetic data in the databases [Tavani 2013].

Ethical concerns of the Human Genome Project revolve around privacy and confidentially of genetic information, psychological impact, and philosophical debate. Many are concerned with privacy of genetic information since government sponsored databanks are supplied to medical research companies. The psychological impact refers to mistrust in reference to race or economic status. The philosophical debate centers around the view of genetic modification as "playing God" in any organism, and whether or not such actions are morally wrong or right [Gibson and Muse 2009] .

With regards to ethical concerns of animal genomics, "*Animal rights advocates also argue that each species should enjoy an inherent, natural right to be free of genetic manipulation in any form*" [Perzigian 2016] .

Ethical concerns in plant genomics center around the "naturalness" of the plants, whether or not a genetically modified plant is "natural" or safe for human consumption [Key et al. 2016] .

5   Conclusion

Bioinformatics is a promising field with the potential to be developed further into a larger opportunity for both computer scientists and biologists. Excellent working examples have been developed and is in use such as the GenBank and the PubMed databases. It is accessible but possess the risk of loss and misuse.

Genomics as a field has already made huge impacts on society including the Human Genome Project and in selective breeding in animals and plants. It has advantages medically and

ISBN: 1-60132-454-5, CSREA Press ©

economically, but it also has disadvantages related to the environmental and consumer health. It also has ethical concerns of privacy, mistrust in racial or economic status, animal rights, plant "naturalness", and the intrusiveness of "playing God".

In summary, bioinformatics and computational genomics have drastically improved the exploration of hereditary qualities, biotechnology, and medicine. We now have the advancements needed to discover new medications and drugs.

6   References

[Barnetche, Gourraud, and Cambon-Thomsen 2005] Barnetche T, Gourraud PA, Cambon-Thomsen A. Strategies in analysis of the genetic component of multifactorial diseases; biostatistical aspects. Transpl Immunol 2005;14:255–266.

[BioPanet 2016] BioPlanet. *What is Bioinformatics?* 2013. Web. 9 June 2016.

[BLAST] [BLAST] Madden, Tom. "The BLAST Sequence Analysis Tool." The NCBI Handbook. http://unmc.edu/bsbc/docs/NCBI_blast.pdf.

[Elston, Olson and Palmer 2002] Elston RC, Olson JM, Palmer L. Biostatistical Genetics and Genetic Epidemiology. 1st Edn. Chichester, John Wiley & Sons, 2002

[Gersbach 2014] Gersbach, Charles A. "Genome Engineering: The Next Genomic Revolution." *Nature Methods* 11.10 (Oct. 2014): 1009-1011. *EBSCOhost Academic Search Complete*. Web. 2 June 2016.

[Gibson and Muse 2009] Gibson, Greg, and Spencer V. Muse. *A Primer of Genome Science*. 3rd ed. Sunderland, MA: Sinauer Associates, 2009. Print.

[Howard et al. 2013] Howard, H. C., et al. "The Ethical Introduction of Genome-Based Information and Technologies into Public Health." *Public Health Genomics* 16.3 (Feb. 2013): 100-9. *ProQuest*. Web. 2 June 2016.

[Kesh and Wullianallur 2016] Someswa Kesh, Wullianallur Raghupathi. *Criticle Issues in Bioinformatics and Computing*. 11 October 2004. Web. 9 June 2016.

[Key et al. 2016] Key, Suzie, Julian K-C Ma, and Pascal MW Drake. "Genetically Modified Plants and Human Health." *Journal of the Royal Society of Medicine* 101.6 (2008): 290–298. *PMC*. Web. 10 June 2016.

[Koonin 2001] Koonin, Eugene V. "Computational Genomics." *Current Biology* 11.5 (2001): R155-158. *Current Biology*. Elsevier Inc., 6 Mar. 2001. Web. 7 June 2016.

[Langmead] Langmead, Ben. "What Are Genomics and Computational Genomics?" Johns Hopkins. http://www.cs.jhu.edu/~langmea/resources/lecture_notes/genomics_comp_genomics.pdf.

[Lappidus 2005] Lappidus, Alla L. "Advances in Bioinformatics and Its Applications." (2005): n. pag. Bioinformaticsinstitute. Web.

[Lesk 2002] Lesk, Arthur M. *Introduction to Bioinformatics*. Oxford: Oxford UP, 2002. Print.

[Lewis and Bartlett 2016] Lewis, Jamie, and Andrew Bartlett. "Inscribing A Discipline: Tensions In The Field Of Bioinformatics." *New Genetics & Society* 32.3 (2013): 243-263. *Academic Search Complete*. Web. 9 June 2016.

[Martensen 2001] Martensen, R. (2001). "The History of Bioethics: An Essay Review". Journal of the History of Medicine 56: 168-175.

[Marturano 2016] Marturano, Antonio. "Bioinformatics and Ethics." *Bioethics* 23.7 (Sept. 2009): ii-iii. *EBSCOhost Academic Search Complete*. Web. 2 June 2016.

[Michael and Jackson 2013] Michael, T. P., and S. Jackson. 2013. The First 50 Plant Genomes. Plant Genome 6. doi:10.3835/plantgenome2013.03.0001in

[MscBio 2016] "MSc in Bioinformatics Master in Bioinformatics Fac. Biocincies, UAB Http://MScBioinformatics.uab.cat Home ." MSc in Bioinformatics Master in Bioinformatics Fac. Biocincies, UAB Http://MScBioinformatics.uab.cat Home . Accessed June 08, 2016. http://mscbioinformatics.uab.cat/base/base3.asp?sitio=ms bioinformaticsen

[OEK 2016] "Online Education Kit: Bioinformatics: Introduction." *Online Education Kit: Bioinformatics: Introduction*. National Human Genome Research Institute, 18 Mar. 2013. Web. 09 June 2016.

[Perzigian 2016] Perzigian, Andrew B. "Brief Summary of Genetic Engineering and Animals." *Brief Summary of Genetic Engineering and Animals*. Michigan State University College of Law, 2003. Web. 09 June 2016.

[Rashidi and Lukas 2000] Rashidi, Hooman H., and Lukas K. Buehler. *Bioinformatics Basics: Applications in Biological Science and Medicine*. Boca Raton, FL: CRC, 2000. Print

[Singh 2012] Singh, V. "What Is the Human Genome Project and What Are Its Advantage and Disadvantages?" *What Is the Human Genome Project and What Are Its Advantage and Disadvantages?* PreserveArticles, 2012. Web. 09 June 2016.

[Tavani 2013] Tavani, Herman T. *Ethics and Technology: Controversies, Questions, and Strategies for Ethical Computing*. Hoboken, N.J: Wiley, 2013. Print.

[Yohe et al. 2015] Yohe, Sophia L., et al. "Standards for Clinical Grade Genomic Databases." *Archives of Pathology & Laboratory Medicine* 139.11 (Nov. 2015): 1400-1412. *EBSCOhost Academic Search Complete*. Web. 2 June 2016.

SESSION

IT SERVICES, SECURITY ISSUES + MOBILE COMPUTING, INTERNET COMPUTING, CROWDSOURCING, TOOLS AND APPLICATIONS

Chair(s)

TBA

Secure Queryable Dynamic Maps

Naresh Adhikari, Naila Bushra, Mahalingam Ramkumar
Department of Computer Science and Engineering
Mississippi State University, MS.

Abstract—**A high degree of confidence in attribution of owner-ship/control of geographic coordinates, or equivalently, confidence in the output of the point-location problem, viz., "in which region does point (x, y) fall?" can substantially improve the scope of Geographic Information Systems (GIS) based services. We propose a novel framework for secure queryable dynamic maps (SQDM), which is borne out of the need for tangible assurances to the point-location problem.**

I. Introduction

A geographic map is a set of polygons, whose sides represent boundaries between adjacent regions. Separation of regions can be on the basis of state, county, wards, and zones for governing purposes, congressional districts for purposes of elections, parcels, for tracking ownership, etc. Real-world maps may have polygons with tens of thousands of sides. Some polygons may also include one or more islands of excluded regions/polygons.

A *dynamic* geographic map permits reshaping of regions by adding new polygons to the map, possibly by dividing/merging existing polygons. A *queryable* map can answer the question *"in which region does point (x, y) fall?"*

A *secure* queryable dynamic map (SQDM) provides *tangible assurances* of *correctness of responses* to queries. Confidence in the correctness of the response can be leveraged for a wide range of practical eGovernment services, and significantly expand the scope of Geographic Information Systems (GIS) [1] based services. The contribution of this paper is a protocol for constructing and maintaining SQDMs.

A. Minimal TCB

Information is only as useful as the confidence in its correctness. The confidence in the correctness of information provided by the SQDM is limited by the integrity of a process $\mathcal{P}$ which

1) takes a set of edges/vertexes of (any number of) closed polygons as input, and
2) pre-processes the data to create an alternate represen-tation, with the goal of simplifying the process of responding to queries.

A complex process $\mathcal{P}$, manipulating possibly millions of sides/vertexes, is highly susceptible to accidental bugs, and/or deliberate attacks. Given the inverse relationship between integrity and complexity, assuring the integrity of any complex process $\mathcal{P}$ has to begin by identifying a minimal *trusted computing base* (TCB) [2].

The TCB for a process $\mathcal{P}$ is "a minimal amount of hard-ware/software that needs to be trusted" to ensure correctness of $\mathcal{P}$. The motivation for identifying a minimal TCB for $\mathcal{P}$ is to narrow the focus of security efforts towards protecting the integrity of the TCB. Specifically, to the extent the integrity of the TCB is guaranteed, no attack on (or bug in) process $\mathcal{P}$ can escape detection.

The *point location problem*, viz., determining the region in which a point (x, y) lies, is an important problem for several application scenarios, like mouse tracking, computer graphics, GIS etc., and has attracted substantial attention in the literature [3]-[5]. Variants that address situations involving dynamic reshaping of regions also exist. However, current strategies in the literature do not address this problem from the perspective of *minimizing the TCB* for assuring the integrity of the process. This is the gap addressed by this paper.

From a minimal TCB perspective, "a minimal amount of software," viz., TCB functions $\mathcal{T}$, will need to be executed inside "a minimal execution environment," say, module **T**, to

1) verify the integrity of process $\mathcal{P}$, and
2) report its findings to any entity that desires to be assured of the correctness of process $\mathcal{P}$.

For our purposes, we desire that a trustworthy module **T** should be able to verify the correctness of the process $\mathcal{P}$, and hence the response (region where a point (x, y) falls), and provide a digitally signed response to the querier.

In this paper we show that a module **T**, with *small con-stant memory size can* execute the necessary TCB functions for assuring $\mathcal{P}$ – irrespective of the size of the geographic region, or the number of polygons, or the number of sides in each polygon. The modest computational abilities required of module **T** are merely the i) ability to execute a cryptographic hash function $h()$, and ii) a function

$$\text{PointOnLine}((x, y), (x_1, y_1)\text{—}(x_2, y_2)) \qquad (1)$$

to determine if a point (x, y) falls on/above/below a line segment connecting points (x_1, y_1) and (x_2, y_2).

Such modest abilities can leveraged by module **T** to track the dynamic integrity of practically unlimited data items stored virtually, by actually storing only the root of a binary hash tree [6]. Specifically, two hash tree based data structures, viz., dictionaries and two-dimensional look-up tables (2D-LUT)[8], are leveraged:

1) dictionaries for storing line segments of polygons, which are inputs to process $\mathcal{P}$, and
2) 2D-LUTs for storing rectangles, viz., outputs of $\mathcal{P}$.

The rest of this paper is organized as follows. Section II describes the SQDM protocol as a 4 step process. The steps are illustrated by considering an example polygon. Section III outlines state-transition models for TCB functions for assuring

ISBN: 1-60132-454-5, CSREA Press ©

the 4 sub-processes. Section IV discusses experimental results in constructing queryable maps from Shapefiles [7] associated with census data, and some of the advantageous implications of a trustworthy SQDM.

II. SQDM PROTOCOL

We shall begin with the assumption that geographical coordinates for any point on the surface of the earth is represented by a tuple (x, y). As a resource limited module $\mathbf{T}$ needs to perform computations based on such coordinates, (for executing PointOnLine()) we shall restrict values like x and y to be m-bit unsigned integers. As coordinates are discrete points, a point (x, y) is said to lie *on* a line (x_1, y_1)—(x_2, y_2) if

$$y = \text{round}\left((x - x_1)\frac{(y_2 - y_1)}{x_2 - x_1}\right) + y_1. \tag{2}$$

The following notations are used in this Section.

1) $\{(x_1, y_1)$—$(x_2, y_2), \langle R_a, R_b \rangle\}$ is a line-segment connecting two points (x_1, y_1) and (x_2, y_2), where $x_1 \leq x_2$, and $y_1 < y_2$ if $x_1 = x_2$ (vertical lines); the line segment divides two regions – R_a above the line and R_b below the line. For vertical lines R_a is to the left of the line;

2) $[x_1, x_2, u]$ is an entry in a 1-D look-up table. This entry conveys that some value u is associated with all points between X-coordinates x_1 and x_2;

3) $[x_1, x_2, [y_1, y_2, v]]$ is an entry in a two dimensional look-up table (2-D LUT). This entry conveys that some value v is associated with all points in the rectangular region bounded by X-coordinates x_1 and x_2 and Y-coordinates y_1 and y_2.

A. SQDM Process $\mathcal{P}$

The input to the SQDM process $\mathcal{P}$ is a set of lines corresponding to closed polygons, where each line is associated with two points and two region labels. Execution of the process $\mathcal{P}$

1) maps each line to a rectangular region $[x_1, x_2, [y_1, y_2, v]]$, and

2) assigns an appropriate value v to all points in the rectangle, where $v = 0$ implies *undefined* value.

Thereafter, responding to a query regarding any point (x, y) boils down to the trivial problem of identifying the rectangle containing (x, y), and using the value v to answer the query.

The process $\mathcal{P}$ consists of four sub-processes:

1) $\mathcal{P}_0$: to i) pre-process input lines and ii) create templates for a 2-D LUT. More specifically, templates are entries of the form $[x_1, x_2, [y_1, y_2, 0]]$ with value v set to 0;

2) $\mathcal{P}_1$, which assigns value v for each 2-D LUT entry;

3) $\mathcal{P}_2$, that utilizes the 2-D LUT prepared by $\mathcal{P}_1$ to answer queries; and

4) $\mathcal{P}_3$, that allows incremental changes to be performed to the 2-D LUT by making batch execution of $\mathcal{P}_1$ possible.

In the rest of this section the 15 sided polygon in Figure 1, which includes an excluded island (4-sided) polygon, will be used as an example for describing process $\mathcal{P}$.

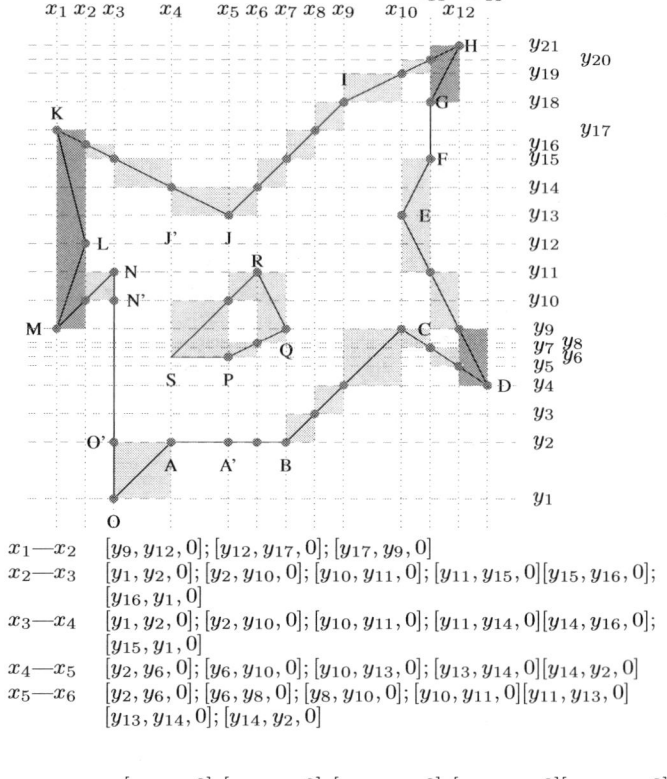

x_1—x_2 $[y_9, y_{12}, 0]; [y_{12}, y_{17}, 0]; [y_{17}, y_9, 0]$
x_2—x_3 $[y_1, y_2, 0]; [y_2, y_{10}, 0]; [y_{10}, y_{11}, 0]; [y_{11}, y_{15}, 0][y_{15}, y_{16}, 0];$
       $[y_{16}, y_1, 0]$
x_3—x_4 $[y_1, y_2, 0]; [y_2, y_{10}, 0]; [y_{10}, y_{11}, 0]; [y_{11}, y_{14}, 0][y_{14}, y_{16}, 0];$
       $[y_{15}, y_1, 0]$
x_4—x_5 $[y_2, y_6, 0]; [y_6, y_{10}, 0]; [y_{10}, y_{13}, 0]; [y_{13}, y_{14}, 0][y_{14}, y_2, 0]$
x_5—x_6 $[y_2, y_6, 0]; [y_6, y_8, 0]; [y_8, y_{10}, 0]; [y_{10}, y_{11}, 0][y_{11}, y_{13}, 0]$
       $[y_{13}, y_{14}, 0]; [y_{14}, y_2, 0]$

$\vdots$

x_{10}—x_{11} $[y_8, y_9, 0]; [y_9, y_{11}, 0]; [y_{11}, y_{13}, 0]; [y_{13}, y_{15}, 0][y_{15}, y_{19}, 0]$
       $[y_{19}, y_{20}, 0]; [y_{20}, y_8, 0]$
x_{11}—x_{12} $[y_5, y_7, 0]; [y_7, y_9, 0]; [y_9, y_{11}, 0]; [y_{11}, y_{15}, 0][y_{15}, y_{18}, 0]$
       $[y_{18}, y_{21}, 0]; [y_{21}, y_5, 0]$
x_{12}—x_{13} $[y_4, y_9, 0]; [y_9, y_4, 0];$

Figure 1: A polygon $ABCDEFGHIJKLMNO$ with 15 sides with an internal island $PQRS$. The X-coordinates of the 15+4 points (x, y) have 13 unique values $x_1 \cdots x_{13}$, creating 12 vertical slabs. Dashed (horizontal) lines represent unique y-values. The figure also depicts of rectangles (2D-LUT items) in selected vertical slabs.

Each process $\mathcal{P}_0 \cdots \mathcal{P}_3$ is associated with a corresponding TCB functionality that assures the correctness of the process. More specifically, from the perspective of TCB functions, the input lines are items of a dictionary, which can be tracked by a module $\mathbf{T}$ by storing a single binary hash tree root p. The output of the TCB functions are rectangles defined by 2D-LUT items. Irrespective of the number of rectangles, module $\mathbf{T}$ needs to store only a single (binary hash tree) root ξ to track all rectangles. The TCB functions are discussed in Section III.

B. Pre-Processing (Process $\mathcal{P}_0$)

Process $\mathcal{P}_0$ consists of the following steps.

1) Similar to [4], identify all unique X-coordinates corresponding to the points (in the figure we have 13 unique points $x_1 \cdots x_{13}$ (dotted vertical lines). These points define 12 vertical strips that can be used to create the first dimension

of the 2-D LUT as

$$[x_1, x_2, 0], [x_2, x_3, 0], \ldots [x_{12}, x_{13}, 0], [x_{13}, x_1, 0], \quad (3)$$

where each item corresponds to a vertical slab. In a 2-D LUT, the values of items in the first (X) dimension, will be replaced with another LUT which has one entry for different intervals corresponding to the second (Y) dimension. The thirteenth item/slab $[x_{13}, x_1, 0]$ is a "wrapped around" slab for all $x > x_{13}$ and all $x < x_1$ – a region that is *not* of interest to us.

2) Split all input lines where they intersect vertical grid lines[1]. Such points are the thick filled circles in Figure 1. The line BC running from x_7 to x_{10}, for example, is split into 3 segments (split at points where the X coordinates are x_8 and x_9). The split segments are (obviously) associated with the same region identifiers as the original line.

At this point we know all unique y-coordinate values across all line segments (horizontal dashed lines). We are now ready to divide each slab vertically to create rectangles, by inserting nested LUT items for the second dimension. For example, nested in the item for slab x_1–x_2 are three items/rectangles with vertical spans y_9–y_{12}, y_{12}–y_{17}, and (the wrapped around rectangle) y_{17}–y_9. For the polygon of Figure 1, the number of vertical rectangles in each of the 12 vertical slabs ranges from 2 to 7.

C. Labeling Rectangles (Process $\mathcal{P}_1$)

Every line segment can now be mapped to a rectangular region $[x_l, x_r, [y_b, y_t, v]]$, where the value v can take 3 different forms

Type I	$v = (d \in \{+, -\}, R_a, R_b)$	
Type II	$v = (c \in \{ll, ul, ur, lr\}, y_c, R_a, R_b, R')$	(4)
Type 0	$v = R$	

Type I (gray) rectangles in which a diagonal is a line segment. For a rectangle $[x_l, x_r, [y_b, y_t, v]]$, the value v conveys information necessary to i) identify the diagonal (positive/negative slope) and ii) the regions R_a, R_b divided by the line. By convention, as the first X coordinate is can not be lower than the second, the diagonal can only be the positive slope diagonal (x_l, y_b)—(x_r, y_t) or the negative slope diagonal (x_l, y_t)—(x_r, y_b). Thus, v conveys values (d, R_a, R_b) where $d = \{+/-\}$.

Type II (dark gray) rectangles (are typically rare) and correspond to *two* line-segments that meet at an acute angle, and overlap in *both* X and Y directions. One line is a diagonal, and the other is a shorter line with a smaller Y-span. The value v of rectangle $[x_l, x_r, [y_b, y_t, v]]$ includes information necessary to identify both lines and the regions divided by the lines. Specifically, value v is of the form (c, y_c, R_a, R_b, R') where

1) $c \in \{ll, ul, ur, lr\}$ indicates the corner of the rectangle where the two lines meet, and
2) $y_1 < y_c < y_2$ is Y-coordinate value necessary to determine the shorter line.

---

[1] For reasons that will become apparent later, some vertical lines may also need to be split.

Note that from the common corner, while the diagonal runs all the way between Y-coordinates y_b and y_t the shorter line runs only till y_c. While each line will be associated with two regions, one will be shared by both lines. R_a and R_b are the regions above and below the diagonal. The third region is R'.

Type 0 (unshaded) rectangles correspond to a horizontal/vertical line that is an edge of the rectangle $[x_l, x_r, [y_b, y_t, v]]$. In such cases, the value assigned to a rectangle is directly a region code like R_a or R_b. Given a line associated with regions R_a, R_b, the value v depends on whether the edge is the bottom or top or right or the left edge, viz.,

$$\text{'bottom/right':} \quad v = R_a \quad \text{'top/left':} \quad v = R_b \quad (5)$$

The need to cut some vertical line-segments arises out of the need to see vertical line segments as sides of rectangles. For example, the line ON (Figure 1) should be cut at O' to map line OO' to the white rectangle to the left, and line $O'N$ to the rectangle to the right. Alternately, it could be cut at N' to map ON' to the left and $N'N$ to the right.

Apart from rectangles associated with input lines, there may exist other Type 0 rectangles that simply happen to fall in-between rectangles associated with lines. An example of such a rectangle in the figure is $[x_9, x_{10}, [y_9, y_{18}, .]]$ between two Type I rectangles. Such rectangles will be marked with a region label that is the same as the region label for a point top-center of the rectangle below and bottom-center of the rectangle above. For Type II rectangles the top-center (tc) and bottom-center (bc) for the four types (ll,ul,ur,lr) are (see Figure 2 (left)) as follows:

$$\begin{array}{ccccc}
 & ll & ul & ur & lr \\
tc & R_a & R' & R' & R_a \\
bc & R' & R_b & R_b & R'
\end{array} \quad (6)$$

If desired, Type II rectangles can be reduced to any desired size by chopping both lines at new X coordinate values. Figure 2 (right) depicts a scenario where a Type II rectangle is reduced to a small fraction of its original size (to the small region in the top left corner) by cutting the lines at X-coordinates x_1, x_2 and x_3.

The coordinate x_1 can be chosen depending on the desired new size of the Type II rectangle. At the point where line x_1 meets the diagonal (say, (x_1, y)), a horizontal line y is drawn till it hits the shorter line at (x_2, y). A vertical is now drawn from (x_2, y) till it hits the diagonal at (x_2, y'). A horizontal line y' is now drawn till it hits the shorter line at (x_3, y') and so on. This process is repeated until the horizontal line from the diagonal can reach the edge of the rectangle without intersecting the shorter line.

D. Answering Queries (Process $\mathcal{P}_2$)

The process for answering queries is as follows. Given a point (x, y), the rectangle $[x_l, x_r, [y_b, y_t, v]]$ that contains the point (or $x_l \leq x < x_r, y_b \leq y < y_t$) is identified. If the rectangle is Type 0, the value v is itself the region label for *every* point inside the rectangle.

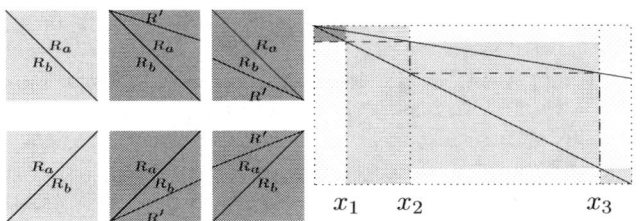

Figure 2: Left: Regions in two types of Type I (+/- slope diagonals) and four types (corner ll,ul,ur,lr) of Type II rectangles. In all types the diagonals separate region R_a above and R_b below. In Type II rectangles the shorter line separates one of the regions R_a / R_b from a third region R'. Right: Type II rectangles can be shrunk to any desired size by chopping both lines at appropriate X-coordinates to create Type I and Type 0 rectangles.

Given a Type I rectangle $[x_l, x_r, [y_b, y_t, v = (+/-, R_a, R_b)]]$ the end-points of the diagonal can be determined. Now, determining " if (x, y) is *below* the diagonal" is sufficient to determine the region in which the point (x, y) falls.

For a Type II rectangle $[x_l, x_r, [y_b, y_t, v = (c, y_c, R_a, R_b, R')]]$, the two lines corresponding to different corners c ('ur', 'lr', 'll', 'ul') are

diagonal	other line	corner	
(x_l, y_b)—(x_r, y_t)	(x_l, y_c)—(x_r, y_t)	'ur'	
(x_l, y_t)—(x_r, y_b)	(x_l, y_c)—(x_r, y_b)	'lr'	(7)
(x_l, y_b)—(x_r, y_t)	(x_l, y_b)—(x_r, y_c)	'll'	
(x_l, y_t)—(x_r, y_b)	(x_l, y_t)—(x_r, y_c)	'ul'	

If R'_a, R'_b are the regions corresponding to the shorter line, for lines meeting in the upper-right and upper-left corners, $R'_a = R'$ and $R'_b = R_a$. For lower-left and lower-right corners $R'_a = R_b$ and $R'_b = R'$ (see Figure 2 (left)). The ability to determine if a point (x, y) is below both lines, or above both lines or in-between the two lines, is now sufficient to determine the region label for any point (x, y) within the rectangle.

E. SQDM Updates (Process $\mathcal{P}_3$)

The process $\mathcal{P}$ can be executed in batches where each batch corresponds to a set of lines to be mapped to rectangles. Once all lines have been utilized to mark-up rectangles, the batch execution is considered complete. A new batch may then be executed to modify current regions, possibly by adding more polygons. As rectangles need to begin and end at X-coordinate points corresponding to input lines, it may be required to split some existing rectangles to incorporate new line segments.

For example, the polygon in Figure 1 could have been incorporated in two batches, where only lines corresponding to the outer polygon were incorporated in the first batch. In this case the first batch would not have had not needed grid line x_6, and two Type I rectangles in line JI between x_5 and x_7 would have been a larger Type I rectangle with diagonal running from (x_5, y_{13}) to (x_7, y_{15}).

A simple strategy to fix this problem is to reverse the labeling process. The line (x_5, y_{13})—(x_7, y_{15}) is added back to the list of lines and the rectangle value is set to zero. Now the line can be split at x_6, and a new vertical division can be created at between x_5 and x_7. All unshaded rectangles can be ignored as splitting such rectangles vertically is trivial (both sides will be assigned the same value as the original rectangle). Now process $\mathcal{P}_1$ can be executed to incorporate two lines (x_5, y_{13})—(x_6, y_{14}) and (x_6, y_{14})—(x_7, y_{15}) into two smaller rectangles.

III. TCB FUNCTIONS

The reason that the correctness of process $\mathcal{P}$ can be verified even by a resource limited module **T** is thanks to binary hash tree based data structures [8]. Specifically, by storing only the root of a binary hash tree, and by performing simple sequences of cryptographic hash operations, module **T** can reliably perform read/write/insert/delete operations in virtually stored dictionaries and look-up-tables (LUT) [8].

A. Dictionaries and LUTs

A dictionary is a collection of key-value pairs (each key in a collection should be unique). For example,

$$\{2, 5\}, \{4, 7\}, \{456, 21\}, \{5, 0\}, \{32, 6\}$$

is a collection of items in a dictionary corresponding to keys 2,4,456 and 32. The item $\{5, 0\}$ with value 0 is regarded as a *place-holder* (it does *not* mean that the value of key 5 is 0).

For our purposes, dictionaries are used for storing line segments, where the dictionary key is a one way function of the coordinates of the end-points, and the item value is a one-way function of the regions separated by the line segment.

LUTs are collections of items of the form $[x_l, x_h, v]$. Together, all items in an LUT collection provide a piecewise definition of a function $f(x)$ over *all* x (a valid LUT should be *complete*). For example, the collection of items

$$[5, 8, 234] \quad [8, 13, 46] \quad [13, 37, 0] \quad [37, 45, 1234] \quad [45, 5, 0]$$

indicates that the value of the function $v = f(x)$ is $v = 234$ for $5 \le x < 8$, 46 for $8 \le x < 13$, 1234 for $37 \le x < 45$. Once again value $v = 0$ has a special interpretation: $f(x)$ is *undefined* for $13 \le x < 37$, and (as per the last item[2]) the function is also undefined for all $x \ge 45$ *and* all $x < 5$. An LUT with a single item $[k, k, 0]$ is complete (although meaningless) as it implies that $f(x)$ undefined for all $x \ge k$ and all $x < k$.

A 2-D LUT can be seen as representation of a function $v = f(x, y)$ of two variables. This can be realized by nesting a LUT for various Y-intervals within each item (for an X-interval). A nested LUT item

$$[x_i, x_{i+1}, [y_j, y_{j+1}, v]], \tag{8}$$

---

[2]Without the item $[45, 5, 0]$ the collection will not be valid LUT as it is incomplete; the function should be specified for independent variable x over the entire domain.

conveys that $f(x, y) = v$ over the rectangular region $x_i \le x < x_{i+1}$ and $y_j \le y < y_{j+1}$. A 2-D LUT with say n intervals for the independent variable x, can have *any* number of Y-intervals in each of the n X-intervals. It can even have zero Y-intervals – for example, if $f(x, y)$ is undefined over a specific X-interval.

The ability of **T** to execute hash tree protocols which demand only a small constant memory size (irrespective of the size of the hash tree) is sufficient to virtually store dictionaries and 2-D LUTs of any size, by storing a single hash inside **T**. By performing such simple operations, **T** can assure the dynamic integrity of the contents of a dictionary and/or 2-D LUT and perform a wide variety of read/write/insert/delete operations on dictionary/LUT items. For a dictionary/LUT with N items, irrespective of the number of nested levels, module **T** has to compute only $\mathbb{O}(\log_2 N)$ hashes for performing a basic read/write operation (30 hashes for a dictionary/LUT with a billion items).

Modifications that can be made to dictionaries/LUTs can be broadly classified into i) *updates* to item values, and ii) *insertion/deletion* of items. Insertion/deletion of items does not affect application specific interpretation of data for the following reasons:

1) Dictionary items are inserted only as place-holders; only place-holders can be removed.

2) Insertion/deletion of items in a LUT merely splits/joins LUT intervals without changing the function represented by the LUT.

Generic (system-independent) functions can be used for inserting/deleting items. Such functions ensure uniqueness of dictionary keys (that place-holders can not be added for a key k if an item/place-holder with key k already exists in the collection), and that an LUT is always complete.

Only updates to item values are governed by system-specific TCB functions. From the perspective of TCB functions, *deleting* an item is the same as setting its value to zero. Adding a new item is the same as modifying the value of a zero valued item (undefined LUT interval, or dictionary place-holder).

B. State Transition Model

For executing SQDM TCB functions, module **T** tracks two roots

1) root p of an input dictionary (containing lines) that triggers process $\mathcal{P}$, and

2) root ξ of a 2-D LUT.

In a dictionary item of the form $\{k, \gamma\}$ corresponding to a line (x_1, y_1)—(x_2, y_2) associated with regions (R_a, R_b) the key k is a line-hash, and value γ is a region-hash, where

$$k = h(x_1, y_1, x_2, y_2) \quad \gamma = h(R_a, R_b) \qquad (9)$$

For Type I rectangles (corresponding to a diagonal line $\{k, \gamma\}$), and for Type II rectangles (two lines $\{k_1, \gamma_1\}$ and $\{k_2, \gamma_2\}$), the value v are (respectively)

$$\begin{aligned} v &= h(k, \gamma) & \text{light gray} \\ v &= h(k_1, k_2, \gamma_1, \gamma_2) & \text{dark gray} \end{aligned} \qquad (10)$$

For Type 0 (unshaded) rectangles the value v directly provides a region code.

As process $\mathcal{P}_0$ splits a line segment into smaller segments, the corresponding TCB function replaces a dictionary item with multiple items with different keys (line-hashes corresponding to smaller line segments), but with the same region-hash γ. The TCB function has to ensure that a segment can be cut *only at a point that lies on the line*.

TCB functions that assure process $\mathcal{P}_1$ delete a dictionary item (line segment) after incorporating it into a rectangle. The process $\mathcal{P}_1$ is deemed complete only when the dictionary is empty. More specifically, unless all lines have been incorporated into the 2-D LUT, queries (process $\mathcal{P}_2$) will not be entertained.

It is useful to see

1) TCB functions as a specification of a *state-transition* model [9], and

2) *execution* of TCB functions by **T** as verification of correctness of such transitions.

A state-transition model is a set of *permitted* transitions that read/write system-specific constrained data items (CDIs) [10]. For our purposes, the CDIs are line-hashes, region-hashes, coordinates of rectangles, and values assigned to rectangles.

Each permitted state-transition can be expressed in terms of

1) triggers,

2) pre-conditions and

3) post-conditions.

Specifically, triggers are unconstrained data items (UDI) [10], provided as inputs to **T**. The UDIs and CDIs need to satisfy some specific pre-conditions for the state-transition to occur. *If* the pre-conditions are satisfied, the post-conditions dictate necessary modifications to values of dictionary/LUT items (CDIs).

As CDIs are stored virtually, verification of CDI pre-conditions will involve

1) execution of binary hash tree protocols, to verify existence of specific dictionary/LUT items against the root stored inside the module, and

2) executing PointOnLine() to determine if a point falls on/below/above a line

Imposing post conditions will involve modifying the root corresponding to the modifications to dictionary/LUT items mandated by post-conditions.

1) State-Transitions for Process $\mathcal{P}_0$: The state-transitions associated with process $\mathcal{P}_0$ can be expressed as follows:

UDIs: $(x_1, y_1, x_2, y_2, x, y, \gamma)$
Pre: (x, y) ON $\{(x_1, y_1)$—$(x_2, y_2)\}$
$k_0 \leftarrow h(x_1, y_1, x_2, y_2)$; $k_1 \leftarrow h(x_1, y_1, x, y)$, $k_2 \leftarrow h(x, y, x_2, y_2)$
Post: $\{k_0, \gamma \to 0\}, \{k_1, 0 \to \gamma\}, \{k_2, 0 \to \gamma\}$

The UDIs provide inputs necessary to unambiguously define pre/post-conditions. In this case the inputs provide end-points of a line $\{(x_1, y_1)$—$(x_2, y_2)\}$, a point (x, y) on the line, and the region hash γ associated with the line. The first pre-condition to be verified is that (x, y) does indeed fall on the line. The UDIs specify the dictionary items $\{k, \gamma\}$ that should currently exist, and the post conditions, that the existing line should be removed ($\{k, \gamma \to 0\}$), and two new

ISBN: 1-60132-454-5, CSREA Press ©

dictionary items should be created ($\{k_1, 0 \to \gamma\}, \{k_2, 0 \to \gamma\}$ corresponding to the two smaller line segments). This function can be invoked again for splitting each of smaller segments further, if necessary.

The other part of process $\mathcal{P}_0$ involves creating rectangular templates with item values set to zero. No state transition model is required for that purpose (generic protocols can be used to create the necessary 2-D LUT with all values set to 0).

2) Process $\mathcal{P}_1$: Assuring process $\mathcal{P}_1$ calls for ensuring that every line in a batch is used to correctly assign a value to a rectangle. Note that if lines can be hidden from the TCB then a gray rectangle can be misrepresented as a green rectangle by untrusted process $\mathcal{P}_1$. Even the very existence of island polygons could be hidden.

The state transition model ensures that a line can be deleted only after it is used to set the value of a 2-D LUT item (rectangle). At the end of the process $\mathcal{P}_1$ the dictionary of input lines will be empty. The TCB is then ready to answer queries and/or commence another batch process.

UDIs: $(x_1, y_1, x_2, y_2, \gamma, v)$//-ve slope diag
Pre: $k \leftarrow h(x_1, y_2, x_2, y_1); v' \leftarrow h(k, \gamma)$
Post: $\{k, \gamma \to 0\}, [x_1, x_2, [y_1, y_2, v \to v']]$

UDIs: $(x_1, y_1, x_2, y_2, R_a, R_b, v)$//left edge
Pre: $k \leftarrow h(x_1, y_1, x_1, y_2); \gamma \leftarrow h(R_a, R_b)$
Post: $\{k, \gamma \to 0\}, [x_1, x_2, [y_1, y_2, v \to R_b]];$

UDIs: $(x_1, y_1, x_2, y_2, y_c, \gamma_1, \gamma_2)$//upper-left corner
Pre: $k_1 \leftarrow h(x_1, y_2, x_2, y_1); k_2 \leftarrow h(x_1, y_2, x_1, y_c);$
$v' \leftarrow h(k_1, k_2, \gamma_1, \gamma_2)$
Post: $\{k_1, \gamma_1 \to 0\}, \{k_2, \gamma_2 \to 0\}, [x_1, x_2, [y_1, y_2, v \to v']]$

The state transition model is represented above for one of the two types of Type I rectangles, one of the four Type 0 rectangles, and one of the four Type II rectangles. In other words, while only three rules are explicitly shown, the complete state transition model will include a total of 2+4+4=10 such transition rules.

3) Process $\mathcal{P}_2$: Process $\mathcal{P}_2$ does not modify CDIs. It merely reports the region associated with a point (x, y). The state model is shown below for two specific cases i) query regarding a point between two lines in Type II rectangle (upper-right corner); and ii) a point *not* below the diagonal of a +ve diagonal Type I rectangle.

UDIs: $(x_1, y_1, x_2, y_2, y_c, R_a, R_b, R', x, y)$//upper-right gray
                                                //in-between lines
Pre: $p = 0; k_1 \leftarrow h(x_1, y_1, x_2, y_2); \gamma_1 \leftarrow h(R_a, R_b)$
$k_2 \leftarrow h(x_1, y_c, x_2, y_2); \gamma_2 \leftarrow h(R', R_a)$
$v \leftarrow h(k_1, k_2, \gamma_1, \gamma_2); [x_1, x_2, [y_1, y_2, v]]$
(x, y) BELOW $\{(x_1, y_c)$—$(x_2, y_2)\}$
(x, y) NOT BELOW $\{(x_1, y_1)$—$(x_2, y_2)\}$
Post: RETURN $\langle \xi, x, y, R_a \rangle$

UDIs: $(x_1, y_1, x_2, y_2, y_c, R_a, R_b)$//+ve diagonal, above
Pre: $k \leftarrow h(x_1, y_1, x_2, y_2); \gamma \leftarrow h(R_a, R_b)$
$v \leftarrow h(k, \gamma); [x_1, x_2, [y_1, y_2, v]]$
(x, y) NOT BELOW $\{(x_1, y_1)$—$(x_2, y_2)\}$
Post: RETURN $\langle \xi, x, y, R_a \rangle$

Some Type 0 rectangles will fall between other types (I/II/0) rectangles. Certificates issued by the TCB function above,

certifying the region code for a point at the top center of the rectangle below, and bottom center of the rectangle above, can be used to mark a rectangle in between. The state-transition model for this purpose is as follows:

UDIs: $(x_1, y_1, x_2, y_2, R, v)$//above and below
Pre: $p = 0; x = (x_1 + x_2) << 1; \langle \xi, x, y_1, R \rangle; \langle \xi, x, y_1, R \rangle$
Post: $[x_1, x_2, [y_1, y_2, v \to R]]$

4) Process $\mathcal{P}_3$: TCB functions for assuring integrity of $\mathcal{P}_3$ simply reverse of TCB functions for $\mathcal{P}_1$. To incorporate new lines with end-points that fall in the middle of a slab, the entire vertical slab (and thus, all rectangles inside the slab) will need to be cut across a new vertical line. Lines corresponding to Type I and II rectangles in such slabs can be moved back to a dictionary, cut as necessary using TCB functions for process $\mathcal{P}_0$, and re-incorporated as rectangles using TCB functions for process $\mathcal{P}_1$.

The state-transition rules for two of the six possible cases (2 Type I + 4 Type II) are shown below.

UDIs: $(x_1, y_1, x_2, y_2, \gamma)$//-ve slope diag
Pre: $k \leftarrow h(x_1, y_2, x_2, y_1); v \leftarrow h(k, \gamma)$
Post: $\{k, 0 \to \gamma\}, [x_1, x_2, [y_1, y_2, v \to 0]]$

UDIs: $(x_1, y_1, x_2, y_2, y_c, \gamma_1, \gamma_2)$//upper-left corner
Pre: $k_1 \leftarrow h(x_1, y_2, x_2, y_1); k_2 \leftarrow h(x_1, y_2, x_1, y_c);$
$v \leftarrow h(k_1, k_2, \gamma_1, \gamma_2)$
Post: $\{k_1, 0 \to \gamma_1\}, \{k_2, 0 \to \gamma_2\}, [x_1, x_2, [y_1, y_2, v \to 0]]$

At every instant of time, the root ξ of the 2-D LUT remains a commitment to the entire SQDM. For scenarios where maps change infrequently, the module **T** need not be on-line to attest responses to queries. The module plays a role only for construction of the SQDM. As answering queries does not modify ξ, the root ξ can be signed by the module for verification by anyone. Any entity can now host the SQDM (the 2-D LUT), and provide rectangles as answers to queries, along with complementary binary-tree hashes to prove consistency against the signed root ξ.

IV. DISCUSSIONS AND CONCLUSIONS

SQDM processes were applied to real-world data for converting polygons in ESRI Shapefile [7] format to an SQDM. Shapefiles representing US states, US Congressional Districts, and MS counties were converted to SQDM representation.

The smallest (in terms of number of sides) polygon was for the US county of Santa Cruz with 40 sides. The largest was the state of Texas with 58568 sides. Figure 3 shows the number of input line-segments, number of line-segments after they are split at unique X-coordinates, and the numbers of the three different types of rectangles in the 2D-LUT representation.

Figure 3 (left) depicts the values for representative polygons from 4 Shapefiles. Figure 3 (right) shows the average numbers. As the number of Type II rectangles is too small to be decipherable in a bar chart, their numbers are shown above each bar. A maximum of 26 Type II rectangles was observed for 33rd congressional district in California. US state of Texas had 58568 line-segments, that were split into 249128 segments, and mapped to 9 Type II rectangles, 198848 Type I rectangles, and 204585 Type 0 rectangles.

ISBN: 1-60132-454-5, CSREA Press ©

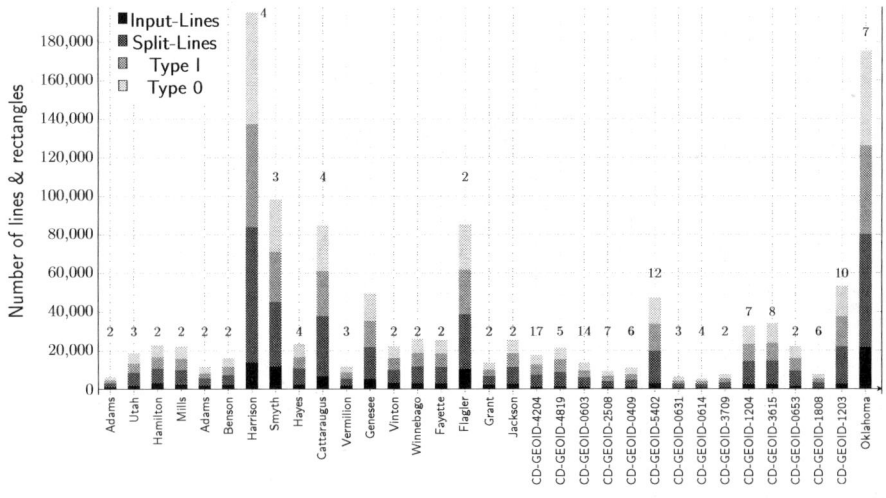
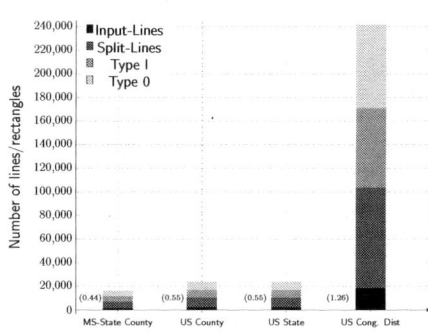

Figure 3: Left: Number of lines and rectangles corresponding to representative polygons from 4 different Shapefiles. Right: Average number of lines and rectangles in each Shapefile. The number of Type II rectangles is shown above the bars.

A. Geography Driven Delegation

Confidence in the attribution of ownership/control of geographic coordinates, is a fundamental requirement for secure delegation of spatial coordinates. A mechanism for secure delegation of geographic coordinates can significantly reduce the "friction" for providing a wide range of useful services. Currently, anyone seeking to provide an (on-line) service is required to

1) purchase a domain name from the domain name system (DNS) [11], and

2) promote the name, with the hope that potential clients will remember the name when they need the service.

3) provide DNS information regarding the name (in the form DNS records) to enable users to contact the service provider.

However, if geographic coordinates can be delegated, service providers need not purchase and promote a name; they already own (or have some control) over a geographic region where the service is provided. Users of service do not need to remember names, as they only need to query for services in and around the location where they need the service.

A restaurant, for instance, does *not* need promote its name, or rely on some better-known service provider (like Google) to promote its name. Anyone looking for services in or near the geographic coordinates (x, y) will be able to determine all services available in and around (x, y).

A world-wide geographic delegation system, akin to the DNS will need to agree on a common geodetic coordinate system (for example, WGS-84 [12]). Delegation of regions can proceed hierarchically into countries, states, and smaller administrative divisions, and finally onto individual owners of parcels, who may also delegate control of regions within a parcel to other entities.

Our current efforts are focused on determining the minimal

TCB for DNS-like services that guarantee the integrity of the response to a query regarding "n-closest services available around coordinate (x, y)."

REFERENCES

[1] https://en.wikipedia.org/wiki/Geographic_information_system

[2] J. Rushby, "Design and Verification of Secure Systems," 8th ACM Symposium on Operating System Principles, Pacific Grove, California, 1981, pp. 1221.

[3] H. Samet, R.E. Webber,"Storing a Colection of Polygons Using Quadtrees,"ACM Transactions on Graphics, 4 (3) July 1985.

[4] D. Dobkin, R.J. Lipton, "Multidimensional searching problems," SIAM Journal on Computing. 5 (2): 181186, 1976.

[5] J Snoeyink, "Point Location," in J.E. Goodma, J. O'Rourke, C.D. Toth (ed.), *Handbook of Discrete and Computational Geometry*, CRC Press, 2017.

[6] R. C. Merkle, "A Digital Signature Based on a Conventional Encryption Function," Advances in Cryptology, CRYPTO '87. Lecture Notes in Computer Science 293. 1987.

[7] "ESRI Shapefile Technical Description," ESRI White paper, 1998. https://www.esri.com/library/whitepapers/pdfs/shapefile.pdf

[8] M. Ramkumar, Symmetric Cryptographic Protocols, Springer, 2014.

[9] C. Landwehr, "Formal Models for Computer Security," ACM Computing Surveys 13 (3): 8, 11, 247278.

[10] D .D. Clark, and D. R. Wilson, "A Comparison of Commercial and Military Computer Security Policies," in Proceedings of the 1987 IEEE Symposium on Research in Security and Privacy (SP'87), May 1987, Oakland, CA; IEEE Press, pp. 184–193.

[11] P. V. Mockapetris, "Domain Names - Concepts and Facilities," RFC Editor, 1987.

[12] https://en.wikipedia.org/wiki/World_Geodetic_System#WGS84, World Geodetic System.

Onto-ITSDM: an Essential Ontology for Decision-Making Support Systems in the IT Service Management Domain

M. Mora[1], J. Marx-Gomez[2], F. Wang[3]
[1]Department of Informatics, Autonomous University of Aguascalientes, Aguascalientes, AGS, Mexico
[2]Department of Informatics, Carl von Ossietzky University Oldenburg, Oldenburg, Lower Saxony, Germany
[3]Information Technology & Administrative Management, Central Washington University, Ellensburg, WA, USA

Abstract *–The design of IT services, provisioned by Data Center Systems, is a mandatory process in several international IT Service Management process frameworks (i.e. ITIL, ISO20K). In this stage 1 (of a 2-year research), we identify the lack of decision-making support for designing such IT services, and based on such scarcity of findings, we report the design of Onto-ITSDM, a frame-based ontology, for supporting the elaboration of high-level decision-making models for DMSS. Our ultimate and specific aim is to support the design of IT services with DMSS that will be both useful and practically feasible to be used for ITSM designers in the praxis. We finally identify further research avenues for improving and empirically testing Onto-ITSDM in stage 2.*

Keywords: IT service design, decision-making support system, ontology, DMSS, ITSM, Protégé

1 Introduction

The design of IT services is a mandatory process in the well-recognized international IT Service Management process frameworks such as ITIL [1], ISO20K [2] and CMMI-SVC [3]. An IT Service is the core output provisioned by modern Data Centers Systems through a Catalogue of IT Services [1, 2, 3].

An IT Service is defined by ITIL [1] as *"a service provided to one or more customers by an IT service provider, based on the use of IT and supports the customer's business processes, and is made up from a combination of people, processes and technology and defined in a Service Level Agreement"*. In particular, ITIL [1] defines a Service as *"a means of delivering value to customers by facilitating outcomes customers want to achieve without the ownership of specific costs and risks"*. To deliver IT services is required a Service System [3], which is defined by CMMI-SVC [3] as *"as an integrated and interdependent combination of service component resources that satisfies service requirements"*. From the three concepts, Service, IT Service, and Service System, we can identify that the provision of IT services demanded by IT users in any organization implies the existence of a Service System composed by Services Component Resources, and that such a Service System can be equaled with the Data Center System in modern organizations. Data Centers are installations specifically built with the primary purpose to house and provide the adequate environmental conditions (space, power, cooling, and physical security) for the computer and telecommunication equipment used in an organization [4]. By extension, Data Center Systems [5, 6] can be defined as the whole system of IT resources, IT people and IT processes for provisioning IT services, and where a core mandatory IT resource is the physical Data Center. The relevance of Data Center is highlighted with industry reports [7, 8] which indicate that 1-hr downtime without provisioning the expected IT services costs from US $10,000 to US $6,000,000 to organizations providing services such as: ATM, cellular services, airline reservations, on-line shopping, package shipping, credit card authorizations, and brokerage operations. Additionally, organizations suffer negative impacts from Data Center downtimes on: image by business disruption, end-user productivity, and third-party operational delays [7, 8]. Hence, the relevance of having IT services and Data Center Systems well-designed, implemented, operated, supported and improved is critical for modern businesses that rely strongly on IT services.

In this research, thus, we focus on the design of IT services in the context of Data Center Systems regarding its decision-making support. Our motivation is based on the scarcity of decision-making support solutions reported in current literature for designing such IT services [9]. Our proposal is the utilization of ontologies with the aim to support the specific process of elaborating high-level decision-making models usable in the design of IT services. Ontologies have been suggested as conceptual aids for supporting the elaboration of simulation models [10, 11]. Our ultimate aim is to support the design of IT services with high-level decision-making models that will be both useful and practically feasible to be used for IT Service designers in the praxis. The remainder of this article continues as follows: in section 2, we review the theoretical foundations on IT Service Design process, on current DMSS support for ITSM, and on Frame-Based Ontologies; in section 3, we report the design of *Onto-ITSDM*, our proposed artifact; in section 4, we discuss succinctly our findings and their implications; and finally, in section 5, we end this article with conclusions, limitations, and final recommendations for further avenues for research.

2   Theoretical Background

2.1   On IT Service Design Process

The main international IT Service Management process frameworks (ITIL [1] and ISO20K [2]; and CMMI-SVC [3]) include an IT Service Design process. It has been recognized as a relevant process in the life cycle of an IT service, before proceeding to its transition-releasing and normal operation [12]. However, this IT Service Design process implies new required knowledge. This is because the new concept of IT service involves all IT components (i.e. hardware, software, dbms, networks, data, applications, environment, and internal and external teams). Consequently, Service Design processes, and their detailed study on how to systematically conduct that emerge as a relevant and current problem [13, 14].

For instance, in ITIL v3 [14] design is an activity that identifies Requirements and then defines a solution that is able to meet these Requirements. Systems (e.g. IT services in particular) must be carefully planned and designed in order to be as expected. An informal design process cannot establish performance, risk-based, security and cost-effective guarantees to users. Design of IT systems helps mainly to avoid costly system disruptions in operational settings caused by design flaws, and to produce expected performances. A high-quality design implies achieving it into the design space caused by the application of constrains (usually bounds on available resources) rather than attaining the maximum or minimums values without consideration to the attached design constrains. In ITIL V3, the Service Design process is essentially conducted with the following activities: 1) gathering service needs and mapping them to requirements for integrated services, and 2) creating the design specifications for the service assets needed to provide services. Similar IT Service Design processes are reported in ISO20K and CMMI-SVC.

Any IT service requires a formal or informal (not recommended) IT service system for its provision. The IT service system is comprised of several components such as: applications (APP), software (SW), hardware (HW), network (NW), data (DATA), environment infrastructure, and internal (IT TEAMS) and external support teams (IT SUPPLIERS). Thus, alongside the concept of IT service, the concept of IT service system also becomes relevant. Figure 1 (adapted from [13]) illustrates a diagrammatic view of IT service and the IT service system concepts.

The Figure 1 shows the following interrelationships: 1) the IT Services are delivered by an IT Service System comprised of IT Components; 2) the IT Services are provisioned to Business Process in the Business Process Layer in conformation to previously defined and agreed

Service Level Agreements (SLAs) between business users and IT service managers; 3) the delivery of IT Services requires additional internal (Operational Level) Agreements and external (Underlying Contracts) technical agreements; 4) the IT Service System includes internal (IT development teams) and external (IT suppliers) teams; and 5) the expected delivered value and warranty metrics from the utilization of the IT Services in the Business Processes layer relies on the IT Service System performance.

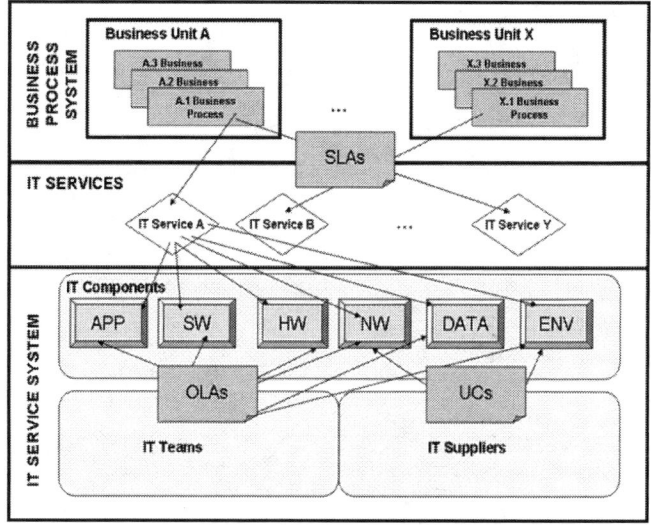

Figure 1. The IT Service System and IT Service Concept

2.2   On Decision-Making Support Systems for Designing IT Services

DMSS are computer-based systems designed for a decisional situation [15]. A decisional situation occurs when at least two courses of action are feasible but it is not clear which of them should be selected. The structured process to analyze such situations is called a Decision-Making process (DMP). In particular, decision makers do not require usually support for simple decisions (e.g., few courses of action, clear distinction of their impacts on the criterion of interest, and a low economic impact of mistakes). However, for moderate and complex decisions, decision makers have used structured DMP and special computer-based support tools (i.e. DMSS) [15]. Such DMSS can be enabled with analytical capabilities or enhanced with intelligent mechanisms. Table 1 (adapted from [16]) reports a sample of decisional situations faced by ITSM practitioners in the IT Service Design process.

In this research, we focus on DMSS of type DSS. A DSS is "*an interactive computer-based system which helps decision makers utilizing data and quantitative models to solve semi-structured problems*" [15]. A DSS offers the following capabilities: what-if analysis of scenarios, goal-seeking analysis, and sensitivity analysis of variables.

ISBN: 1-60132-454-5, CSREA Press ©

Table 1. A sample of decisional situations found in IT Service Design process

ITSM ACTIVITY	EXAMPLES OF DECISIONAL SITUATIONS
Service Level Management Process. ITSM implementers need to negotiate suitable SLAs, OLAs and UCs.	1. To select best options from a set of alternative SLAs jointly with users. 2. To select best options from a set of alternative OLAs for supporting a particular SLA. 3. To select best options from a set of alternative UCs for supporting a particular SLA.
Capacity Management Process. ITSM implementers need to select best architecture of CIs in designed IT services for achieving the expected capacities levels. **Availability Management Process.** ITSM implementers need to select best architecture of CIs in designed IT services for achieving the expected availabilities levels. **IT Service Continuity Management Process.** ITSM implementers need to select best architecture of CIs in designed IT services for achieving the expected continuity levels.	1. To select best architectures of CIs from a set of alternative schemes for normal services. 2. To select best architectures of CIs from a set of alternative schemes for critical services. 3. To select a particular and critical CI for supporting a critical IT service. 4. To evaluate several schemes for IT teams for achieving the expected levels of service. 5. To evaluate options for external (on the cloud) extra IT capabilities for achieving the expected levels of service.
Supplier Management Process. ITSM implementers need to select best IT suppliers for IT assets or as external service providers under UCs or SLAs.	1. To select best IT suppliers for acquiring normal IT assets. To select best IT suppliers for acquiring critical IT assets. 3. To evaluate the overall performance of IT suppliers.

Figure 2 (adapted from [16]) shows the high-level view of any DSS.

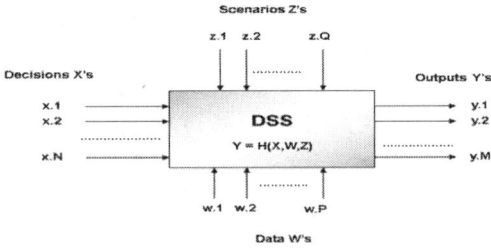

Figure 2. A Generic DSS Architecture

Figure 2 reports four types of variables: 1) decision variables X's; 2) known or controlled parameters W's; 3) uncontrolled risk-based scenarios variables Z's; and 4) output variables Y's. These four categories must be interrelated (quantitatively and/or qualitatively) with an underlying model $H(X,W,Z)$ that can be quantitative or/and qualitative, for producing face-validity outputs Y's when specific decisions X's are fixed under specific scenarios Z's and parameters W's.

The DSS model (identified as $Y=H(X,Z,W)$) can use different modeling approaches. In particular, four ones are identified as most used in the context of ITSM: 1) Analytical Hierarchical Process (AHP) [14]; 2) System Dynamics (SD) [16]; 3) Discrete-Event Simulation (DES) [17]; and 4) Agent-based Simulation (ABS) [18].

2.3   On Frame-Based Ontologies

2.3.1   The Ontology Concept

In the Artificial Intelligence discipline [19, 20], the need was realized to share and reuse knowledge bases, which are hindered by the used monolithic knowledge representations mechanism (e.g. rules, or logical propositions). Gruber [19] suggested the utilization of ontologies (e.g. agreed essential definitions of the things to be represented in the intelligent system) as a potential solution. In summary, ontologies are "... *content theories about the sort of objects,, properties of objects, and relations between objects that are possible in a specified domain of knowledge.*" [20].

2.3.2   A Review of Frames-based Ontologies

Knowledge Representation mechanisms [21] are essentially: 1) surrogates for the things under reasoning; 2) implicit decisions on the visible world by an intelligent system (e.g. through ontological commitments); and 3) a conceptual partial specification of a theory of intelligent reasoning. Frames/OKBC based mechanisms [22] and 2) First-order Logic (FOL) based mechanisms [23] are two of the main Knowledge Representation mechanisms [21] used to represent ontologies due to their power expressivity, completeness and soundness of inferential algorithms, as well as their pragmatic utility. In this research, similar to [24], we select Frames as the most suitable scheme for a better power expressiveness (structured/composite concepts, and n-arity relationships), pursued reasoning issues (natural reasoning capabilities), and pragmatic issues.

3   The Design and Building of Onto-ITSDM

The design and building of Onto-ITSDM was conducted with a simplified version of Noy and McGuiness' methodological guidelines [24, 25]. The activities conducted were: A1) definition of domain, scope, competency, and design goals of the ontology; A2) identification of knowledge sources; A3) initial identification and organization of ontological components (concepts, hierarchy of concepts, interrelationships); and A4) building and testing of ontology. While there are other methodologies for designing ontology-based systems [26], we selected and adapted Noy and McGuiness' methodology due to the following reasons: 1) balance between completeness of core activities and level of detail by activity; 2) adequacy for the system's scope; and 3) theoretical and empirical effectiveness of the methodology.

3.1.1 Definition of Domain, Scope, Competency, and Design Goals of the Ontology

The domain refers to the knowledge layers to be represented in the ontology Onto-ITSDM. Ontologies can be designed from scratch or derived from generic high-level ontologies. In this research, we adapt and simplify four previous ontologies reported in Mora et al. [24, 27] regarding the following knowledge layers: 1) a top-level ontology of essential things; 2) a system ontology; 3) a business system ontology; and 4) service system ontology. On these previous ontologies (adapted and simplified for our main research aim), we define an IT service system ontology in layer 5, and a DMSS ontology in layer 6. Scope of an ontology refers to the boundaries fixed on the set of concepts, attributes and interrelationships to be defined in the ontology. The scope fixed for Onto-ITSDM is declared as the set of minimal concepts, attributes and interrelationships used in IT Services Systems.

Competency of an ontology refers to its functional capabilities for responding relevant user inquiries. The generic required inquiries for Onto-ITSDM are the following ones: 1) what is a an IT service system service?; 2) how an IT service system is comprised?; 3) what is an IT service?; 4) what are the outcomes/measures of an IT service?; 5) what are the inputs/outputs to/from an IT service system?; 6) how can the resources used in an IT service system affect the IT service measures/outcomes?; 7) what is the structure of a DMSS artifact?; and 8) how the values of output Y variables can be estimated?. Finally, design goals must be established to establish generic evaluation criteria and design guidelines. According to [19] the following ontology design goals should be pursued: 1) clarity, 2) coherence, 3) extendibility, 4) minimal encoding bias, and 5) minimal ontological commitment. For 1, 2 and 4 design goals, we use conceptual maps (see Figure 3) for elaborating an initial ontology.

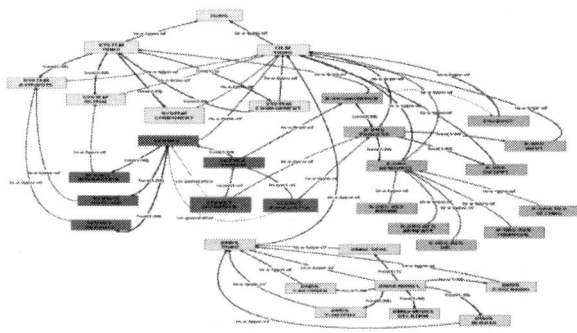

Figure 3. Conceptual Map for Onto-ITSDM Design

On design goal 3, we used a balance strategy design for having generic and specific concepts in the ITSM domain. For design goal 5, we privileged usefulness on generality of the Onto-ITSM ontology.

3.1.2 Identification of Knowledge Sources

In this task, it is required to locate knowledge sources (human, documents). For Onto-ITSDM we consider IT service design process and IT service concepts reported in main ITSM literature [12, 14], and DMSS foundations reported in [15].

3.1.3 Initial Identification and Organization of Ontological Components

In this task, a list of potential concepts is required at the first step. We generated one table by each knowledge layer that reports their concepts and main attributes. As examples, we reported here the Tables from 2 to 5 for Organization, Service System, IT Service, and DMSS chunks of knowledge.

Table 2. List of Initial Concepts for Organization Ontology

CONCEPT	SUPER CONCEPT	CORE SLOTS (ATTRIBUTES)
b-organization	system-thing	• name • comprised-of(b-org-process1, …) • generates (product1,…, service1, …) • …
b-org-process	system-component	• name • is-part-of(b-org-function1, …) • has-inputs(b-org-inp1, …) • has-outputs(b-org-out1,…) • has-resources(b-org-res1,…) • …
b-org-resource	system-component	• name • type(human, artifact, dik, financial, setting) • …
b-org-input	system-component	• name • …
b-org-output	system-component	• name • …

Table 3. List of Initial Concepts for Service System Ontology

CONCEPT	SUPER CONCEPT	CORE SLOTS (ATTRIBUTES)
service-system	b-organization	• name • comprised-of(service-appraiser, service-facilitator) • has(serv1, serv2, …) • …
service- appraiser	b-organization	• name • cogenerate(serv1, serv2, …) • …
service-facilitator	b-organization	• name • cogenerate(serv1, serv2, …) • …
service	item-thing	• name • has(services-outcomes, service-measures, service-interactions) • …
service-outcome	system-attribute	• name • …

ISBN: 1-60132-454-5, CSREA Press ©

service-measure	system-attribute	• name • …
service-interaction	system-action	• name • …

Table 4. List of Initial Concepts for IT Service System Ontology

CONCEPT	SUPER CONCEPT	CORE SLOTS (ATTRIBUTES)
it-service-system	service-system	• name • comprised-of(serv-appraiser, serv-facilitator) • has(serv1, serv2, …) • …
it-service- appraiser	b-org-process	• name • cogenerate(it-serv1, it-serv2, …) • …
…	…	• …
it-service -interaction	system-action	• name • …

Table 5. List of Initial Concepts for DMSS Ontology

CONCEPT	SUPER CONCEPT	CORE SLOTS (ATTRIBUTES)
dmss-tool	dmss-thing	• name • type(DSS, EIS, KBS, IDMS, BA) • purpose • has(dmss-model) • …
dmss-model	dmss-thing	• name • type(AHP, ODE, SD, ABS) • has(x-decision1, …) • has(y-output1, …) • has(z-scenario1, …) • has(w-data1, …) • has(dmss-model-relation1, …) • …
dmss-model -relation	dmss-thing	• name • specification • …
dmss-x-decision	dmss-thing	• name • …
…	…	• …
dmss-z-scenario	dmss-thing	• name • …

3.1.4 Building and Testing of Ontology

We used the Protégé 4.3 version tool for frames for building the *Onto-ITSDM* ontology. It was a 7-iteration process conducted by the first author. Second and third co-authors conducted a final checklist of concepts, attributes and interrelationships. We conducted a checklist of competency questions by using a logical reasoner (Algernon). The final Onto-ITSDM ontology produced 42 classes, 47 slots, and P interrelationships. Figure 4 shows the final conceptual map of

ones are integrated in the *Onto-ITSDM* ontology

the designed *Onto-ITSDM* ontology, and Figure 5 shows the concepts, slots and interrelationships of IT service system and DMSS thing, both of which are core concepts in *Onto-ITSDM* ontology.

4 Discussion on Implications

Several studies have identified: 1) the relevance of the IT service design process, 2) the need of supporting this process with DMSS tools; and 3) the lack of such support currently. This research aims ultimately to provide useful, user-friendly, compatible and valued support to ITSM practitioners and academicians interested in the design of IT services aligned with the IT Service Management process frameworks recommendations, and thus to address the aforementioned three research issues. Our solution strategy is based on the design and building of an Ontology-based Knowledge Management System (KMS) with an IT Service and a DMSS Tool ontologies. In this article, we have reported the design of the core ontology named *Onto-ITSDM*. The next research effort will be focused on using this *Onto-ITSDM* ontology in a KMS that provides explicit knowledge-based support for elaborating DMSS models and DMSS tools for the specific activities in the IT service design process.

Hence, while the final artifact (i.e. the KMS), has not been yet built, we consider that the design of the core ontology *Onto-ITSDM* provides interesting contributions for the theoretical knowledge and praxis of the ITSM domain. For the conceptual side, this research: 1) advances previous studies on conceptual but not implemented services systems ontologies with the design and implementation of an IT service ontology with a computer tool (i.e. Protégé); 2) accumulates previous reported knowledge on conceptual service systems ontologies by reusing (and adapting) them; and 3) innovates with a DMSS tool ontology, as similar ones were not found in the literature. For the practical side, this research: 1) builds a usable computer-based artifact (i.e. the *Onto-ITSDM* ontology) with an IT service system and DMSS tool ontologies; 2) promotes and fosters the design of DMSS for supporting IT service design activities; and 3) presents evidence on the feasibility of these kind of artifacts.

5 Conclusions

In this research, we have reported the need of counting with DMSS tools in the ITSM domain, and in particular for the IT service design process. The main ITSM frameworks suggest the utilization of DMSS tools for supporting the design of IT services, but the literature review found a scarcity of evidences on it. Thus, in this research, we addressed such a problematic situation, and we reported the design and building specific ontologies on IT service system and DMSS tool. Both.

ISBN: 1-60132-454-5, CSREA Press ©

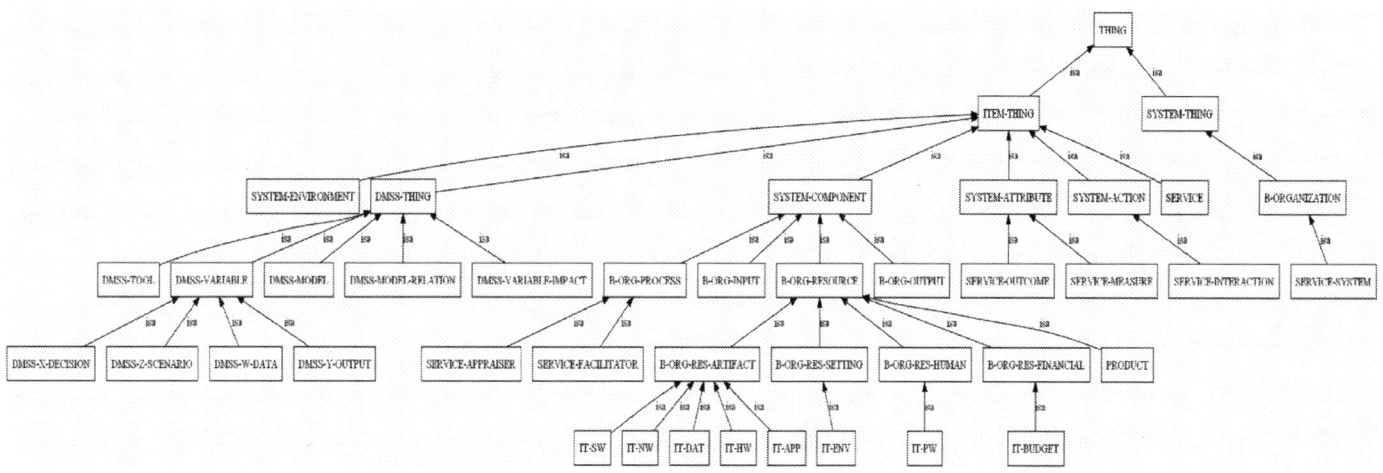

Figure 4. Conceptual Map for final *Onto-ITSDM* Ontology

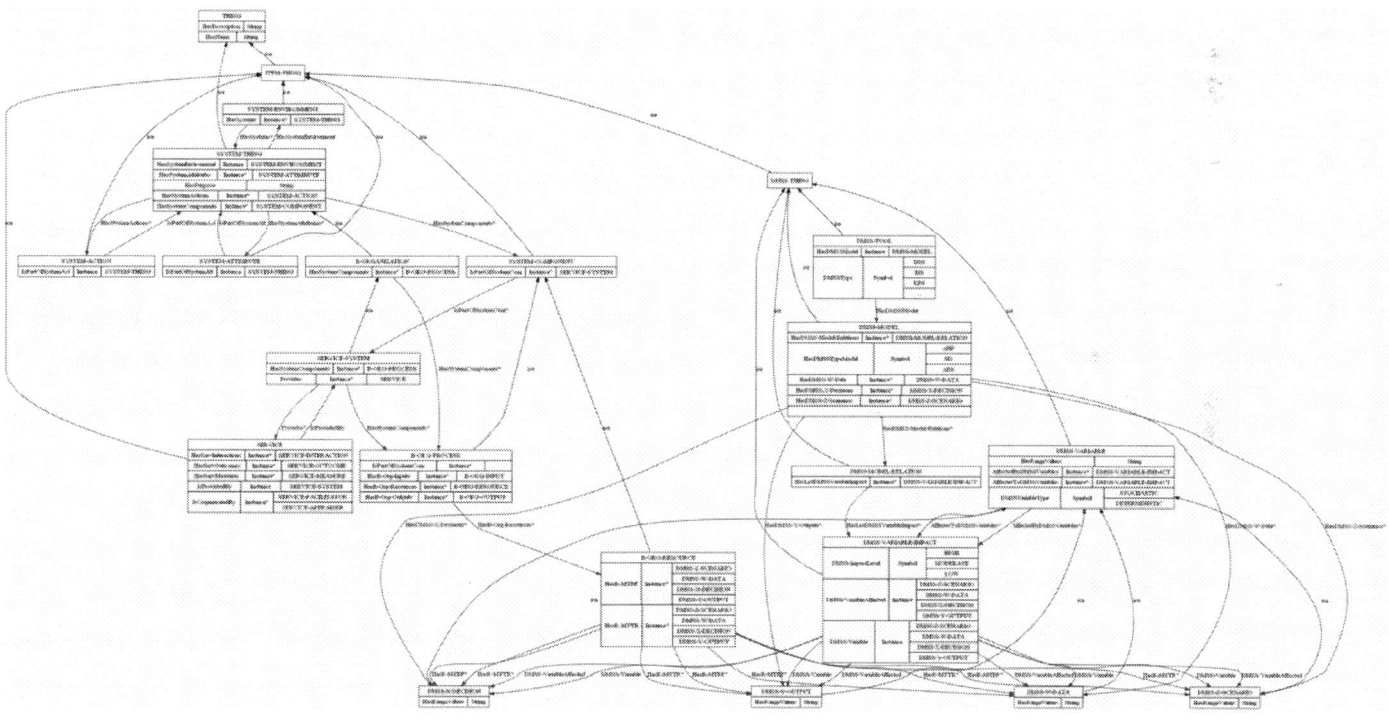

Figure 5. IT Service System and DMSS-Thing Core Concepts in *Onto-ITSDM* Ontology

Protégé Frames 3.4 was used for implementing it. Face validity and competency inquires tests were conducted by the authors. Hence, we consider that this research and produced artifact contributes with theoretical and practical advances in the ITSM domain. Next research effort will be focused in the building and empirical test of a KMS tool using the *Onto-ITSDM* ontology for supporting the design of DMSS models and DMSS tools for IT service design tasks.

6   References

[1] J. van Bon et al. "Foundations of IT Service Management based on ITIL v3". Van Haren Publishing, 2007.

[2] ISO. "ISO/IEC 20000-4 Information Technology–Service Management Part 4 Process Reference Model". International Standards Organization, 2010.

[3] SEI. "CMMI® for Services - Version 1.3". Software Engineering Institute, 2010.

[4] R. Snevely. "Enterprise data center design and methodology". Prentice Hall Press, 2002.

[5] B. Holtsnider and B. Jaffe. "IT Manager's Handbook: Getting your new job done". Elsevier, 2012.

[6] M. Mora et al. "Toward an integrated conceptualization of the service and service system concepts: A systems approach"; International Journal of Information Systems in the Service Sector (IGI), Vol. 1, Issue 2, 36–57, Apr 2009.

[7] ENP. "Understanding the cost of data center downtime: an analysis of the financial impact on infrastructure vulnerability". Emerson Network Power, 2011.

[8] PIR. "Cost of Data Center Outages". Ponemon Institute Research, 2016.

[9] M. Mora, G. Phillips-Wren, J. Marx-Gomez, F. Wang and O. Gelman. "The role of decision-making support systems in IT service management processes"; Intelligent Decision Technologies (IOS Press), Vol. 8, 147-163, Apr 2014.

[10] M. Hoffman. "Ontologies in Modeling and Simulation: An Epistemological Perspective". In A. Tolk (Ed.), "Ontology, Epistemology and Teleology for Modeling and Simulation". Springer, (59-87), 2013.

[11] M. Leon, E. Huang, and K. Kwon. "Ontologies and Simulation: a Practical Approach"; The Journal of Simulation (Palgrave), Vol. 5, 190-201, May 2011.

[12] M. Mora, M. Raisinghani, R. O'Connor, J. Marx and O. Gelman. "An Extensive Review on IT Service Design in Seven International ITSM Processes Frameworks: Part I"; International Journal of Information Technology and Systems Approach (IGI), Vol. 7, Issue 2, 85-109, Jul 2014.

[13] P. Weist. "An AHP-based Decision Making Framework for IT Service Design". MWAIS 2009 Proceedings Paper 11, 1-7, 2009.

[14] C. Rudd and V. Lloyd. "ITIL Version 3 Service Design". The Stationery Office, 2007.

[15] G. Forgionne, M. Mora, J. Gupta and O. Gelman. "Decision-making support systems". In M. M. Khosrow-Pour (Ed.), Encyclopedia of Information Science and Technology. IGI, (759-765), 2005.

[16] E. Orta, M. Ruiz, N. Hurtado, and D. Gawn. "Decision-making in IT service management: a simulation based approach"; Decision Support Systems (Elsevier), Vol. 66, 36-51, Jun 2014.

[17] A. Kieninger, F. Berghoff, H. Fromm, and G. Satzger. "Simulation-Based Quantification of Business Impact Caused by Service Incidents". In IESS 2013 Proceedings, Springer, (170-185), 2013.

[18] A. Puvvala, V. Kumar, and R. Patil. "Governance Policies in IT Service Support"; in Australian Conference on Information Systems Proceedings, (1-10), 2016.

[19] T. Gruber. "Toward Principles for the Design of Ontologies Used for Knowledge Sharing". Technical Report KSL 93-04, Knowledge Systems Laboratory, Stanford University, 1993.

[20] B. Chandrasekaran, J. Josephson and V. Benjamins. "What are ontologies, and why do we need them?"; IEEE Intelligent systems (IEEE), Vol. 14, Issue 1, 20-26, Jan 1999.

[21] R. Davis, H. Shrobe and P. Szolovit. "What Is a Knowledge Representation"; AI Magazine (AAAI), Spring, 17-33, Apr 1993.

[22] R. Fikes and T. Kehler. "The Role of Frame-Based Representation in Reasoning"; Communications of the ACM (ACM), Vol. 28, Issue 9, 904-920, Sep 1985.

[23] A. Borgida. "On the relative expressiveness of description logics and first order logics"; Artificial Intelligence (AAAI), Vol. 82, 353-367, Jan 1996.

[24] M. Mora, R. O'Connor, M. Raisinghani and O. Gelman. "Design, Build and Evaluation of an Ontology-Based KMS for Supporting CMMI-DEV Understanding: Benefits and Limitations"; International Journal of Software Engineering and Knowledge Engineering (World Scientific), Vol. 23, Issue 7, 999–1032, Jul 2013.

[25] N. Noy and D. McGuinness. "Ontology Development 101: A Guide to Creating Your First Ontology". Stanford University, 1–25, 2008.

[26] O. Corcho, M. Fernandez-Lopez, and A. Gomez-Perez. "Methodologies, tools and languages for building ontologies: where is their meeting point?"; Data & Knowledge Engineering (Elsevier), Vol. 46, 41–64, Oct 2003.

[27] M. Mora, M. Raisinghani, O. Gelman and M. Sicilia. "Onto-ServSys: A service system ontology". In H. Demirkan, J. Spohrer and V. Khrisnas (Eds.), The Science of Service Systems, Springer, (151–173), 2011.

ISBN: 1-60132-454-5, CSREA Press ©

A WCF & WPF based Chat Application

S. Narayanaswami and D. Yoon
CIS Department, University of Michigan, Dearborn, MI, USA

Abstract - *We present a chat system based on Windows Communication Foundation (WCF) and Windows Presentation Foundation (WPF) with emphasis on security aspects of WCF. As the name indicates, WCF lays down the foundation for the communication between server and client, while WPF is a graphical user interface system in .NET. Through the chat system, we explore the security measures implemented in X.509, which include the contracts, endpoints and the usage of the service. This is then presented by developing an application which implements the WCF security aspects in a client-server architecture and effectively handles the security. WCF provide a very rich and easy configurable environment to implement security. The client and server will communicate by using xml messages. WCF provides two mechanisms for transfer security which is transport security and message security. We will make use of these security mechanism provided by the WCF in our application.*

One common use of the WCF is to provide a way to distribute and collect data and information to and from multiple clients at the same time, with no hassle in the user experience on the client side.

The four core security features that WCF addresses are Authentication, Authorization, Confidentiality, Integrity and auditing. WCF supports a variety of authentication options including user name, Windows, and certificate authentication which will be studied in detail.

Keywords: Security, X509, Client, Server, cloud system

1   Introduction

A chat system is an internet communication system in which a client asks questions and the server answers them.   It is a relatively simple system, yet contains all aspects of the client- server model.

A client logins into the system with the valid id. The server checks the clients certificate and allows a chat session if the client has the legitimate certificate. The activities of the system is briefly summarized below.

- Allows the registered users to Login using their Credentials.
- Allow users to join a peer-peer chat

- Display Online users/contact list
- Allow sending and receiving message from and to Contact
- Server records user login and logoff time.
- User list updated when user goes offline
- Secure message using Certificate

2   System Architecture and Design

Service
- Interface IChattingService
  Login, Logoff, Send Message
- Interface IClient
  GetMessage, GetUpdate

Host
- Define Endpoints
- Define Bindings
- Define the Security-Message Level-Certificate (Reliable Sessions)

Client
- Implement IClient in Client Callback

Others
- Allows user to login with proper Credentials

3   Implementation of the System

This system was built on WCF and WPF using .NET framework 4.5.2 in Visual Studio 2015. The WPF acts as a wrapper around the WCF making the Application look nicer that ordinary windows form or console application. The WPF is the library that provides us with all GUI elements and user interactions. We have secured the Application by making use of Certificates, one for the Client and Server using makecert.exe. (*Makecert.exe is a free tool provided by Microsoft which helps to create X.509 certificates that are signed by a system test root key or by another specified key*) [6].

WCF is used to build service oriented applications using which we can transfer messages and data asynchronously from one service end point to another.[3]. In WCF when we think about service, we are going to create a class of service and Interface called Service Contract. Some of the key terminologies to know on WCF include:

Service: The service is the implementation for things that are exposed to the outside client. Every client starting a session does not initiate a new instance of the service

Service Contract: Service contract is what is exposed to the outside world which specifies the methods that need to be implemented. (Login/Send Message/List Users)

The Client sees what the server has to offer through the Service Contract. Service contract is marked with the [ServiceContract] attribute. The Operation Contract attribute defines an operation and is part of the service contract and is decorated with [OperationContract] attribute. The service and the service contract need to be connected or hosted to make use of the features provided by them.

Endpoint: An endpoint of WCF service acts as a gateway for communicating with the outside world. An endpoint is composed of

Address: Every service has unique address which is of the format

[Transport] :// [Domain Name]: [Port]// [Service Name]

Binding: *Binding indicates the protocol ·that are supported by the service (TCP/HTTP/NET*CP)

Contract: This defines the Operations/or what the service can do.

3.1 Client

The Client is implemented using the WPF (Windows Presentation Foundation). The client pages consist of the MainWindow.xaml. This is the screen where users will exchange messages. The right side list holds the list of users online. We have use the dictionary data structure to hold the users and we remove the user from the dictionary when the user goes offline.

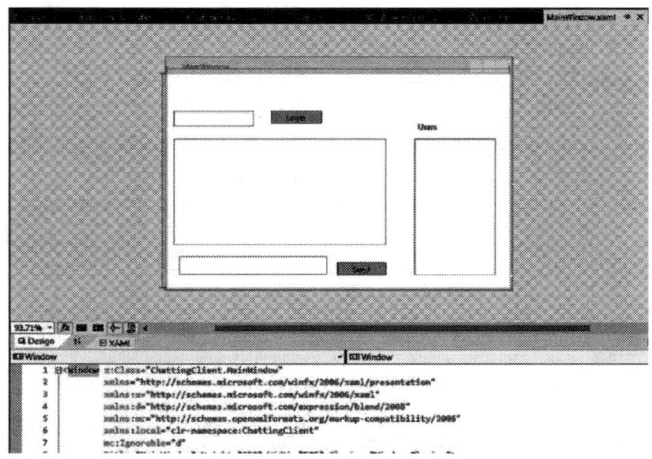

Figure 1 A login window and the code behind

3.1.1 Server

The server is split into two parts. The first is the Interface which has the Contract, methods and properties and the second part being the implementation of the Interface. The server contains a contract that determines the Service behavior.

The ChattingInterfaces is where we have defined the OperationContract, which includes:

1. Login- this accepts the parameter username, which is used to login with the desired name to join the chat window.

2. SendMessageToAll- this operation accepts the message and username as parameter and is used to distribute the message across the active clients

3. Logout-this operation Logs the client out of the chat window/application

4. GetCurrentUsers – This returns a list of String which holds the Current active users in the application

In the Chatting Server, we define the Operation Contract methods. In the chatting server, we create a Dictionary to hold the list of logged in users in the Application. On user exit, the user is removed from the dictionary.

The ChattingServer code is pretty straight forward. It establishes the connection and prints the client's status.

4. Securing It Using Certificates

Certificates are a type of Identification to ensure that the communication is known and reliable. Technically a Certificate binds together a name and a public key [6].

(Makecert.exe is a free tool provided by Microsoft which helps to create X.509 certificates that are signed by a system test root key or by another specified key)

To have a secured communication between the Client and Server, I have used the X509 certificate authentication. This consist of the WCF Services-clients should be authenticated by X509 certificate. Client should validate the service using this certificate.

Steps to be followed to create the certificate [7]:

Step 1:
Open Visual Studio Command Prompt and go to the location where you want to save the certificate.

Step 2:
Execute the below command

makecert -n "CN=RootCATest" -r -sv RootCATest.pvk RootCATest.cer

You will be prompted to enter a password and hit OK.

Step 3:
The next step is to install the Root Certificate Authority in Client and Server machine

For the Certificate to be made a trusted one, we need to import this to the Trusted Root Certification Authority Store. The Microsoft Management Control (MMC), can be accessed by typing MMC in the command prompt. In the MMC dialog box, we have to click the Add or Remove Snap in from the File menu and select Certificate from the available Snap-in and Add the certificate.

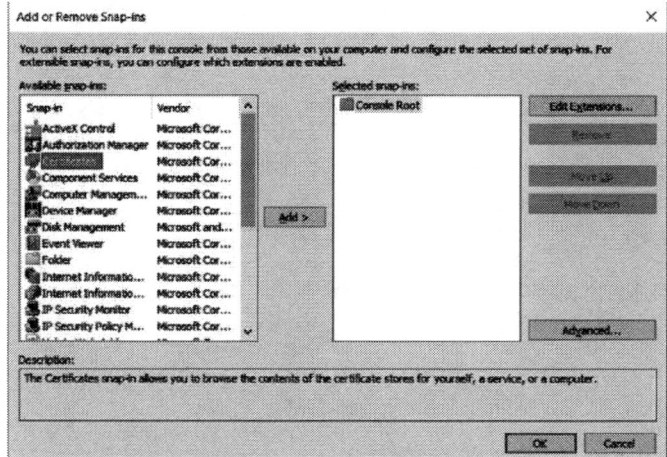

Figure 2 Microsoft Management Control Dialog box)

This will prompt the Certificate Snap in dialog, Select the Computer account and use the default option in the following steps and hit Finish.

Step 4:
We now need to add the Certificate to the Store by importing it. To Import the certificate, go-to the Console Root and expand the Certificates menu item.
Expand the Trusted Root Certificate Authority, right click and select 'All Task' and 'Import' (Fig 6.5).
The welcome wizard appears the one below (Fig: 6.6)

Step 5:
The next step is to install the Temporary Service Certificate to the Server machine. We follow the same steps as we followed to the Client machine.

makecert -sk <<UniqueKeyName>> -iv RootCATest.pvk -n "CN=<<MachineName>>" -ic RootCATest.cer -sr localmachine -ss my -sky exchange -pe

Configuring the Temporary Service Certificate in IIS

Step 6:
Once the certificates are installed in the Client and Server machines, we need to update our configuration files of the Client and Server. In the config, we add the client and server credentials to the respective project config and specify the certificate name in the find value and the store location will be of that of the current user.

5   Putting It Altogether

After creating the Certificates and updating the config file, this section has the screenshot of the application. We will be using two instance of the client and see how the message transfer is achieved.
The below screen is the Login screen of the application. The user has to provide the login information and this is validated with the stored values in the backend. If the authentication is successful, the User is taken to chat window

6   Conclusions

WCF Chat application has been implemented successfully. The following service functions have been verified:

- Allows only authenticated users to login to thapplication
- Allow multiple instances of the Client with single server
- Peer to peer message transfer
- Update Active user list
- Secure the message transfer with Certificate at both the client and server
- Server records all the information about the client instances login and logoff

It can be concluded that the implementation of WCF is simple but versatile in its effectiveness. It is a powerful way of establishing a secured communication either using transport or message level security. WCF inherently provides authentication, authorization, integrity and confidentiality for any application built on the WCF framework. The implementation of the service was smooth and the created service worked as intended.
The application was developed using the best practice of coding standard.

7   References

[1] https://msdn.microsoft.com/en-us/library/ff648498.aspx - Creating and installing temporary Certificates

[2] http://weblogs.asp.net/psheriff/create-a-login-window-in-wpf-2013 - Creating a login window in WPF

[3] http://www.c-sharpcorner.com/UploadFile/16101a/a-beginners-tutorial-for-understanding-windows-communicatio/   - Great tutorial to understand the basics of WCF

[4] https://msdn.microsoft.com/en-us/library/cc179585.aspx - Understanding Windows Communication Foundation

ISBN: 1-60132-454-5, CSREA Press ©

[5] https://msdn.microsoft.com/en-
us/library/bb690929(v=vs.90).aspx – WCF chat sample by
MSDN

[6] https://msdn.microsoft.com/en-us/library/ff647171.aspx
-   Creating and installing Temporary Certificates in WCF for
Message Security

[7] http://www.yangsoft.com/blog/?p=105   - How to use
makecert.exe to generate Certificates for WCF service in
Windows

[8] https://blogs.msdn.microsoft.com/theothersteve/
2010/04/19/how-to-create-a-peer-to-peer-chat-application-
using-wpf-and-wcf-in-visual-studio-2010/   - Sample peer to
peer chat application

ISBN: 1-60132-454-5, CSREA Press ©

Digitization of companies
- understanding IT as an enabler -

Isabell Schrader
best-practice innovations GmbH
Norbertstr. 32
50670

mail: isabell.schrader@b-pi.com

Olaf Droegehorn
University of Applied Sciences Harz
Department of Automation & Computer Science
Friedrichstrasse 57-59
38855 Wernigerode, Germany
mail: odroegehorn@hs-harz.de

Papertypye: Regular Research Paper

Abstract – *The digitization of the business world is changing the role of IT: its strategic importance is expanding. The IT can, will ad, should be the central design element for new business elements. This results in new challenges for IT departments, but more than this also for business units and strategic business plan developers. In the past the focus of updated IT approaches was set on cost and stability. However, IT nowadays needs to meet additional requirements as adaptability and agility. When rethinking IT strategies within the context of business digitization the following questions need to be answered: Is IT just a tool to deliver faster business? Or can it be an enabler for new business opportunities and business models. Is it enough to think about how the necessary services can be provided or which methods are suitable for which requirements? It seems that moreover a new holistic strategy including IT and business in an interactive, bi-cyclic development process might lead to new business opportunities and customer satisfaction. But this demands also for a new set of management principles and mind-sets to enforce digitization on all levels of a company and to help the enterprise maximize returns from technology investments. In this paper an employee oriented approach is suggested, leading towards a manamgement attitude that can implement digitization by empowering the own work force. This leads towards an inhouse capability that is inevitably unparalleled to any consultancy solution. Therefore each company, striving to touch upon digitization, should allow itself to reach out towards this self-empowering strategy.*

Keywords: Digitization, innovative management structure, new mind-sets, digital generation, IT as enabler

1   Introduction

The digital transformation of companies is a demanding task, which is nowadays a necessitiy but in several cases embodies the risk of failure. For instance, in the recent past there are striking examples in which the IT has been updated technology as well as strategic wise but the business, using the capabilites, has stayed the same. Deutsche Bank, for example, redesigned its major future project of a new "digital bank". One reason is for sure the lack of competences and understanding for new digital processes and technologies. The Frankfurt-based energy supplier Mainova AG had to restructure its IT in recent years completely. Apart from the fact that IT should be restructured every 3 to 5 years, due to technological updates, should the business stay the same? DHL has announced a new "IT Renewal Roadmap" [4], but no "Business Renewal Roadmap" was announced to make use of the new technological capabilities.

Since the end of the 20th century, the 4th industrial revolution has begun. But is it just a technical update of tools, or is it a ground breaking new enabler of business opportunities? The focus here is on the increasing digitization of previous analogue processes and the integration of cyber-physical systems [12], and therefore the challenges that arise in the business divisions from new opportunities enabled by new technlogies. Instead of "pre-production" many products and/or services are manufactured on demand or according to actual requirements [12]. As a result, new business models have been created and IT-strategies have been developed in order to deal with fast changing requirements, new markets and visions that can be met by innovative IT solutions. In the IT sector new challanges like "Cloud Computing", "Design Thinking", "Big Data", "Outsourcing", "Migration", "Workplace Transformation", "Collaboration" and "MSS (Managed Security Service)" are nowadays daily business [6] but it seems that the business divisions are not responding to it. The common aim seems to always be: IT needs to change, IT needs to be flexible, IT needs to adapt and become agile, but business stays the same. But instead, a new opportunitiy of a bi-cyclic process, empowereing both sides with new seeds can lead to a much faster business, of course supported and maintained by IT, but only driven by enhanced, tuned and revolutionized business ideas from the business divisions.

Within this paper several aspects, tools and approaches are presented to change the mind-set of employees and managers in the related divions. Under the assumption that IT can be an enabler to improve not only business performance but developes new business models as well as processes, components are outlined that are necessary for the business in order to understand IT as enabler.

ISBN: 1-60132-454-5, CSREA Press ©

2   Motivation – Many approaches without a supporting mind-set

Revolutionary approaches for the IT have been developed to change the entire IT landscape in companies. For example, "Agile IT", "Adaptive IT", "digital transformation", "Business-IT-Alignment" and other terms include concepts and steps on how IT can be enabled in order to support business processes more efficiently. This has led to a new, quite agile mind-set of IT personell, enabling the teams to react on new, enhanced business requirements in a spontaneous manner.

Typically, those changes are not driven by technological updates but within reorganization-projects from the business divisions. Reviewing the aforementioned digitization projects, it can be shown that business development is limited to the use of faster IT provisioning instead of enabling new business models and opportunities by new IT technologies.

Given the fact, that IT departments are delivering new, faster and demand-related services, the IT personell has been trained to support their business customers already in a just-in-time, focussed to business, meaning service uptime in terms of IT, manners for quite a while. But thinking this concept ahead in terms of business digitization, the business, in the need of developing new IT based service offerings, needs to respond in a similar updated and enhanced manner to its customers as the IT personell did beforehand.

But the initial roadblock in this design process stems from a former time where business an IT departments were serverly seperated and using different "languages" to run its operations [10].

From the authors point of view business people involved are often impressed by technological possibilities.

But instead of just being impressed by technological advances it is of upmost importance for modern companies that business people understand at least the business possibilities stemming from those IT updates. By making use of these advances, may it be as short term market leads or enhanced customer online services, this could lead in a longer run to an enhanced and more comprehensive business delivery concept than it has ever been developed before.

Looking into the former business organizations the typical question would be: Who actually runs whom?

But pushing the well known hurdles and hirarchie beside it may not even be a question of who depends on whom. Because undoubtly there is no IT without a business and in these days there is no business without IT. Therefore, it is meaningless to ask if we just follow the latest technological developments. But on the other hand we should not inevitably and unconsciously adapt to the new conditions without understanding an analyzing its opportunities.

As a consequence, a bi-cyclic process between business and IT, educating, enabling and developing both sides at the same time coud provide a possible answer to this problem.

The 21st-century or the generation Y is denoted to raise up with digital technology. This bears of course the risk that this generation follows up inconciously new technological advances, but enables mankind also to be the creator of our own reality in which we consciously and sensibly use possibilities at our disposal.

We need to "develop and use technologies that helps us and which is useful to us. In this case, technologies are tools" resulting in digitization of society and companies, which should be actively self-designed and self-determined [1].

In order to make this happen parameters, tools, mind-sets and organizational structures are needed.

In addition, a certain kind of competence in the digital environment is needed to overcome the pure helplessness when digital innovations occur to make business related meaning out of it.

Employees need to be aware of their inner attitude, their values and their mental models regarding IT- in short, their mind-set. According to the Project manager Baehr [1] our mind-set is shaped by:

- Our feelings and our thoughts
- Our mental models and beliefs
- Our personal values and settings

Everyone has their own individual mind-set regarding IT. It is characterized both by our personality as well as by our previous experiences with IT. Furthermore, family, school and education, culture and their values have an impact on the personal mind-set. "The perception about the importance of our mind-set has increased strongly in recent years. Science it is increasingly proving that we can consciously change and develop our mental attitude. Just as we wish. And what impact this has on our behavior, our actions, our satisfaction, our health and our relationship with other people" [1].

3   How mind-sets can affect collaboration

The mind-set affects behavior, actions and communication with others. In terms of digitization, it can be explained in more detail with the following example - permanent availability, constant interruptions.

Many employees have the feeling to be interrupted at their work all the time and just do not get anything done. If one starts with a task for which all attention is needed, such as the elaboration of a concept, it needs a lot of time after an interruption to get back into the topic. In the case of multiple interruptions, the time for the creation is considerably increased. Permanent interruptions are seen to stem from digitization, Smartphones, Social Media and Tablets that offer simply a lot of interruptions, especially during working hours. But looking very carefully into these issues it can be denoted, that it is still a free choice if people are immediately reacting on digital triggers or not.

A study on the burnout risk of project managers in 2013 shows that constant interruptions are a major risk factor that correlates significantly with a high burnout risk. 80% of the interviewees are often interrupted, most of whom feel that they are actually burdened [2]. So this kind of mind-set is characterized by a regular interruption culture.

Constant interruptions have their causes both in external circumstances and specific behavior of employees. In the case of external conditions there are all the networking possibilities that stem from digitization which play an important role. One of the internal factors is, above all, our mindset, which determines the way we use these possibilities above. Here are a few examples:

- People are afraid that they might miss something important or urgent if they do not react immediately to incoming SMS, emails or calls.
- People are afraid of the consequences if the boss or the customer has a concern and if they do not answer immediately.
- People are afraid that they will lose recognition in the team if they do not react immediately and help.
- People interrupt others simply because they want to answer a question immediately or they are under pressure and it has to go fast.
- People drive themselves and others, according to the principle: "Time is money". And so they make sure that they do not come to their senses or even fear, Smartphone-times off [1].

The problem that derives from such behavior becomes a routine when employees constantly practicing it. It becomes automatism and they do not even think about when they jump up again and get started. And so each individual contributes daily to the creation of a regular interruption culture. The lack of awareness, our lack of consciousness, is steadily increasing the vicious circle.

A suitable solution is to be aware of this behavior and the underlying patterns of feelings and thoughts. Only when people recognize and let go of these underlying patterns they are able to master the situation again.

However, another factor is the working culture within a company. The cooperation between IT- and business unit is still difficult and underperforming, it needs to be redefined as outlined in "Process-oriented IT-Management as management approach to face digitization" [10]. Kelleher quoted Britain's Winston Churchill: "Never have so few, been asked to do so much, for so many, with so little." In this context Kelleher summarizes significant trends and challenges just focussed on the IT-Management of companies [3], missing out the business management. They certainly face similar challanges, to achieve more with reduced ressources, delivering just-in-time to consumers as well as to adapt to changed business environments. A lot of approaches for dealing with any kind of new technology trends have been developed and the consequence always sounds like "innovative companies are forced to enhance their IT-Management processes and tools" [9]. Certainly these kind of approaches are essential, but they are nothing without a strong business counterpart that understands IT-Processes and new possibilities that technology is able to create. The business needs to adapt their understanding of IT and learn to understand IT as an enabler.

4   Approach to understand IT as an enabler

Digitization must be the key issue "a matter of the boss" [11]. No matter how big a company is, digital change should be the focus of the companies' strategy. All hirarchy-levels of the company need to be involved. The management level should not stick to old patterns but should rather inspire employees to uptake digital changes and take actively part themselves. The basis for a digital change is permanent availability of data via the Internet and access to it via browsers. This sole of an infrastructure and additional platforms must not only subordinate software, but also products, business processes and business models in the future, if they are to be used meaningfully or to be successful in competition [7]. In short, only those who ultimately focus everything on IT strategy and structure remain in the market.

Furthermore, digitization requires resources such as budget and manpower. A digital transformation process can not take place without adequate budgets, sufficient skilled employees and the necessary knowledge. The business needs to understand that the goal of digitization should not be primarily to increase efficiency, but also to establish new business models for the benefit of customers.

It is of utmost significance that employees are involved at an early stage. Networking and digital data opens up opportunities for new work and management models. This can create anxiety among employees. Here, it is important to involve the employees as early as possible in shaping new working environment. Only with understanding and enthusiasm new structures can be created and established. Ideas and creativity need to be encouraged. In order to create something entirely new, one needs corresponding ideas and creative solutions. Thinking outside the box and understanding the increasing complexity of modern technology and modern business is essential. Companies need to establish room and space in order to do out of the box thinking. Companies are most likely able to find true innovative approaches through the intensive, knowledge-driven cooperation in cross-functional teams (e.g. process-oriented IT-Management). It is therefore important to reduce functional silos in the company in order to link employees and their knowledge [10]. Innovation processes should be implemented not only within IT and business units but cross-departmental. Digital business transformation is a real innovation task. In order to enhance both the development of approaches as well as creating a sustainable basis for a transformation, these tasks have to be established and managed as an innovation process. The aim is to find an optimal balance between rules and freedom, each individually according to the needs of a company, employees and requirements of their workplace. A good orientation could be process models like Stage-Gate or elements from original digital methods like Lean Startup, Design Thinking or the clear service-related service design. What connects these methods is a user-centered, cooperative conceptual and developmental process as well as the permanent review of the assumptions and the results achieved [7]. An innovation culture needs to be built. Encouraging creativity and introducing innovation processes is necessary but not yet sufficient. Without a top-management

ISBN: 1-60132-454-5, CSREA Press ©

innovation culture, these measures remain ineffective, because employees need to see a good example and get encouraged when having innovative ideas. Only where the digital transformation is wanted in the whole company it also takes place. It is the task of the companies' management to productively combine traditional and digital experiences. In short: "Nerds" and "Suits" on the same level. An innovation culture also includes freedom of discretion for the employees as well as the necessity that everyone can make mistakes and is allowed to make mistakes. Only those who have the courage to fail also take necessary risks [7]. In the light of involving employees at an early stage, Jon Kolko, the vice president of design at Blackboard, characterized the term design-centric culture. "Design-centric culture transcends design as a role, imparting a set of principles to all people who help bring ideas to life" [5]. Those principles are:

- Focus on users' experiences, especially their emotional ones.
- Create models to examine complex problems.
- Use prototypes to explore potential solutions.
- Tolerate failure.
- Exhibit thoughtful restraint.

Kolkos conclusion is: "Design thinking is an essential tool for simplifying and humanizing. It can't be extra; it needs to be a core competence" [5].

In addition, design technology with man for mankind can make a huge difference and create acceptance from the start. To master the digital transformation, it is not enough to overload the employees with a 300 pages strong manual. They need practical encouragement. Employees can, for example, playfully acquire new technology competences with so-called "Serious Games" or with the help of real or virtual learning factories [11]. "Specifically, people need their interactions with technologies and other complex systems to be simple, intuitive, and pleasurable" [5]. For example, the Microsoft Operations Framework (MOF) 4.0 provides relevant, practical, and implementable guidlines to align business and IT objectives. The framework encompasses "the entire IT service management lifecycle, providing organizations with the knowledge to seamlessly blend business and IT goals while establishing and implementing reliable, cost-effective IT services" [14].

Employees need further education regarding frameworks like MOF as well as methods like Design Thinking. But they do not only need it, they need to want it since it needs experts to embed the digitization into a company. Training can be done with experts within a company but also with external coaches. Another opportunity could be to acquire knowledge through crowdfunding. Here the focus is the exchange of knowledge of experts via a digital media, because networking is a core element of digitization. During the digitization process individual companies and production sites can be linked and become a network, so they are able to link their value chains maybe even exchange data and benefit from synergies, generate competitive advantages and generate joint growth. However they should keep in mind to always keep the customer in focus. Of course it is a matter of time to change a corporate culture and mind-sets of people, therefore companies should start as

early as possible. Identification with a company and its culture starts from day one when working for a company. Hence the onboarding-process should be well prepared. From own experience companies take a lot of time for the recruiting process but typically forget the importance and the relevance an onboarding process can have on an employee. The first impression counts and it is decisive for the picture a new employee receives about the corporate culture. The potential replacements for specialists and executives should understand from the beginning that the IT can also be understood as an enabler. This is, however, only possible if a rethinking has already taken place on the executive level. Since it not only needs a bottom-up understanding, but also a top-down understanding of the possibilities that IT and new technologies can bring to the company. So far business units see IT as support to their processes, a functional unit that is necessary, because letters have gone out of fashion, are too expensive and the business is running worldwide and therefore needs digital means of communication. Functions like enterprise resource planning, financial- & human resources as well as e-mail systems have to work, but in the long run they are not something that brings the big advantage to organizations. However even though an accounting system is quite important, most businesses are not a key player on the market because they have a better accounting system. Business units need to understand IT as enabler to enhance business opportunities and stay competitive on the market. Figure 1 shows components that may help the business to change their way of thinking about IT and to see IT as enabler.

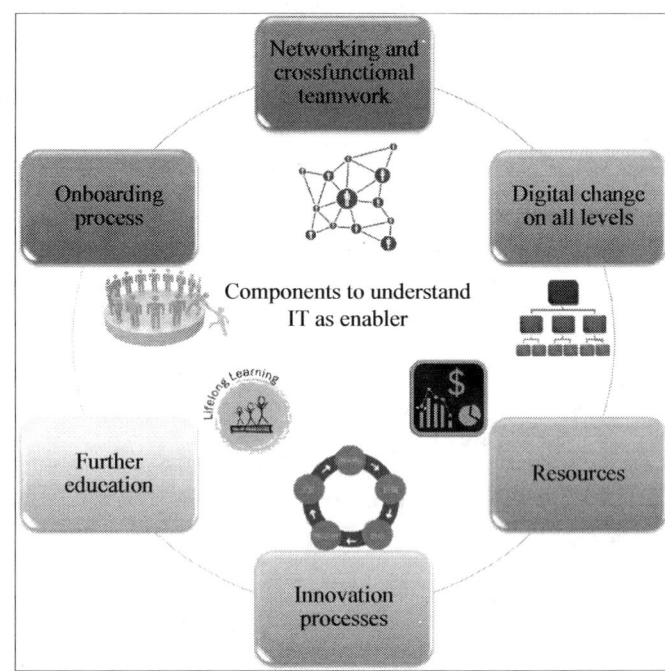

Figure 1: Components to understand IT as enabler

Including digital change in business strategies and therefore on all levels of a company puts IT and business units into a collaborative position. IT budgets of course need to be optimized as any other costs, but the management should consider to rather invest in respective ressources instead of cutting them. Creating and shaping new working environments by including innovation processes need to be self-evidently. Which in turn leads to an innovation culture in which people want to learn and are supported by the top-management. In this case top-management wants and supports a change in corporate culture and is able to understand IT as enabler. A top-management needs to go a step beqond making only decisions, it needs to act accordingly.

Richard Skriletz a manager and management consultant described already in 2013 how IT can be transformed into a business enabler:

- Identifiying and pursuing opportunities for improving and enhancing business process performance
- Providing business design standards, controls, and compliance
- Reducing the resources required for IT infrstructure

5   Conclusion & Outlook

Looking into digitizaion approaches of modern companies it gets obvious that a certain demand towards IT departments are formulated without updating the business sectors accordingly. By just requiring an agile IT development and a just-in-time IT service delivery strategy no new business models are created. The classic, well known business just happens faster. But IT departments, especially incorporating up-to-date technologies, are capabale to boost new business models and provisioning opportunites never seen before. Therefore, new management approaches as well as inclusion of business personell is of upmost importance to open up these new opportunities for well established companies.

Within this paper several components and principles have been discussed and outlined in order to be able to understand the IT as an enabler for new business opportunities. Under the assumption that IT is not only a functional support for business processes, different alternative actions to change mind-sets and corporate culture have been presented in order to face digitization not only with agile, flexible and adaptive IT, but with a different point of view on how business needs to change their way of thinking as well.

Because only by a simultaneous development of business departments together with the IT a bi-cyclic process, empowering and enhacing both sides at the same time, can be done. This will lead towards new business opportunities, enabled and driven by new IT-technologies leading towarrds business chances, which were unthinkable before.

6   References

[1] Baehr, M., Digitalisierung im Business – Brauchen wir ein neues Mind Set?. Available: http://barcamp.corbusiness.de/digitalisierung-im-business-brauchen-wir-ein-neues-mind-set/ (2017, March 13).

[2] GPM Deutsche Gesellschaft für Projektmanagement e.V., Burnout bei ProjektmanagerInnen. Available: https://www.gpm-ipma.de/fileadmin/user_upload/Know-How/studien/2014Kurzfassung_Homepage_web_final.pdf (2017, March 14).

[3] Kelleher D., The six most significant trends in IT management. Available: http://www.gfi.com/blog/the-sixmost-significant-trends-in-it-management/ (2016, March 09.)

[4] Keller, A.; Neumann, F., IT-Strategie – neue alte Perspektiven: Digitale Transformation ist keine Selbstverständlichkeit. Available: http://ap-verlag.de/it-strategie-neue-alte-perspektiven-digitale-transformation-ist-keine-selbstverstaendlichkeit/28431/ (2017, March 9).

[5] Kolko, J., Design Thinking Comes of Age. http://www.henleyleadership.com/uploads/pdf/designthinkingcomesofage.pdf (2017, March 21).

[6] Kullus, K., Sprechen Sie IT? 9 Buzzwords, die jeder kennen sollte. Available: https://www.techtag.de/netzkultur/sprechen-sie-9-buzzwords-die-jeder-kennen-sollte/7/ (2017, March 13).

[7] Neugebauer, T., Wie Unternehmen transformieren. Available: http://www.computerwoche.de/a/wie-unternehmen-transformieren,3064296 (2017, March 13).

[8] Niersmann, K., Niemann, F., Die Digitalisierung erfordert wandlungsfähige Business-Software. Available: http://www.godesys.de/fileadmin/user_upload/Support/Downloads/Whitepaper/godesys-PAC_Trendstudie_Digitalisierung.pdf (2017, March 13).

[9] Olufs D., Strategisches IT Management. Available:https://www.sysedv.tuberlin.de/fileadmin/fg161/hp/lehre/StratITM/02-Strategisches_IT_Management_part_1.pdf (2017, March 09).

[10] Schrader, I., Drögehorn, O., Process-oriented IT-Management as management approach to face digitization. Available: Proc. of the 15th International Conference on e-Learning, e-Business, Enterprise Information Systems, and e-Government (2017, March 13).

[11] Sowa, T., Digitalisierung muss Chefsache sein. Available: http://www.erfolg-und-business.de/business-von-morgen/digitalisierung-muss-chefsache-sein (2017, March 13).

[12] Industrie-wegweiser, Von Industrie 1.0 bis 4.0 – Industrie im Wandel der Zeit. Available: http://industrie-wegweiser.de/von-industrie-1-0-bis-4-0-industrie-im-wandel-der-zeit/ (2017, March 13).

[13] Skriletz, R., How to Make IT a Business Enabler. Available: http://www.b-eye-network.com/view/16788 (2017, March 21).

[14] Solution Accelerators, Microsoft Operations Framework. Available: https://technet.microsoft.com/en-us/library/dd320379.aspx (2017, March 21).

A Solution to the Long-Hours Working of Self-Employed Teleworking or Crowdsourcing

Hodaka NAKANISHI

Technology Transfer Center, Teikyo University, Itabashi-ku, Tokyo, Japan

Abstract - *In Japan, long hours working of self-employed teleworkers and freelancers is a serious problem. To clarify the mechanism of long hours working of teleworkers, a model which explains the relation between working hours and several factors concerning labor related matters such as worker's character, worker's skill, regulation of working hours, and so on is developed. Based on this model, four scenarios based on the presence or absence of regulation on working hours and the clarity of required quality of products are developed. For each scenario, the relationship between the worker's preference and skill and the working hours is examined. The introduction of regulation on working hours is effective as a countermeasure for the long hours working, but workers with low technical capabilities may lose their jobs. The clarification and revelation of required quality of products also has a prevention effect of long-hours working. The improvement of worker's skill is an important strategy for the stabilization of teleworkers' work. Providing opportunities of vocational training for workers can be an effective approach for the prevention of long-hours working.*

Keywords: telework, crowdsourcing, long-hour working, Work Life Balance, worker's skill

1 Introduction

"Workstyle Reform" is promoted as a government policy in Japan. Workstyle Reform is a policy which enable women and men, elderly people and young people, those with disabilities and intractable diseases to realize a satisfying workstyle that meets everyone's needs. Telework or crowdsourcing, which is a way of flexible working without restrictions on time and place by utilizing ICT, is promoted as a strategy of Workstyle Reform by the Japanese Government. Characteristics of this workstyle are that the worker is responsible for the management of their working hours and that the worker is evaluated by the outcome.

The working conditions of teleworkers vary from country to country, but in Japan it is reported that self-employed teleworkers and freelancers suffer low income and long hours of working [1]. As working hours of self-employed teleworkers and freelancers are self-managed, their workstyle is not simple but various. Some people go for fun soon after they accomplish their ordered job, but others will keep working and aim for quality improvement. Some workers want to achieve higher income, and some workers are aiming

for a free workstyle even with low income. The workstyle of self-employed teleworkers and freelancers is various and strategies for preventing long hours working depend on their character and preference. Since it is hard to discuss the paths for optimizing working hours and income with a single story, multiple scenarios should be set based on the institutional and business requirements surrounding the workers and should be discussed how teleworkers and freelancers take actions for each scenario in this research.

Although several measures are being taken against long hours working by strengthening regulations on companies and showing guidelines by the government, these measures are for employee of companies. For a self-employed teleworker, working condition is determined by the contract between company and teleworker, and effective countermeasures have not been taken. For instance, amendments to the Subcontractor Promotion Law which is to protect subcontractors are proposed [1] [2], but they have not been realized.

Evidence based policies are promoted and evidences are required for policy planning to promote self-employed teleworkers and freelancers as Workstyle Reform. There are many statistics on employment type teleworkers. But there are few statistical data on how self-employed teleworkers or freelancers work. The relationship between working style of teleworking and working hours is not clear.

The purpose of this research is to indicate that self-employed teleworking and crowdsourcing tends to cause long hours working by examining the relationship between working style of teleworking and working hours, and to suggest solutions for the long hours working. As mentioned above, there is no single solution. Therefore, in this paper, four scenarios are developed depending on the clarity of the required quality of outcomes and the presence or absence of time constraints, and for each scenario, depending on the characteristics of workers (work preference and technical capability). The worker's workstyle in each scenario is examined.

In chapter 2, working hours' decision model is developed to analyze the mechanism by which worker's working hours are determined. In chapter 3, two policy factors related to long hours working of teleworkers are set: limitation of working hours and clarity of required quality of outcomes. In chapter 4, the attitude towards working and the skill as a characteristic of the worker are discussed. In Chapter 5, four scenarios by combining two kinds of policy are presented and discussed with characteristics of workers. Chapter 6 summarizes measures to prevent long hours working in self-employed type teleworking or crowdsourcing, and makes policy recommendations.

2 Working hours' decision model

In this chapter, a model to decide working hours for one given job is developed to consider the working hours of self-employed teleworkers and freelancers. The cost and benefit of self-employed teleworkers and freelancers are analyzed from a viewpoint of working hours. A worker keeps working if the benefit of from the job is larger than the cost of the job and the worker stops working if the cost exceeds the benefit.

In this model, it is assumed that the quality (q) improves as work hours (t) increases, and that the increase of quality is diminishing over time (1)(2)(3).

$$q = U(t) \qquad (1)$$
$$dU/dt > 0 \qquad (2)$$
$$d^2U/dt^2 < 0 \qquad (3)$$

The teleworkers or freelancers should work until required quality level (Q_r) is attained at t_r(Fig.1). The required quality level is previously presented to the workers by the employer as a specification of the job. The workers are paid a predetermined fixed reward when the product is turned in. As the quality level of the product corresponds to the reward and the reward is equal to the benefit of the worker, Y axis of graph in Fig.1 (quality) can be regarded as benefit and U(t) can be regarded as benefit line.

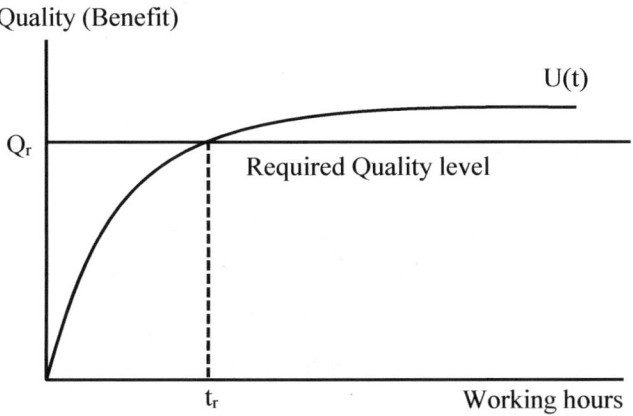

Fig. 1 Quality of product and working hours

The cost of the worker increases as the working hours become longer (Fig.2). Working hours are decided by a comparison of benefit and cost associated with "sense of burden" of workers. This sense of burden includes physical and mental fatigue and lost chances due to time constraints. The benefit of workers is increasing (2), but marginal benefit decreases as working hours increase (3). In contrast, the cost of workers increases as working hours increase. When the cost of worker exceeds the benefit of workers at t_e, the worker's profit (benefit minus cost) becomes negative, then the worker stops working. In case t_r is smaller than t_e, the worker may stop working at t_r and can get some profit. But in case t_r is larger than t_e, the worker stops working before the required quality is obtained or keeps working even though he/she suffers a loss for the job.

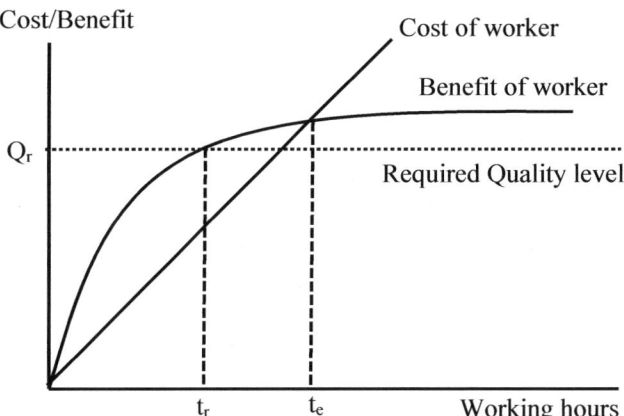

Fig.2 Cost and benefit of worker and working hours

3 Possible Strategies

In this chapter, strategies to prevent teleworkers from long hour working are examined. There can be two kinds of strategies; compulsory strategies and voluntary strategies. Compulsory strategies include a regulation to limit working hours. Voluntary strategies are measures to change workers' behavior by themselves.

3.1 Limitation of working hours

The length of working hours should differ depending on whether workers' working hours are legally limited or not. In Japan, the upper limit of regular working hours is determined to 40 hours a week, 8 hours a day by the Labor Standards Act. As for overtime work, it is determined that less than 45 hours per month is preferable, but the limit is not applied if the workers and the employer conclude a special agreement. To prevent "death from overwork (karoshi)", the Japanese government have recently decided to hold overtime hours to less than 100 hours per month. Therefore, employees' working hours are now limited. As for self-employed teleworkers and freelancers, however, they work through contracts with companies or clients and are not subject to the protection of Labor Standards Act. The workers should control their working hours by themselves. They work as much as they think they need, so long hours working easily occurs. To prevent the workers from long hour working, the introduction of new regulation to limit working hours might be a strategy, but there are side effects. Possible side effects can be examined with the working hours' decision model presented in Chapter 2.

Let us consider a case where the working hour is compulsorily limited to t_{Max} (Fig.3). If the necessary time to attain the required quality is shorter than t_{Max}, the worker can accomplish the products with required quality level in the limited time and can deliver the products. But if required quality is high and cannot be attained within t_{Max}, the worker cannot finish the work within the time limit and cannot deliver the products with required quality. It is a breach of the contract and the worker loses his/her trust. The introduction of the limitation of working hours may deprive self-employed teleworkers or freelancers of working chance.

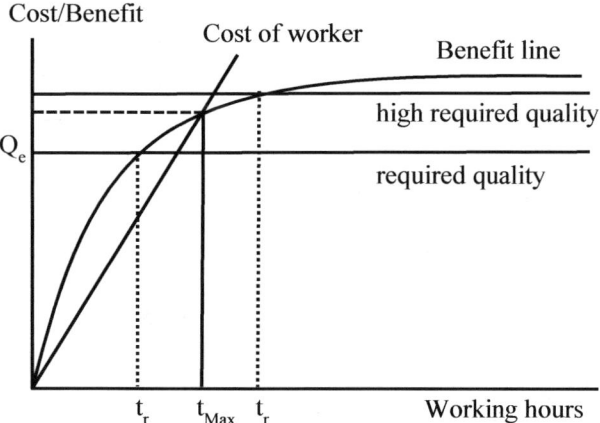

Fig.3 Limitation of working hour

3.2   Visibility of the Quality Requirement

The specification of work products is usually clear but sometimes there is another hidden specification. A worker may work long hours to submit the product of higher quality than is previously presented because he/she expects a long-term return such as repeated order or additional order by getting good reputation or evaluation from clients. As "required" quality level where higher long-term return can be obtained in the long run is not obvious, the worker keeps working until he/she thinks the quality of the product meets the expected quality level. Overtime working is said to relate to the increase of long-term income of workers [3].

Data entry is an example of working with obvious specification. The goal of the job is clear. After they finish inputting and checking the data, overtime work does not lead to the improvement of the quality. It is meaningless to keep working. Since the evaluation for the work is confirmed at the time of delivery and inspection, the worker does not have to guess the implicitly required quality.

However, the required level for the products is not clear for some cases. There are jobs that the quality of the products will improve as the worker works longer. A design proposal is an example of this type of job. The longer considering the design over time, the higher the quality becomes and the worker will be highly evaluated. Even if the required quality of the job is determined in advance, there is a possibility of getting the next job by getting high evaluation with overtime work without pay. In crowdsourcing, a high evaluation brings long-term revenue increases to freelancers. Freelancers always feel uneasy about the continuity of their work.

In the model, the implicit quality level (Q_i) is higher than the explicit quality level (Q_e) which is presented in the order by the employer (4) and the working hours to attain implicit quality level (t_i) is longer than the working hours to attain explicit quality level (t_e) (5)(Fig.4).

$$Q_e < Q_i \qquad (4)$$
$$t_i < t_e \qquad (5)$$

As for workers who do not ask for long-term return, they stop working at t_e with quality level of Q_e, and go to another work or enjoy leisure time. However, when workers expect a long-term return, they will continue working until they believe that they have reached at the sufficiently high level of quality. Since there is no payment for the work after achieving Q_e, this work becomes an unpaid work. Although it seems to be an irrational action, unpaid overtime work will improve the wages in the long run [3]. In the survey on crowdsourcing, it is shown that the stability of income is one of the most concerned issues for self-employed teleworkers and freelancers [4].

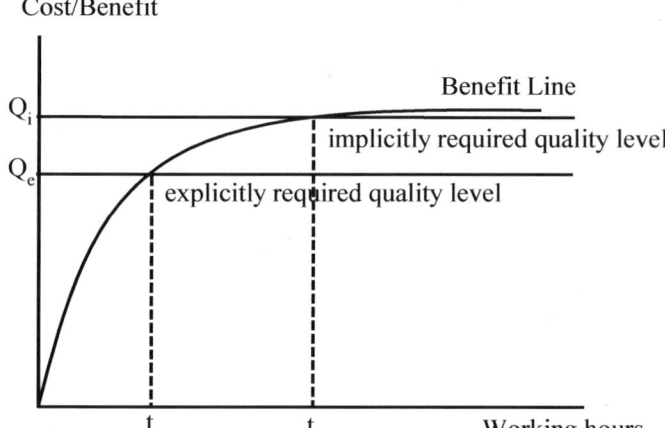

Fig.4 Two kinds of required quality levels

4   Character of workers

The way of implementing the work which is closely related to working hours depends on worker's character. The character includes attitude towards working and technical ability of the worker.

4.1   The attitude towards working

There are two types of workers regarding attitude towards working; one is hard working and enjoys working (herein after HW) and the other is a person who places emphasis on work life balance (hereinafter WLB).

HWs get involved in work and lose track of time. They are eager to improve the quality of the outcome and want to achieve the results beyond the required quality level. They are sometimes workaholic. In hearing against self-employed teleworkers who are engaged in tapescript with enthusiasm, they say, "Tapescript is fun, it's tough but I can feel a sense of accomplishment when I completed the work," "I do not think so much to earn money, but I am doing it because it's fun," "I want to understand the contents rather than just making

ISBN: 1-60132-454-5, CSREA Press ©

transcript." Many remarks indicate that they are enjoying their work [5].

On the other hand, WLBs value leisure time. They are concerned about the length of working hours. Once the quality of the outcome meets the required level, they do not work anymore to improve the quality of outcome.

For WLBs, increasing rate of working cost by working hours is higher than HWs because WLBs feel a burden of long hours working much more than HWs feel. The line which represents the relationship between working hours and sense of burden (cost) for WLBs (Line B) is then steeper slope than that for HWs (Line A) in Fig.5. Let t_A be the working hours when Line A exceeds Benefit Line and t_B be the working hours when Line B exceeds Benefit Line, then $t_B < t_A$. This shows that workers who place emphasis on work-life balance stop working earlier. If the worker can deliver the product satisfying the required quality at t_Q and t_Q is smaller than t_B ($t_Q \leqq t_B < t_A$), both WLBs and HWs can attain the required quality level, but if the required quality level is so high and t_Q is between t_B and t_A ($t_B < t_Q < t_A$), this is the case shown in Fig.5, HWs can deliver the products with required quality but WLBs cannot deliver the required products.

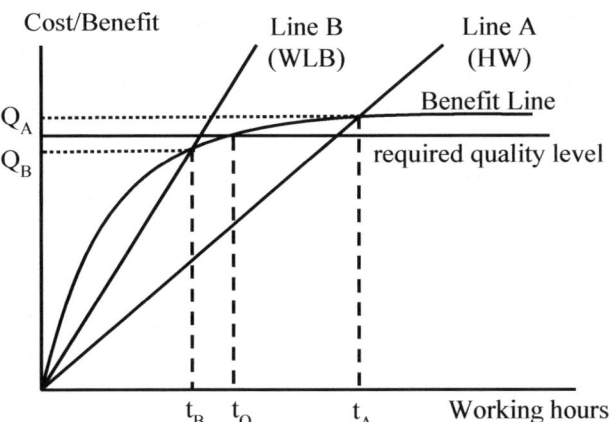

Fig.5 Worker's preference and work hours

4.2 Skill of workers

Regarding technical capabilities of workers, "High Skill worker (HS)" which has technological capabilities beyond the average technical skill required for business and "Low Skill worker (LS)" which does not reach the average technical skill required for business are considered.

In the field of self-employed teleworking, there are cases where people with low technical skill enter and have delivered the products with required quality by working very long hours. When Nakanishi (2010) [4] interviewed eight groups of teleworkers in Kochi prefecture, Japan, members of the groups said, "It took 8 or 9 hours to make a transcript of 30 minutes recording," "It took 4 hours to make a transcript of 12 minutes speech," and "It took me 20 days to dictate 133 minutes recording." In this way, there are cases where workers with high motivation but with low skills work for a long time and they have extremely low income per hour.

The relation between worker's skill and working hours is examined (Fig.6). The effect of the regulation which limits long hours working for workers is also considered. Let the working hours to satisfy the required quality level (Q_e) be t_H for the high skill worker and t_L for the low skill worker. As high skill worker can achieve the required quality with shorter working hour than low skill worker can, t_H is smaller than t_L ($t_H < t_L$).

Let us consider a case where the working time is compulsorily limited to t_{Max} between t_H and t_L ($t_H < t_{Max} < t_L$). The high skill worker can achieve the required quality level before t_{Max} and deliver the product, but the low skill worker cannot achieve the required quality level within the time limit. Therefore, the low skill worker cannot deliver the product with required quality. It is a breach of the contract and the worker loses his/her trust.

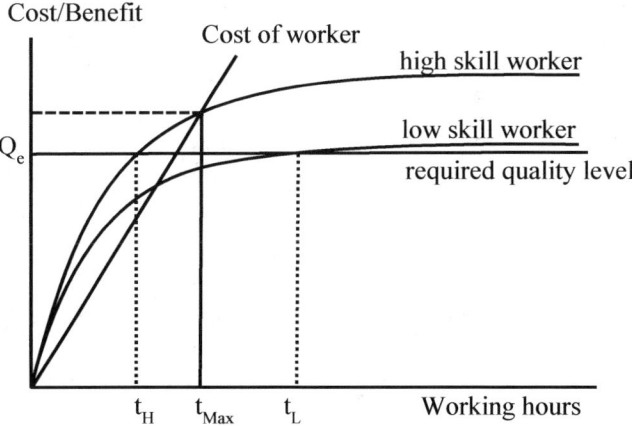

Fig.6 Working hours and worker's skill

5   Setting Scenarios

Four scenarios are set depending on the two kinds of strategies: setting an upper limit on working hours and clarification of quality requirement. These four scenarios are:
- No limit on working hours, requirement unclear
- No limit on working hours, clear requirement
- Limited working hours, requirement unclear
- Limited working hours, clear requirement

Each scenario is analyzed with characters of workers argued in Chapter 4 because the working hours may vary based on the characters of workers. Although excessive workload is considered as a major cause of long hour working, the amount of labor is assumed to be appropriate in this research because the aim of the study is to clarify the relationship between working style as telework and working hours.

5.1   Scenario 1

No limit on working hours, requirement unclear

HWs keep working until they are satisfied with the result because the required quality level is not clearly presented. Since they are pleased to work and they worry about the evaluation from the clients, they tend to work for a long time as their physical and mental strength allows. If their skill is high, their outcome may be highly evaluated and they can get the chance to work repeatedly and they are expected to get high income. In case of low technical skill, they fulfill the contract by raising the quality of outcome to the required level with long hours working. They can get orders again only after a lot of effort but they don't care long hours working. The low skill worker can be found often in part-time workers of housewives in Japan. Their income per hour tends to be very low.

WLBs stop working and enjoy leisure when they think that they attain enough quality. If the workers' skill is high, the quality of the outcome will reach the requested quality and the order will be repeated as they can gain high appraisal. Although stable income is obtained, income is not high because they place emphasis on leisure time rather than income. On the other hand, when the skill is low, it is inevitable to work long hours to achieve the required level. Work-life balance cannot be attained and complaints of the workers increase. Because the quality requirement level is unclear, they may stop quality improvement effort by their own judgment. But if the client is not satisfied with the quality, there is the possibility of losing the job next time.

5.2 Scenario 2

No limit on working hours, clear requirement

HWs can finish working and earn a certain income by delivering the product with required quality. If their skill is high, they can complete their work in a short time, not working for a long time. In addition, there is a possibility of trying to increase income by receiving orders from other clients in the surplus time due to finishing work in a short time. On the other hand, when the skill is low, the work should be continued until the required quality is achieved, so they must work for long hours. But HWs don't care long hours working because they are hard-working and enjoy the working.

WLBs finish the job with required quality and enjoy leisure time. When the skill is high and the work ends in a short time, leisure time becomes long and their work life balance can be achieved. But in the case of low skill, they are forced to work for long hours to obtain the minimum income for living. Since the required level of quality is clear, they should keep working until reaching the required level at the expense of their life.

5.3 Scenario 3

Limited working hours, requirement unclear

HWs with high skill can complete their job within the time limit and receive a reward. It is possible for them to carry out high quality work corresponding to their high technical skill. They work until limited hours to obtain higher

evaluation and to earn high income in the long term. For HWs with low skill, it is impossible to obtain the required quality within the time limit. They cannot get job from clients.

WLBs can also work within the time limit and get a certain income. Because emphasis is placed on securing leisure time rather than income, WLBs with high skill finish their work earlier than time limit. Income is not so high, but satisfaction with their life is high. If the skill of the worker is low, it is impossible to obtain the necessary quality within the time limit. They cannot achieve sufficient results and lose their job.

5.4 Scenario 4

Limited working hours, clear requirement

HWs with high skill can deliver the product of required quality within the time limit and can receive a reward. They can complete the required level in a short time and they don't work anymore because the required quality is obvious. They may try to increase their income by getting orders from other clients within the limited hours but they are not legally allowed to work for long hours. As for HWs with low skill, they can understand that it is impossible for them to attain the required quality within the time limit because the required quality is obvious. They will not enter the work.

WLBs with high skill can complete the requested quality within the time limit and enjoys their leisure time. In case their skill is low, they understand beforehand that it is impossible for them to attain the required quality within the time limit. Therefore, they will not enter the work.

The above scenarios are summarized in Table 1. In the case without any countermeasures for long hours working (scenario 1), HWs with high skill work for long hours and get high income, while WLBs with high skill can enjoy their life and can get some income. WLBs with high skill are satisfied with their life even though legal protections for workers from long hours working do not exist. If work-life balance intention is strong but technical skill is low, they should work for long hours to get minimum income to live despite their preference of working. Furthermore, they may lose their job because of the gap between self-evaluation and evaluation from clients.

In the case of limiting working hours (scenarios 3 and 4), both HWs and WLBs do not have to work for long hours. However, people with low technical skills cannot attain the required level within the limited time. Thus, they will lose their job in an unintended manner.

By clarifying the required quality level (scenario 2, 4), workers can recognize in advance whether they can respond to the request of clients. They can prevent unintended loss of their job by the inconsistency with the request of clients. Workers with low technical skills will not enter the work as they are aware of the level of their own skill. They can make efforts to improve their technical skills.

ISBN: 1-60132-454-5, CSREA Press ©

Table 1   Working hour and income by the Scenarios

Scenarios	HW type workers	WLB type workers
Scenario 1 No limit on working hours, requirement unclear	HS: They work long hours expecting high evaluation and can get high income. LS: They try to meet the required quality by long hours working.	HS: They can finish the work in a short time and enjoy leisure time. LS: They are forced to work long hours to meet the required quality level. But they may not get next job.
Scenario 2 No limit on working hours, clear requirement	HS: They finish their work in a short time and can get other orders. They work for long hours in total. LS: They should work for long hours but they don't care long hours working.	HS: They can finish the work in a short time and enjoy leisure time. LS: They are forced to work for long hours to reach the required quality level.
Scenario 3 Limited working hours, requirement unclear	HS: They finish their work in a short time but work until the time limit expecting high evaluation and long term high income. LS: They cannot achieve sufficient results within the time limit and lose their job.	HS: They work within the time limit and get a certain income. They are satisfied with their life. LS: They cannot achieve sufficient results within the time limit and lose their job.
Scenario 4 Limited working hours, clear requirement	HL: They finish their work in a short time and work until the time limit. But they are not allowed to work for long hours. LS: They will not enter the work.	HL: They can finish their work within the time limit and enjoys their leisure. LS: They will not enter the work.

6   Conclusion and Proposal

In order that a self-employed teleworker and freelancers can work soundly without getting into long hours working, the limitation of working hours and clarification of the quality requirement of the job are considered as measurements. The regulation to limit working hours can be an effective measurement because the regulation can control working hours directly, but this measurement has serious side effects. If the regulation is introduced, low skill workers will fail in attaining the required quality of the products within the time limit. Low skill workers may therefore lose their job. Furthermore, it is difficult for governments to regulate working hours because working hours of self-employed teleworkers and freelancers are self-managed.

Regarding the clarification of the quality of the products, the ordering party should clarify the long-term evaluation criteria. The criteria include whether the excess of required quality level is evaluated or not, and whether good evaluation results in repeated order or not.

As self-employed telework and crowdsourcing emphasizes the autonomy of workers, it is important to change the mind of workers. It might be effective for self-employed teleworkers and freelancers to promote the awareness of the importance of work-life balance and to suppress working hours voluntarily. However, there is a possibility of losing work if their technical capability is low, so it is necessary to implement some measurements to improve the worker's skill at the same time. It is important to prepare the system for improving worker skill such as vocational training.

7   Acknowledgements

This work was supported by Grants-in-Aid for Scientific Research, Grant Number 25380532, awarded by Japan Society for the Promotion of Science.

8   References

[1]   Sato, A (2008), Telework, Iwanami-shinsyo, 1133. (in Japanese)

[2]   Japan Telework Society (2015), Telework ga mirai wo tukuru (Telework create the future), Impress R&D. (in Japanese)

[3]   Pannenberg, M (2002), Long-term Effects of Unpaid Overtime: Evidence for West Germany, IZA DP No.614

[4]   Freelancers Union & Upwork (2016), Freelancing in America: 2016.

[5]   Nakanishi, H (2011), Regional Development Model for Any Municipality, Sairyu-sya. (in Japanese)

UU5: Open Source Library for User Interface Development

M. Beránek[1], and V. Kovář[1]
[1]Information Technology Department, Unicorn College, Prague, Czech Republic

Abstract - *Methods and tools for developing cross-platform user interfaces for mobile applications have been the subject of recent research interest both in academia and by industry practitioners. A common problem with front-end User Interface (UI) frameworks is their closed architecture forcing designers to implement the UI using a limited set of components. This lack of extensibility limits the usability of the interface and can result in poor user experience. In this paper we describe the UI component of the Unicorn Application Framework and illustrate its features using a simple online store scenario.*

Keywords: HTML5, User Interface Development, Unicorn Universe 5 Framework

1   Introduction

A common problem with UI (User Interface) frameworks is their closed architecture forcing designers to implement the user interface from a limited set of components. This lack of extensibility limits the usability features of the UI and may result in an unappealing UI, impacting on the sales potential for the entire application system. It can be argued that from the point of view of customers, good user experience is more important than the functionality of the application. UU5 (Unicorn Universe & HTML5) framework makes the development of specialized components that improve the user experience easy to implement and to integrate with React (https://facebook.github.io/react/) and other UI libraries. The UU5 application development process assumes that the initial design proposal is performed by creative UX (User eXperience design) experts, usually sourced from an external agency that specializes on creative marketing. The UU5 framework is an integral part of the recently released Unicorn Application Framework (UAF) designed to support rapid development of reliable and scalable cloud-based mobile applications.

In this paper we focus on the user interface component of the UAF (*uuUserInterface*) and describe the UU5 library designed for the implementation of user interfaces based on HTML5. The next section (section 2) is a review of related work and section 3 describes the requirements for a cloud-based solution architecture focusing on the features of the Unicorn Application Framework. Section 4 describes the UU5 library, and section 5 presents a case study that illustrates UU5 features using a simple online store scenario. Section 6 presents our conclusions.

2   Related Work

Methods and tools for developing cross-platform user interfaces for mobile applications have been the subject of recent research interest both in academia and by industry practitioners [1], [2], [3-5]. Tom Melamed and Ben Clayton from Hewlett-Packard Labs have investigated the use of pervasive computing to deliver applications and services on mobile phones evaluating a number of platforms including J2ME and native Smartphone development [1]. The paper introduces HTML5, describes its advantages and disadvantages and concludes that HTML5 is a good solution for creating and distributing pervasive media applications. Available cross-platform frameworks and mobile development tools are discussed by Smutny et al. illustrating the application of HTML5 for the development of mobile English-Czech dictionary translation intended for bachelor and master students of automation and technical cybernetics study program [2]. Andre Charland and Brain Leroux compare native code vs. web code development for mobile applications and conclude that hybrid solutions will play an important role in the future [3]. In another recent publication the authors report on a comparative analysis of cross-platform development approaches for mobile applications and conclude that HTML5 will play a major role in the future [4]. Experiences during an industrial project concerned with building user interfaces for database access are discussed in [6]. The authors describe a systematic approach to analysis of standards and conventions for the design of user interfaces for various mobile platform, focusing on interoperability of different systems, including HTML5, Java and .NET. Philippe Kruchten described the 4+1 Architectural View Model for the Rational Unified Process [7]. One of the views, *Scenarios* consists of a set of use cases that describe sequences of interactions between objects and processes. UML 2.5 specification describes use cases that capture behavior of systems. Users and IoT devices that interact with a system through use cases are represented as Actors [8]. Literature review indicates that there is a trend towards the use of HTML5 based technologies for the implementation of cross-platform mobile applications.

3   Cloud-based Solution Architecture

Software architecture has crucial impact on success of software projects. There is an urgent need for enterprise applications to take advantage of the massive increase in the use of mobile and web technology and the emergence of IoT (Internet of Things) making applications available anywhere and anytime for both end users and smart devices. These trends are placing increasing demands on the performance of ICT infrastructure, and are driving the adoption of cloud computing.

Most mobile applications that we use in our personal life are cloud-based and have a high quality user interface. The situation is different for enterprise applications that are mostly operated on-premise. Institutions such as banks, insurance companies, energy companies, and other industrial enterprises are still reluctant to migrate their applications to the cloud, and the user interfaces associated with such applications often do not meet the high expectations that users have today.

Based on our experience at Unicorn with designing and developing of hundreds of large-scale information systems for our clients we are convinced that cloud deployment of enterprise applications together with ensuring high level of user experience and satisfaction will play a key role in the near future. As users of enterprise applications demand the same level of usability and functionality as they are used to from personal applications on mobile devices, software architecture that supports effective development of applications that can interact with end users as well as IoT devices is becoming essential.

Software system consists of a set of use cases, with some directly supporting various business processes (e.g. accommodation reservation, purchase order processing, etc.), and others dedicated to essential infrastructure functionality - *infrastructure use cases* (e.g. user authentication, logging, multilingual support, UI support, etc.). It is often the case that the infrastructure use cases are re-developed for each project separately. Unicorn has recently released the Unicorn Application Framework (UAF) - a cloud-based, mobile-first IoT ready architecture that incorporates standard infrastructure services and allows application developers to focus on use cases that support business functionality.

The UAF includes the following five key standards and components [9]:

- *uuUserInterface* - a standard and the corresponding framework components for the development of Graphical User Interfaces (GUI) for large range of application requirements that can be deployed on all widely available modern devices, including mobile phones, tablets, notebooks, smart TVs, desktop computers, etc.
- *uuIoT* - a standard and the corresponding framework components that can control a very large number of IoT devices and various appliances interacting with enterprise applications.
- *uuAppServer* - a standard and the corresponding framework components for developing cloud-based application server components that encapsulate a range of application requirements and interact with persistent cloud storage.

- *uuCloud* - a standard and the corresponding framework components that support elasticity and autonomic provisioning of cloud services delivered from a reliable data center that can support tens of thousands of virtual containers and servers.
- *uuBT and uuMT* - a standard and the corresponding framework components that support the development of large-scale information systems for organizations (uuBT) and individuals (uuMT).

In this paper, we focus on user interface component of the UAF (*uuUserInterface*). More specifically, we describe the UU5 library designed for the implementation of user interfaces based on HTML5.

4 UU5 Library

UU5 is a platform and a library for building user interfaces based on HTML5 and JavaScript. The library integrates React and Bootstrap frameworks. The library assists in developing responsive, *mobile-first* applications, with UI that adapts to a specific device, ensuring user experience that is comparable with native applications, i.e. applications designed to run on the given platform (e.g. iOS, Android). The UU5 library can be used for all devices such smartphones, tablets, desktops, laptops or smart TVs that support a web browser. UU5 is ideal for developing Single Page Applications [10, 11] and produces applications that can be easily controlled by keyboards, mouse or touch. The UU5 library is an open source library and its license is derived from the standard BSD license [12].

4.1 Basic UU5 Areas

Figure 1 depicts areas that are addressed by UU5, and are typically required by any modern web application.

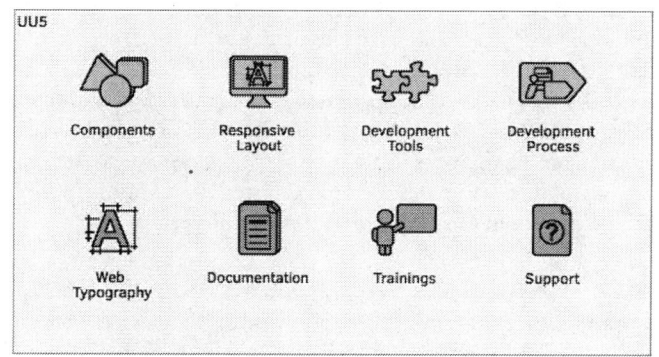

Figure 1: Key areas of the UU5 library [9]

The library provides a basic set of visual components that are used as UI building blocks. All components work with any standard screen resolution, from smart phones to 4K screens. The UU5 library includes all standard visual components, exceeding the range available in the standard Bootstrap component set [13]. The development of responsive application layouts is very easy thanks to UU5. In addition to the visual appearance, application behavior and content can be adapted for a specific type of device. The toolkit for component development and the development process are part of the library, and are described in detail in section 4.3.

Typography is concerned with different types of fonts. In the context of UU5, the library applies similar rules for all visual components. Basic visual style of the application is carefully balanced to optimize usability on all devices. Procedures and tools that directly support adaptation of the UI to reflect a specific visual style of an application or corporate design are available.

The UU5 library contains documentation, training materials and a set of ready to use examples. Support for developers is also available, allowing people with basic knowledge of HTML5, JavaScript and CSS3 to learn to work with UU5 in a few days.

The UU5 library supports navigation between application components without the need to reload pages. Navigation is performed using the address bar and web browser history; this enables, for example, to send a link to individual application components via e-mail, even in Single Page Applications. Mobile web applications are fully supported by the UU5 library; an icon and a link to a web application can be placed directly on the home screen of the smartphone or tablet, so that the web application looks like a native iOS or Android application. The UU5 library is multilingual and supports dynamic switching of languages at runtime without the need to reload pages.

4.2   UU5 Technical Concepts

UU5 is based on Bootstrap (http://getbootstrap.com) and React (https://facebook.github.io/react) open source frameworks. Bootstrap was chosen because it is the most widely used standard for responsive web applications. Bootstrap is a HTML/CSS/JavaScript framework created by Mark Otto and Jacob Thornton at Twitter [14]. React is a powerful JavaScript library for building user interfaces developed by Facebook. React has a powerful rendering engine and supports the latest web development standards. UU5 integrates and extends both frameworks enabling development of responsive, *mobile first* applications even by less experienced developers. Based on our experience, we believe that development using UU5 is faster and more flexible than using Bootstrap and React libraries directly.

Unlike most other HTML and JavaScript frameworks, UU5 emphasizes component-based development, as we believe that this approach brings long-term benefits for software development. Well-structured, independent components make development and maintenance of software faster and easier, and at the same time reduce the number of software defects. Another major benefit is that applications running on different devices share the same code base, avoiding complex release management. Furthermore, the need to synchronize deployment of different versions of front-end and back-end applications, and performing multiple bug fixes across different web and mobile applications is alleviated. Our experience with component-based development indicates that in the long-term the development costs are reduced by at least by 50% compared to traditional approaches that do not use

components. The use of the UU5 library results in reduced number of lines of code, better code readability, and consequently fewer errors. These savings occur both during the initial development and during maintenance activities such as code refactoring and making code changes.

Benefits of UU5 and component-based development are illustrated by the following example that compares code complexity of plain Bootstrap code (Figure 3) and UU5 library component-based code (Figure 4) of the implementation of modal window shown in Figure 2.

Figure 2: An example of the modal window implementation

```
1    <div class="modal fade" id="myModal" role="dialog">
2        <div class="modal-dialog">
3            <div class="modal-content">
4                <div class="modal-header">
5                    <button type="button" class="close" data-dismiss="modal">&times;</button>
6                    <h4 class="modal-title">Modal Header</h4>
7                </div>
8                <div class="modal-body">
9                    <p>Some text in the modal.</p>
10               </div>
11               <div class="modal-footer">
12                   <button type="button" class="btn btn-default" data-dismiss="modal">Close</button>
13               </div>
14           </div>
15       </div>
16   </div>
```

Figure 3: An example of code using Bootstrap

```
1    <UU5.Bricks.Modal header='Modal Header' ref_={(r) => this._modal = r}
2        onClose={ (object) => {object.component.close(false);}}
3        footer={(<UU5.Bricks.Button content="Close" onClick={() => this._modal.close()} />)}>
4        <UU5.Bricks.Paragraph>Some text in the modal.</UU5.Bricks.Paragraph>
5    </UU5.Bricks.Modal>
```

Figure 4: An example of code using UU5

The difference in number of lines of code is evident even for this very simple example.

The latest version of JavaScript ES6 (Ecmascript 6) is used for development of UU5 applications. Browser compatibility is ensured by automatic transpilation using the Babel transpiler [15]. UU5 implements the front-end application layer and can be easily integrated with any back-end technology that supports standard web protocols (i.e. RESTful APIs) for interacting with the front-end layer. The UU5 library can be used either in new development projects or to redevelop front-ends for existing applications. The library supports dynamic and lazy loading of components and data to ensure fast user interface response times. UU5 is compatible with all major web browsers and operating systems.

4.3   UU5 Components

As illustrated in Figure 5, UU5 components are grouped into four modules. Documentation of the components is available online and is freely accessible [16].

ISBN: 1-60132-454-5, CSREA Press ©

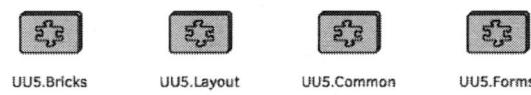

Figure 5: UU5 component modules

UU5.Bricks module contains 62 basic visual components provided by the library. Each component has properties and an API (Application Programming Interface). The properties are used to access parameters or data passed from the parent component during the rendering process. State is used in components that need to dynamically manage data. State is private and fully controlled by the component [17]; other components can use the interface to pass control commands. The concept of properties and interfaces is derived from React, and is a common feature of component-based development.

UU5 library contains components such as alert, badge, button group, dropdown, jumbotron, navigation bar and modal window derived from Bootstrap and more complex components such as camera, data table, file viewer, Google maps, rating, slider, swiper and tree.

Figure 6: An example of UU5.Bricks.Slider

Figure 6 illustrates an example of Slider component (UU5.Bricks.Slider). The Slider component has six properties listed in Table 1 and four interface methods listed in Table 2.

Table 1: Properties of UU5.Bricks.Slider

Property	Description
min	Minimum possible value of the range
max	Maximum possible value of the range
step	Value to be added to or subtracted from the value of the range
value	Current value of the range
onChanged	Method invoked when the value is changed

Table 2: Interface methods of UU5.Bricks.Slider

Method	Description
getValue	Gets the current value of the range
setValue	Sets the current value of the range
increase	Increases the value of the slider by a value
decrease	Decreases the value of the slider by a value

UU5.Layout components are used for defining the layout of the page (user interface screen). There are six main Layout components (Table 3).

Components such as UU5.Layout.Container, UU5.Layout.Row and UU5.Layout.Column support responsive behavior which is fully based on Bootstrap's grid system [12]. UU5.Layout module includes more advanced components such as collections and mixins. Collections are used for implementing columns, containers, rows and wrappers (e.g. UU5.Layout.ColumnCollection). This type of a component is useful when implementing multiple components of the same type (e.g. column) and the developer wants to avoid encapsulating it in the parent component. Mixins enable components to have implicit behavior as required by the application. In UU5.Layout module, there are mixin components for column collections, columns, container collections, containers, flc, root, row collections, rows, wrapper collections and wrappers.

Table 3: UU5.Layout components

Component	Description
UU5.Layout.Root	Top-level component, root of the visual use case
UU5.Layout.Row	Component derived from Bootstrap; represents row in Bootstrap's grid system [18]
UU5.Layout.Column	Component derived from Bootstrap; represents column in Bootstrap's grid system [18]
UU5.Layout.Container	Component placed at the root, and used to wrap single UU5.Layout.Row components
UU5.Layout.Wrapper	Component placed in the column and used to wrap a single UU5.Layout.Flc components
UU5.Layout.Flc	Component placed in UU5.Layout.Wrapper and used to wrap single component whose type is not layout

UU5.Common module contains only mixin components, which implement common behavior, properties and interface methods of various types of components. For example, UU5.Common.ScreenSizeMixin is used to determine the screen size in the visual use case. If the screen size is changed, a corresponding event is triggered. UU5.Common.SwipeMixin enriches components with properties and interface methods that support touch gestures. Mixins become very handy in development of more complex components and user interface in general. Very special and important component in UU5.Common is UU5.Common.VucMixin which represents a visual use case - application logic executed on end user devices such as mobile phones, tablets, smart TVs, desktop computers, laptops, etc.

UU5.Forms module contains form inputs such as checkboxes, datepicker, file browser, number inputs, text inputs, radios, selects, text areas, text buttons or text glyphicons that are used to build various types of forms. Inclusion of mixins in the UU5.Forms module enables components to support useful functions such as validations, on change events, displaying messages to the user, providing properties for defining glyphicons within the input component, font size, label or read only property. In addition, inputs can be wrapped by UU5.Forms.FormMixin; this enables easy access to values from all inputs in the form, to getting a collection of inputs, checking if inputs are valid and resetting values of form inputs.

4.4   Development Process and Toolkit

An integral part of the UU5 library is the software development process and a toolkit that fully supports this process. As JavaScript is a dynamic programming language, it is extremely important to use coding tools, i.e. linters, code analysis tools and syntax analyzers. These tools help programmers to detect most defects during coding and compilation, minimizing runtime errors. The configuration of these tools can be time-consuming; to alleviate this issue the library includes UU5 Development Workspace that provides developers with a fully configured workspace for the development of new user interfaces (it takes about 10 minutes to install the workspace). UU5 Development Workspace requires Node.js (https://nodejs.org) - JavaScript runtime built on Chrome's V8 JavaScript engine. The workspace is platform independent and can be used on any Windows, macOS or Linux computer. The pre-configured development environment consists of a set of recommended tools, guidelines and prepared scripts that assist with the development of user interfaces. The UU5 user interfaces can be developed using any source code editor or IDE (e.g. Eclipse, Microsoft Visual Studio, Microsoft Visual Studio Code, Sublime Text). We have very good experience with JetBrains (http://www.jetbrains.com) IDEs, for example WebStorm.

The UU5 applications development process includes requirement analysis, design and development phases. *Mock components* created during the requirement analysis and design phases serve as templates for graphic designers. UU5 basic components are used to create the mock components, and together with the final graphic design and schemas of component structure are the main deliverables of the design phase. Examples of these deliverables are shown in the case study description in Section 5.

Web browsers such as Google Chrome and Mozilla Firefox support debugging of source code in ES6, but without transpilation. Different types of configurations (e.g. development, production) are included in the UU5 development environment. It enables data mocking and flexibility in creating test scenarios during the development process. Pre-configured scripts and tools enable the creation of distribution packages for the production environment that meet the policies for optimization within page loading (minification) and web browser cache (versioning). Another benefit of the UU5 development process is that large projects can be split into separate modules that are loaded into the web browser as required, making the application faster to run.

The UU5 environment fully supports creating separate libraries, their build and distribution via npm packages. npm (http://www.npmjs.com) is the default package manager for the JavaScript runtime environment Node.js [19]. Preferred distribution channel of the UU5 library for the development environment is a npm package, alternatively the Content Delivery Network (CDN).

5   UU5 Case Study

In this section, we describe the use of the UU5 library in a demo application called Goodymat illustrating the Unicorn mobile-first IoT-ready cloud architecture. The application implements a simple online store offering three products. From the user interface point of view there are three visual use cases as listed in Table 4.

Table 4: Goodymat application visual use cases

Visual use-case	Description
Eshop	implements the online store and enables the user to buy a selected product
BackofficeOrders	enables the merchandiser to process orders
BackofficeShopLocker	enables the merchandiser or the administrator to close the Eshop

We have selected the Eshop visual use case (VUC) to illustrate the use of the UU5 library. Following the UU5 application development process described in section 4.4, we begin with component decomposition schema illustrated in Figure 7, depicting the hierarchy of components. We use the Unicorn Universe Business Modelling Language (uuBML) to draw the schema. uuBML is a tool for visual modelling and communication based on the principles of Unified Modelling Language (UML) and includes guideline for creating diagrams and models [20].

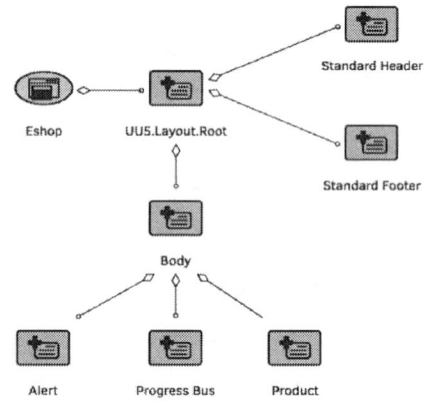

Figure 7: Eshop VUC component decomposition

The UU5.Layout module UU5.Layout.Root component is used as the root component in the Eshop VUC. The root consists of three unique components: Standard Header,

Standard Footer and Body (i.e. there is only one standard header, one standard footer and one body in the root). The Body component consists of an Alert component, Progress Bus and one or more Product components.

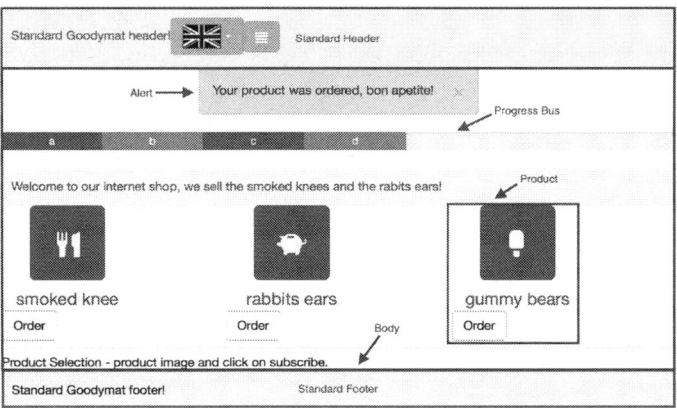

Figure 8: An example of mock components

Following decomposition, the mock components are created sketching the desired appearance of the user interface and allowing the prototyping of basic functionality of the interface. The mock components of the Eshop VUC are shown in Figure 8. Based on the mock components, the graphic designer creates the final graphic design as shown in Figure 9.

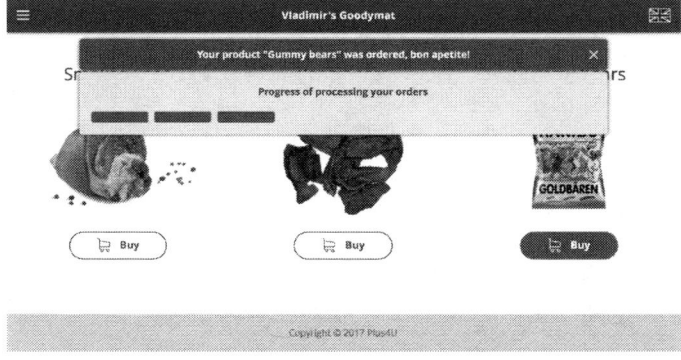

Figure 9: Final graphic design

The final phase of the development process is the implementation that produces the runtime version of the Eshop VUC.

6   Conclusions

In this paper we have argued that most front-end UI frameworks suffer from a lack of extensibility, forcing designers to implement the UI using a limited set of components, potentially resulting in poor user experience. We have described the user interface component (*uuUserInterface*) of the Unicorn Application Framework and the UU5 library designed to support the implementation of cross-platform user interfaces based on HTML5 and JavaScript. The use of well-structured, independent components makes the development and maintenance of software faster and easier, and reduces software defects.

Another major long-term benefit is that applications running on different devices share the same code base, avoiding complex release management. Our experience indicates that in the long-term the development costs can be reduced by as much as 50% when compared to traditional approaches that do not use components. Furthermore, the use of the UU5 library results in reduced number of lines of code, better code readability and fewer software defects.

7   References

[1] Tom Melamed, Ben Clayton, "A comparative evaluation of HTML5 as a pervasive media platform," *International Conference on Mobile Computing, Applications, and Services.* Springer, 2009.

[2] Pavel Smutný, "Mobile development tools and cross-platform solutions," *13th International Carpathian Control Conference (ICCC).* IEEE, 2012.

[3] Andre Charland, Brian LeRoux, "Mobile application development: web vs. native," *Communications of the ACM*, 2011, vol. 54, issue 5, p. 49-53.

[4] Spyros Xanthopolous, Stelios Xinagalos, "A comparative analysis of cross-platform development approaches for mobile applications," in *Proceedings of the 6th Balkan Conference in Informatics.* ACM, 2013.

[5] Johan Harjono, et al. "Building smarter web applications with HTML5," in *Proceedings of the 2010 Conference of the Center for Advanced Studies on Collaborative Research.* IBM Corp, 2010.

[6] Andreas Holzinger, Peter Treitler, Wolfgang Slany, "Making apps useable on multiple different mobile platforms: On interoperability for business application development on smartphones," *International Conference on Availability, Reliability, and Security.* Springer, 2012.

[7] Philippe Kruchten, "Architectural Blueprints - The "4+1" View Model of Software Architecture," *IEEE Software* 12 (6), November 2006, p. 42-50.

[8] OMG. (2015) OMG Unified Modeling Language^{TM}, version 2.5. [Online]. Available: http://www.omg.org/cgi-bin/doc?formal/15-03-01.pdf

[9] Unicorn. (2017) UAFV01 – Design. [Online]. Available: https://www.plus4u.net, document code: UU-BT:SI/UAFV01/DESIGN

[10] Flanagan, David. *"JavaScript - The Definitive Guide,"* 5th ed. O'Reilly, Sebastopol, CA, 2006, p. 497.

[11] Michael S. Mikowski, Josh C. Powel. (2012) Single Page Web Applications. [Online]. Available: http://deals.manningpublications.com/spa.pdf

[12] Unicorn, "UAF License for the uu5 software". [Online]. Available: https://cdn.plus4u.net/uu-uu5g04/0.0.0/uu5g04.min.js

[13] Mark Otto, Jacob Thornton. (2017) Components – Bootstrap. [Online]. Available: https://getbootstrap.com/components/

ISBN: 1-60132-454-5, CSREA Press ©

[14] Mark Otto, Jacob Thornton. (2017) About – Bootstrap. [Online]. Available: https://getbootstrap.com/about/

[15] Kyriakos-Ioannis D. Kyriakou, Ioannis K. Chaniottis, Nikolaos D. Tselikas, "The GPM meta-transcompiler: Harmonizing JavaScript-oriented Web development with the upcoming ECMAScript 6 Harmony specification", in *Proceedings of the 12th Annual IEEE Consumer Communications and Networking Conference (CCNC)*, Las Vegas, January 2015.

[16] Unicorn. (2017) Unicorn Application Framework Documentation. [Online]. Available: https://uuos9.plus4u.net/uu-uu5doc/84723967990073193/public/

[17] Facebook. (2017) Add-Ons – React. [Online]. Available: https://facebook.github.io/react/docs/addons.html

[18] Mark Otto, Jacob Thornton. (2017) CSS – Bootstrap. [Online]. Available: http://getbootstrap.com/css/

[19] Node.js Foundation. (2017) Node.js. [Online]. Available: https://nodejs.org/en/

[20] Unicorn. (2017) uuBML Draw Documentation, version 2.11.3 [Online], Available: https://www.plus4u.net, document code: VPH-BT:UUAPPKNH.UUBMLDRAW/DOC

SESSION

LATE PAPERS - BANK RISK MANAGEMENT

Chair(s)

TBA

ISBN: 1-60132-454-5, CSREA Press ©

Modeling and Analysis of Contagion Dynamics and Bank Risk Management using System Dynamics

Ramesh G. Kini

Professor of ISM at the Faculty of IT, Kazakh British Tech. U. Room 277, FIT, KBTU, 59 Tole Bi, Almaty 050000, Rep. of Kazakhstan (kinirameshg@gmail.com)

Kairat Tokpaev

Recent graduate of BSc in IS program, Faculty of IT, Kazakh British Tech. U. in Almaty, Kazakhstan

Abstract - Over the last nine years or so, different parts of the world have suffered from a host of seemingly unending financial and economic trials and tribulations, and political upheaval, the after-effects of the global financial crisis (the "Long" or "Great Recession") that officially started in September 2008 and lasted less than a couple of years. Using system dynamics and discrete event simulation approaches, we seek to model and analyze how the interconnectedness (on the assets and liabilities sides of their balance sheets) between banks in a financial network, and between financial networks in turn, can result in a failure of a single bank triggering other defaults and spreading as a contagion through the global financial networks, generating cascades of defaults.

Keywords-bank risk, financial contagion, default cascades, housing, interest rates, rating agencies

1. INTRODUCTION

Warning about "…'tipping points', 'thresholds and breakpoints', 'regime shifts'…all…terms that describe the flip of a complex dynamical system from one state to another" (e.g., the Wall Street Crash of 1929 and the Great Depression), and which make "… increasingly complicated and globally interlinked financial markets …no less immune to…system-wide (systemic) threats," three biologists, May, Levin and Sugihara (May, et al., 2008), had asked very presciently, "Who knows, for instance, how the present concern over sub-prime loans will pan out?" in early 2008. Nearly nine years and a whole host of seemingly unending financial and economic trials and tribulations later, all we can truly say in response is that while the global markets have supposedly recovered from the recession, we still do not know for sure how long the after-effects of the global financial crisis (the "Long" or "Great Recession," henceforth, the LoGR) will really last.

Most analysts see the LoGR as having had its genesis in:

- the massive global credit expansion that has taken place over the last three decades or so, and especially after 2001 when Alan Greenspan, the chairman of the board of governors of the US Federal Reserve, launched a low interest rate regime during George W. Bush's first term as the President of the US, in order to re-inflate the economy that had been sent into a tailspin by the dot.com crash;
- the role of securitization which enabled banks to move illiquid assets, or groups of illiquid assets, off their balance sheets by transforming and combining them into securities through financial engineering, e.g., a mortgage-backed security (MBS), a type of asset-backed security secured by a collection of mortgage;
- the "liar's loans," or "no-docs" loans, that were written by mortgage firms to meet the demand for them by individuals and institutions whose only purpose was to securitize and sell

- subprime mortgage products based on these questionable loans, designed to fail (and yet provided attractive enough ratings by the three ratings agencies, namely, Fitch, Standard and Poor's and Moody's, so as to find buyers somewhere, somehow -- this is why some analysts would like to hold the ratings agencies as chiefly responsible for precipitating the crisis), and then make a fortune betting against them;
- the very significant increase in leverage or the amount of debt taken on by the banks and financial institutions relative to their equity or "capital" stocks;

the moral hazard and potentially disastrous consequences associated with the manner in which banks, and especially the larger, more global players – secure in the tacit understanding that they would be bailed out by the taxpayers if they "blew" themselves up and hence more inclined to take on far more risks than they could have been expected to bear – managed to parlay the gains in leverage, that was mentioned above, into continued growth beyond sustainable limits, till they became "too big to fail" or TBTF. In hindsight, it is now obvious that as these massively overleveraged financial institutions had, over the last three decades or more and especially over the first seven years of this century, become increasingly reckless, rather than merely less-than-prudent, in their drive to become big enough to be deemed TBTF, they not only threatened their own continued existence but also ensured that their self-destruction would ruin not only their own balance sheets but also those of the countries that had "backstopped" them by guaranteeing their sovereign debts.

Figure 1 below depicts how a combination of causes came together in a super-additive way to unleash a "perfect" financial storm, an "ice-age"-type freezing of global trade and financial flows, and in turn a recession that all but threatened to become a full-blown depression. Some of these had their roots in the poorly governed financial sector, others with roots in the cyclical residential and commercial real estate sector, yet others that were related to the inability of a significant number of manufacturers and service providers in the US and Europe to withstand the winds of globalization that were blowing in from Asia, for instance, and lastly, a few that stemmed from the simmering discontent that was brewing for a while in the Middle East and North Africa on the one hand, as well as in the "periphery" rather than the "core" of the European Union, on the other hand.

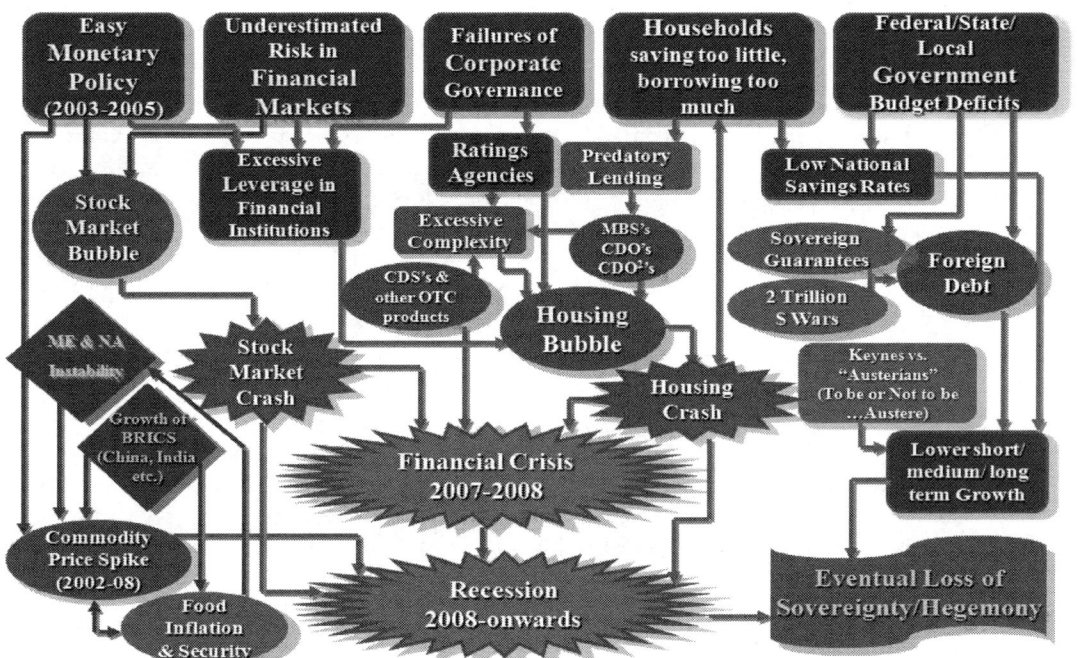

Figure 1: The Origins of the Financial/Economic Crisis and its After-effects (Adapted from HBS source http://siteresources.worldbank.org/EXTPREMNET/Resources/489960-1338997241035/Growth_Commission_Workshops_Financial_Crisis_Impact_Frankel_Presentation.pdf)

Many like the writer Nessim Taleb see rare "black swan" events (with fat tailed probability distributions) as the causes of bank failures. We, on the other hand, see a system that is finely tuned and usually in balance but not robust or resilient enough to absorb the shocks from one or more minor events that can then propagate throughout the system, and hence prone to being subject to upheavals and boom-bust cyclicality as a result. In what follows, we will try to make the case that the interaction between households, the private sector comprising of financial and nonfinancial players and the government and other public sector entities, in general, leads to macro-economic growth spurts and slowdowns. More specifically, we focus on the role of the various players in the construction industry or the housing sector in triggering off the boom-bust cyclicality over time.

2. DEMOGRAPHICS, DEBT, DEFICITS & FINANCIAL DISASTERS

To provide deeper insights into the impact of the cyclical ups and downs, i.e., the boom and bust cycles, of the real estate sector on the macro-economy, consider the following extension

of the analysis of demographic factors offered by Kini and Melnikov (2016), comprising of various players in the macro-economy (primarily, the household sector, the private sector and the government, including public sector entities), in which they play a number of different roles, with a number of macroeconomic linkages between them, as depicted in Figure 2 below.

2A: The Household Sector: The ordinary men and women (and their dependents, *viz.*, their young children and retired parents, etc.) in the household sector play a number of roles simultaneously, as:

parents of families or procreators (mothers and fathers) and as heads of households who earn either by working as employees in the private or public sector or as landlords or members of the producer class, and thus look after the procreated (their children) as well as other dependents (e.g., their own parents): here the two halves (male and female) of the nation's population pyramid depicted in Figure 3, the age-groups or cohorts, and the segments who are either of working age or too young -- or too old -- and hence dependent on their parents or children, change dynamically over time, through aging itself, the net accretion process (the net effect of the birth and death rates, as well as the net effect of the immigration and emigration processes);

participants in the labor force who are of working age:
(i) who provide their labor inputs to: the private sector producers; the capitalists; the financial institutions; the government and public sector employers; as well as landlords;

(ii) who, in return, get paid wages and salaries;

(iii) who spend part of what they earn on goods and services provided by the other macroeconomic players;

(iv) who pay direct and/or indirect taxes to, or are provided subsidies by, the government;

(v) who save the remainder of their wages and salaries, which they could:

- deposit in their accounts with one or more of those financial institutions and get paid interest in return,
- invest in real estate (this could entail occupying a home they partly or wholly own, in which case they would save on the rent that they would otherwise have to pay to some landlord, or buying additional properties, which could elevate them to the rent-seeking landlord class),
- or invest in the stocks, shares and bonds issued by the private sector producers, the capitalists, the financial institutions and the partially privatized public sector

entities, some or all of who pay dividends to their shareholders and interest to their bondholders; and

(vi) who may borrow money over the short-, medium- and long-term from banks and other financial institutions to cover their credit card payments, their university tuition fees, their mortgage payments, and so on, and who would very likely pay the principal back and the interest due to their creditors over time;

- consumers of the various goods and services provided by the other players in the macroeconomy;
- tax-paying, voting citizens, members of various "publics" and as stakeholders as far as the government and the other players are concerned;
- rent-payers, savers, investors and borrowers as mentioned above; and
- perhaps, as members of the producer- or capitalist- class (if they launch and grow their own companies), or as rent-seeking landlords, if they have invested in real estate, or as elected or unelected members of the legislative/parliamentary bodies, government ministries and agencies, and so on.

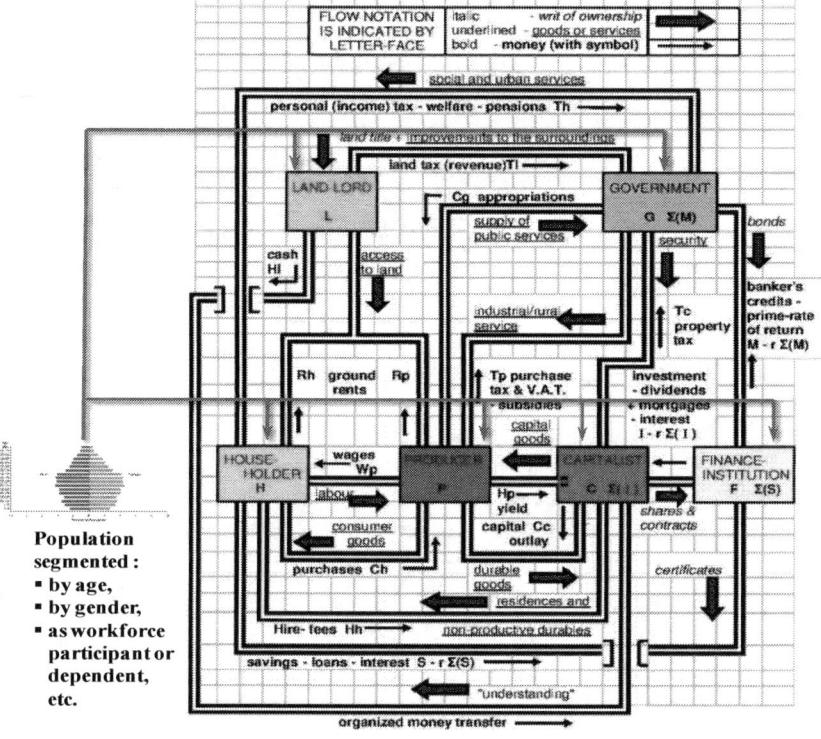

Population segmented :
- by age,
- by gender,
- as workforce participant or dependent, etc.

Figure 2: The Role of Ordinary Male and Female Citizens and their Dependents in the Macro-Economy. (Adapted from the figure provided in Wikipedia, the free encyclopedia: https://en.wikipedia.org/wiki/Macroeconomic_model)

We should note that demographic effects are primary economic growth and development drivers in a number of different ways:

(i) marriage rates (new family "starts" in turn drive housing "starts" over time, if not immediately), birth and death rates and aging population dynamics (through a combination of the birth

and death processes and immigration and emigration processes, some countries grow and are relatively young in terms of the average age of their populations, e.g., India and Iran, while others shrink and age rapidly, e.g., Japan and Germany);

(ii) workforce participation rates (i.e., the fractions of the males and females in the population who are of working age, say in the 15 to 65 age group, and that are actually gainfully employed in productive activities);

(iii) the family-related workforce dropout and reentry rates (these are much less critical for males than for females, who in the child bearing age groups may drop out of the workforce to bear and raise children – this could be temporary, if the mothers return to the workforce when their children have reached an age where they can be looked after by child care providers, or be admitted to nursery and then primary school – or permanent, as in the case of Japan, where mothers seldom return to the workforce even after their children go to school, attributable perhaps to the some-what patriarchal and chauvinistic attitudes adopted by their male colleagues and by employers in general);

(iv) the unemployment-related workforce dropout and reentry rates (given that male workforce participation rates fell during the LoGR, and did not recover long after, unlike in the case of the rates for females, especially where young males were disproportionately employed in sectors hardest hit by the recession, e.g., construction, mining, etc., the effect of unemployment has to be taken into account since discretionary and non discretionary expenditures by the household sector and investments of savings in bank deposits, stock and commodity markets, or in real estate, education, and so on, which are vital drivers of growth in the macro economy, would be either severely curtailed or even missing pieces of the puzzle in the case of unemployment);

(v) aging and retirement (since retirees are generally no longer in the workforce and draw down, rather than build up, their savings to cover their living and medical costs, its is vital that safety nets, Social Security and other pension schemes remain viable for the foreseeable future – these could be traditional PAYG, or Pay As You Go, defined benefits-type or the defined contribution-type schemes that are being increasingly used more recently, especially during the transition from the former to the latter); for instance.

2B: The Financial and Non-Financial Sectors:

While the non-financial sector serves to mostly employ the people in the household sector and to produce the goods and services which individual consumers and other private and public sector customers consume in general, the construction industry has a central role to play in making the global financial system more vulnerable, as we argue below. While the financial sector comprises of the banks, pension funds, VCs, etc., act as financial intermediaries who channel funds from savers to borrowers, our analysis is specifically centered around the financial sector's exposure to both commercial and residential real estate markets, which are affected by different business drivers, and this also affects the risks associated with those loans. People in the household sector who are gainfully employed by private or public sector firms earn, bear the usual household expenditures (rent, food and sustenance, travel, interest on automobile and personal loans, etc.), save what is left after spending, and invest these savings in bank deposits, equity markets, i.e., shares of companies through IPOs, FPOs, and secondary markets, and also in bond and commodity markets. While they also borrow to cover personal debt and for credit card payments, education loans, and so on, we focus only on the impact of real estate mortgages on the financial system.

We note that there is a built-in asymmetry *vis-à-vis* real estate boom-bust cycles, in that the appreciation in value during the boom portion of the cycle accrues to the borrower as a capital gain (while the bank's valuation is capped off at the level of the loan principal plus unpaid interest if any), but the drop in value during the bust portion of the cycle, which should normally have been absorbed by the borrower as a capital loss, may have to borne by the bank in case the borrower were to choose to abandon the underwater mortgage[1] (leaving the bank to absorb the difference between the yet to be paid portion of the loan principal plus unpaid interest if any, and the value of the asset on its books, as "marked to market," as a capital loss and this could escalate as more underwater mortgages get surrendered). This serves to attenuate or limit the banks' share of the real estate valuation gains during the boom period and amplify the losses that accrue to the banks during the downturns in the real estate markets.

Changes in the residential real estate stock and the related loan portfolio would depend on: (i) the # of new housing starts, and so on, which would depend on the population, its growth rate (net effects of birth and death, immigration and emigration), and its distribution; (ii) sales of older units on the secondary market (this in turn would depend on sales by the owners or the banks in case of repossessed dwelling units); (iii) the fraction of the units at the rental versus ownership ends of the spectrum and the fraction of loans by borrowers who borrow to buy, own and occupy and those who borrow to buy, own and rent out to others; and (iv) the interaction between these market segments (for instance, if more people rent, then the demand for housing units on an ownership basis would be lower, and vice versa).

2C: Government and the Public Sector: The government earns revenues (through the taxes it collects, including indirect taxes such as sales taxes, VAT, excise and duties, and direct taxes such as individual and corporate income taxes, wealth taxes and estate duties, etc.), spends, borrows (through treasury bills and "munis"), invests, and so on, just like any other player in the financial system. More importantly, it has a critical regulatory

oversight role and it controls the macro-economic framework through its fiscal and monetary policies (e.g., setting tax rates and controlling money supply which in turn affects inflation, setting of interest rates which affects the ability of households and corporations to borrow money and service existing debt, etc.) and its budgetary exercises (since most governments rarely enjoy surpluses, government deficits have to be financed and these attempts by the government to borrow in the markets tends to crowd out private sector borrowers). Governments, along with the public sector entities, are also employers who provide salaries and wages to a significant fraction of the workforce (who spend, borrow and repay, save and invest, etc., just like private sector employees) and also consumers and customers for goods and services offered by other public sector enterprises and private sector corporations. For traditional defined benefits-type pension schemes, governments also honor an intergenerational compact, by financing the pensions and Social Security payouts to retirees as well as their medical expenses through taxes levied on current working group adults (as mentioned earlier, aging populations which are also shrinking like Japan's lead to much higher dependency ratios and excessive government debt levels).

Additionally, since exports and imports determine the current account balance and in turn the foreign exchange conversion rates between any country's currency and internationally traded currencies such as the USD, the Euro, the British pound, the Japanese yen, and increasingly the Chinese yuan, governments and central banks pay substantial attention to exchange rates and act decisively to prevent steep declines (which may make exports more competitive but also end up impoverishing their citizens) or steep gains (which can make exports less competitive and domestic producers incapable of fighting off cheaper imports) in their respective currencies.

These are vital monitoring and control measures as far as the economy is concerned. Take interest rates, for example: when the economy is struggling to overcome factors that tend to depress the economy, low interest rates can be used (as Alan Greenspan did in the wake of the dot.com bust) to jump start the recovery or "unleash" the animal spirits, and when real estate prices have reached unaffordable levels and asset bubbles seem to be forming, then high interest rates can be used to keep "irrational exuberance" in check (Alan Greenspan was also held responsible for the housing asset bubble that led to the LoGR because he did not act soon enough to raise interest rates and deflate the asset bubbles that were forming before they reached dangerous proportions).

Governments also enter into treaties that bind successive governments to act in certain ways that citizens may or may not find conducive to their welfare. If, for instance, several sovereign countries in a region wish to form a union, they have different routes to one: (i) a political union, which would entail complete loss of sovereignty for the members (a worthy goal but not one that can be achieved easily except through a long drawn out process of mutual adjustments and compromises made by equal partners); and watered down versions such as: (ii) a banking union (where the banks are subject to the same set of rules and oversight by a common regulator – perhaps, with the benefit of hindsight, Europe should have started with this as first step); (iii) a fiscal union and monetary (in which an elected

---

1 In some countries, laws relating to full recourse prevent borrowers from walking away from real estate deals that are currently under water and leaving the lenders to absorb any capital losses -- they can proceed against borrowers and guarantors to recover any difference between the loan amount on the books (principal plus unpaid interest) and the current valuation of the asset as marked to its market price.

parliament and other bureaucratic entities, such as a central bank for instance, would control most of the decisions that would have otherwise been made by sovereign countries, including money supply and interest rates, taxation and outlays and all the other aspects of the budgetary calculus that parties, aiming to form sovereign governments at the member rather than at the unified level, take into account when making promises to voters, e.g., public sector jobs that are more like sinecures offered to supporters, generous pension levels, early retirement ages, and so on.

Single currency unions like the Euro region with otherwise sovereign members having no control over foreign exchange rates, money supply, and interest rates (and in turn the degree to which some of them can compete on their own with the others within the union and other countries outside the union) and only partial control over taxes, fiscal expenditures and deficits budgetary revenues and outlays or expenditures, etc., can be difficult to hold together if economic growth is somewhat two paced (a faster growing North versus a slower growing or even stagnant South, hamstrung by having a currency out of its control, as it struggled to recover from the recession). Furthermore, if the richer members (who had benefited disproportionately from the currency union in the first place, e.g., Germany) mistakenly mandate austerity and internal adjustments for the weaker members of the union, rather than the Keynesian approach to preventing sovereign defaults as countries, this will cause further contractions, much higher unemployment levels (and especially for the youth, fresh out of schools and universities, who need the early on-the-job training, exposure and experience in order to succeed over the rest of their careers), and in turn even more political upheaval and instability in Greece, Portugal and Spain, for instance. If the "have-nots" in the EU's periphery, or the PIIGS, see their duly elected governments perforce having to tighten their belts and recant on the promises made earlier in the with respect to public sector jobs and pensions, etc., in accordance with the dictates of the "haves" in the core of the EU, this can lead to wide-spread street protests and the instability of elected governments.

This misplaced emphasis in Europe on austerity, has left a vast majority of the citizens, and especially the younger generation of employment seekers who found their degrees were worthless in the job market, feeling increasingly disenchanted in the wake of the financial turmoil in the West, and susceptible to what was on offer from a host of hitherto-marginal or even fringe political parties and movements. These erstwhile fringe parties and movements, with a litany of ultra-right-wing and ultra-left-wing causes to espouse, have become increasingly strident and on the ascendant since the onset of the LoGR and who are displacing the more moderate centrist groups. Analysts have started to equate the political upheaval as we recently witnessed with the Brexit referendum in the UK and the elections in the US as a

backlash against globalization and expect a raft of protectionist measures to be adopted by governments in the future.

3. MODELING FINANCIAL CONTAGION BETWEEN BANKS

Bank balance sheet problems resulting in bank defaults are contagious. If banks in a financial network, and those financial networks in turn, are more closely interlinked with each other on the assets and liabilities sides of their balance sheets, the failure of a single bank (say Lehman Brothers at the start of the crisis on Sept 11, 2008) can trigger other defaults and spread through the global financial networks, generating cascades of defaults. A number of analysts and authors hailing from various fields, e.g., natural and social sciences, have sought to an analyze the causes of financial contagion and the efficacy of measures to prevent the spread of contagion effects and cascading defaults.

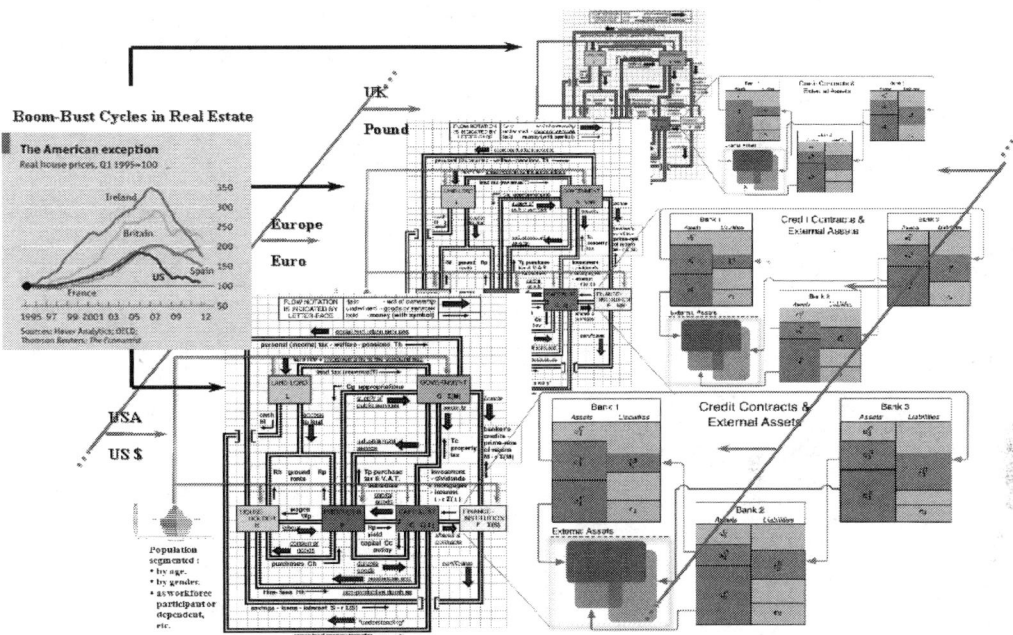

Figure 2: Interconnectedness between Banks and Financial Networks and linkages to the Real Estate Boom-Bust Cycles (extending a concept from Battistona, 2016 and incorporating a plot from http://www.economist.com/node/21553459)

To more fully comprehend the genesis and after-effects of the LoGR, we will seek to bring in the role of boom-bust-type cyclicality in, and multi-year lagged effects of, the residential and commercial real estate sectors, as well as the functions of the central banks in inflating and deflating the economy, along with the government departments such as treasury, and so on.

As depicted in Figure 2, we extend the basic model of interconnected banks to interconnected financial networks, where the interconnectedness between banks in a region, country and across continents (in the latter case, foreign exchange fluctuations can amplify or attenuate the shocks transmitted from one bank to another across national boundaries) can lead to the contagion spreading locally/nationally/globally as it did in the days following Lehman's bankruptcy. The trigger event could be the boom-bust cyclicality in the housing sector, as shown, or the

ISBN: 1-60132-454-5, CSREA Press ©

possibility of one or more banks in a region being defrauded either by an internal or external actor.

Noted analysts, e.g., Pozsar, et. al (2013) blame shadow banking for the recurring financial sector problems and define shadow banks as "financial intermediaries that conduct maturity, credit, and liquidity transformation without explicit access to central bank liquidity or public sector credit guarantees." While we agree that the nature of financial intermediation has changed substantially since the mid-1980s with the advent of market-based financial system, and that shadow banks which have played a key role in the market-based financial system, particularly in the run-up to the financial crisis, can be expected to be an important part of the financial system for the foreseeable future, we feel that our model cannot be easily extended to incorporate the "plumbing" of the shadow banking system – we will present a simpler analysis of financial system interlinkages. Future extensions may help point towards reform efforts that seek to remediate credit bubble excesses and to change capital and liquidity standards for the sector as a whole.

4. DISCUSSION: THE AFTERMATH OF LoGR

We now focus on the after effects, and especially those that become manifest over the medium to long term basis, of a severe downturn triggered off by a contagious string of bank failures such as the one we witnessed in 2008-2009.

Consider what happens when the loss of employment opportunities in the short run persists over the longer haul for a number of different reasons. As a result of longer term and hence skill-atrophying levels of unemployment especially for young fresh male[2] graduates, they could become increasingly addicted to the Internet and games. This has a sort of "double whammy" effect in that because they fail to acquire the skills valued in the employed and employable in the first place, they are severely at a disadvantage relative to the employed males, Notice that as males drop out of the workforce (either because or because they were too), *vis-à-vis* their ability to perform some or all of the functions and roles earlier in Section 2).

---

2 We have more or less resorted to stereotyping unemployed and increasingly unemployable youth, most vulnerable to becoming gaming addicts, as males. Research indicates that addicts can be of any race or gender, generally falling between 18 and 55, with an average of 15 years of education. We however, believe that younger males are more at risk in the current environment, and will continue our analysis based on this assumption.

In the absence of policy initiatives by governments, unemployed youth, more susceptible to getting addicted to Internet gaming, for instance will grow in size over time, as addicts in each cohort grow older and "infect" their peers in the same cohort, as well as their juniors (abelow above, as younger addicts grow older, they could become more addicted, more socially isolated, less employable (since they may lack skills that their non-addicted cohort mates had picked up in schools & universities, while they were getting their online "fixes") and hence, or otherwise, less attractive to potential mates. If the younger unemployed and unemployable males (being jobless and addicted) cannot find spouses because they cannot support families in the first place, new household formation levels as well as new housing starts will be depressed -- one of the main drivers and leading indicators for GDP and GDP growth.

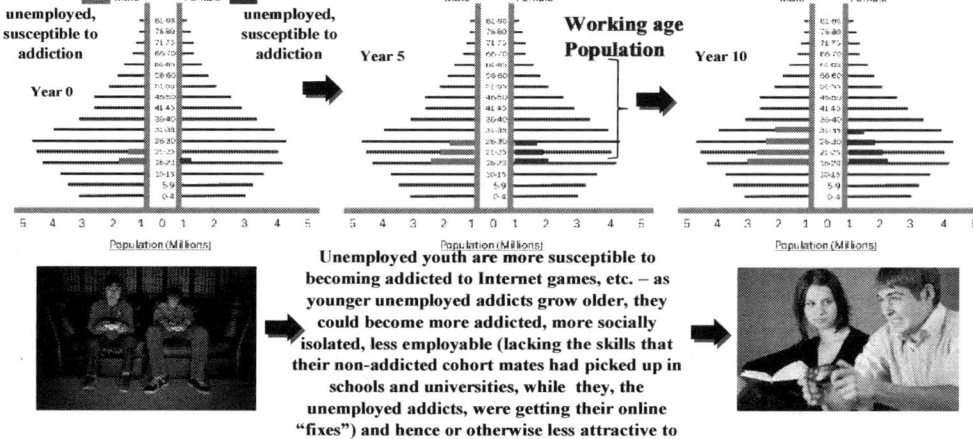

Figure 3: Interaction between Youth Unemployment and Gaming Addiction over Time (adapted from Kini and Melnikov, 2016)

We can think of this as having a "multiple whammy" negative economic impact over time (as depicted in Figure 5 below):

- incomes, otherwise earned by younger unemployed and unemployable men, will be missing as far in the GDP and GDP growth rate calculus;

- the multiplier effects of the money they would have otherwise spent (if they had stable incomes), would be missing and this would depress most if not all of the goods and services markets over time;

- the inability to start and form stable households would translate either into a drop in birth rates over time (and this would have ripple effects over time, when the missing contribution of the unborn next generation to the GDP and GDP growth rates, two decades or more later, is taken into account), or worse; and

- the local, state and federal governments would have to ramp up their law and order and criminal system related expenditures heavily over time to tackle the concomitant social problems, crime rates, and so on (as the old saying goes, "an idle mind is the devil's workshop").

This can have significantly adverse socioeconomic implications for society and the nation as well, in the "here and now" sense, and it could get worse over time. Why? As shown in Figure 4, the population of unemployed youth, who could potentially get addicted, can be expected to grow over time, in the absence of any policy initiatives by the government, since addicts in each cohort, as they grow older, will most likely "infect" more of their peers in the same cohort, as well as their juniors (and perhaps seniors, too), in the same unemployment "boat").

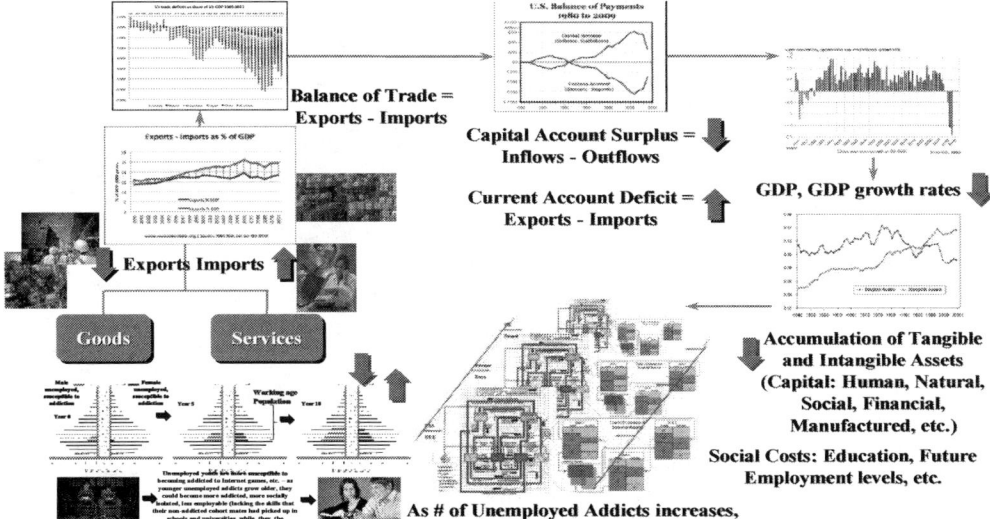

Figure 4: As the population of unemployed addicts grows over time, the Macro-Economy gets adversely impacted in numerous ways (adapted from Kini, 2016 and a diagram available at https://drjah.wordpress.com/research/graphics-page/visualising-economic-entities/).

As the population of unemployed youth, who are susceptible to becoming gaming addicts for instance grows over time, the macroeconomy gets adversely impacted in an inter-temporal sense, as depicted in Figure 5 above. In a direct sense, as explained above, the economy will suffer adverse consequences in three or four different ways as the population of unemployed potential addicts grows over time. Indirectly, there could be just as many and just as deleterious side-effects, namely:

- the balance of trade or the current account deficit (imports minus exports) will become increasingly adverse to the nation facing a serious and growing youth unemployment problem, because imports will increase and at the same time exports could decrease because of a growing shortage of skilled and committed human resources over time;
- the capital account deficit (capital outflows minus inflows) could also become increasingly adverse, with FDI and FII (foreign direct and indirect investment, respectively) flows finding their way to other nations that can have adequate resources, including human resources, and which are therefore more growth oriented;

- lower GDP growth rates, in turn, translate over time into lower investments in accumulated tangible and intangible capital stocks, or conversely increases in the tangible and intangible liabilities, for the future (this includes human capital, social capital, financial capital, manufactured capital, and even natural capital), and this could trigger off a vicious, rather than virtuous, cycle, with even more serious negative externality effects.

5. CONCLUSIONS

We have to recognize that there are a number of functions and roles that we all play for nost of our lives, if the economy is to grow sustainably and equitably, and if we are to attain what we all aspire for, i.e., a better life for ourselves and for our children, and so on. Our home ownership-related roles, along with several financial and nonfinancial factors with lagged or leading effects, do end up driving boom-bust cycles in the housing sector, which in turn adversely affects the financial sector.

Using system dynamics and discrete event simulation approaches, we model and analyze the impact of inter-connectedness (on the assets and liabilities sides of their balance sheets) between banks in a financial network, and between financial networks in turn, on the financial sector, and show how a failure of a single bank can trigger other defaults – this could spread as a contagion through the global financial networks, generating cascades of defaults.

REFERENCES

Battistona S., G. Caldarelli R. M. Maye, T. Roukny, and J. E. Stiglitz, PNAS, September 6, 2016, vol. 113, no. 36,10031–10036, www.pnas.org/cgi/doi/10.1073/pnas.1521573113)

Kini R. and I. Melnikov, "The Gaming Addiction Problem and its Economic and Social Consequences: A Comprehensive, Dynamic Approach," Appl. Math. Inf. Sci. 5, No. 3, 1-10 (2016)

May, R, Levin, S and Sugihara, G (2008), 'Ecology for bankers', Nature, Vol. 451, pages 893-95.

Pozsar Z., T. Adrian, A. Ashcraft and H. Boesky "Shadow Banking," Federal Reserve Bank of New York Staff Reports, Staff Report No. 458, July 2010, Revised February 2012 https://www.newyorkfed.org/medialibrary/media/research/epr/2013/0713adri.pdf; accessed on June 28th 2107 at 22:02

(see also Shadow Banking FRBNY Economic Policy Review / December 2013 https://www.newyorkfed.org/medialibrary/media/research/staff_reports/sr458.pdf).

Author Index